Frontiers of Developmental Psychopathology

Frontiers of Developmental Psychopathology

Edited by

Mark F. Lenzenweger

Jeffrey J. Haugaard

New York Oxford
OXFORD UNIVERSITY PRESS
1996

Oxford University Press

Oxford New York
Athens Auckland Bangkok Bombay
Calcutta Cape Town Dar es Salaam Delhi
Florence Hong Kong Istanbul Karachi
Kuala Lumpur Madras Madrid Melbourne
Mexico City Nairobi Paris Singapore
Taipei Tokyo Toronto

and associated companies in
Berlin Ibadan

Copyright © 1996 by Oxford University Press, Inc.

Published by Oxford University Press, Inc.
198 Madison Avenue, New York, New York 10016

Oxford is a registered trademark of Oxford University Press

All rights reserved. No part of this publication may be reproduced,
stored in a retrieval system, or transmitted, in any form or by any means,
electronic, mechanical, photocopying, recording, or otherwise,
without the prior permission of Oxford University Press.

Library of Congress Cataloging-in-Publication Data
Frontiers of developmental psychopathology / edited by Mark F. Lenzenweger, Jeffrey J. Haugaard.
p. cm.   Includes bibliographical references and index.
ISBN 0-19-509001-2
1. Mental illness—Etiology.
2. Developmental psychology.
I. Lenzenweger, Mark F.
II. Haugaard, Jeffrey J., 1951–
[DNLM: 1. Mental Disorders.
2. Models, Psychological. WM 100 F9345 1955]
RC454.4.F76   1995   616.89′071—dc20
DNLM/DLC   for Library of Congress   94-23362

1 3 5 7 9 8 6 4 2
Printed in the United States of America on acid-free paper

Preface

Developmental psychopathology is "coming of age" as a scientific approach and the collective efforts of those working within the developmental psychopathology framework have begun to shed light on a variety of psychopathologies. Whereas 20 years ago Thomas Achenbach noted in his 1974 text *Developmental Psychopathology* that his was a "book about a field that hardly yet exists," one can now surely observe a thriving subdiscipline of scientific psychopathology research. For example, the approach now has its own specialty journal—*Development and Psychopathology*—two handbooks that review the extant literature (e.g., Cicchetti & Cohen, 1995a, 1995b; Lewis & Miller, 1990), and, indeed, Achenbach's *Developmental Psychopathology* (2nd ed.) is viewed by many as the standard text for an approach that is now firmly rooted and growing.

As developmental psychopathology enters its "early adulthood," so to speak, it seemed to us an ideal time to critically take stock of the development observed thus far, with an eye toward the future and unresolved issues. In doing so, it became readily apparent that clearly identifiable trends were emerging within developmental psychopathology, both in terms of substantive areas of concern as well as methodologies. These trends are well documented in the works noted above. However, we were also struck by themes that have remained somewhat inadequately developed and explored in developmental psychopathology, and this led us to convene a symposium at Cornell University to focus on such matters. In short, we thought that this was an ideal time to explore the more uncharted territories in psychopathological development in an attempt to gently prod and influence this emerging scientific approach.

To date, developmental psychopathology has been predominantly, though clearly not exclusively, concerned with understanding less severe forms of psychopathology, and characterized by a relative preponderance of research best described as "psychosocial," whereas genetic influences, neurobiological systems, and brain development have been less well explored and integrated. Although there is no denying the relevance of psychosocial factors in the determination and maintenance of all forms of psychopathology, we believe developmental psychopathology must more fully embrace a wider spectrum of psychopathology for scientific inquiry if it is to genuinely assist us in understanding those forms of illness that pose major public health concerns. Whereas the study of deviant social attachment patterns, behavioral competence (or lack thereof), and dysfunctional parent-child relations have all provided valuable insights, greater developmental clarity is needed in our understanding of *clinically significant psychopathology*—for example, autism, schizophrenia, anxiety disorders, depression, antisocial personality, eating disorders, and other noteworthy conditions like attention-deficit disorder. These disorders, which spring from complex dynamic and interactive processes, fill our clinics, hospitals, and other clinical service agencies. A fuller understanding of the complex and more severe forms of psychopathology will yield important etiological and developmental information and may ultimately result in better treatment and prevention efforts, but will also provide us with an understanding of normative psychological development and functioning.

The degree to which developmental psychopathology has been "underbiologized," so to speak, is clearly evident when perusing the research literature and probably is somewhat reflective of the extensive influence of psychosocial models in normative developmental psychology—what David Rowe (1994), the noted developmental behavioral geneticist, has called "socialization science." Whereas many reports on developmental psychopathology focus on parent-child interactions, childrearing attitudes, dysfunctional parenting, and putatively related dysfunctional outcomes (e.g., maltreatment leading to impaired competence), few genuine attempts have been made to integrate genetic factors, neurotransmitter models, and neuroscientific processes, which as yet remain a relative rarity in the modal developmental psychopathology article or chapter. In the interest of not being *misunderstood*, we should like to emphasize that we are observing a relative imbalance in developmental psychopathology in favor of psychosocial models of pathological development over more biologically influenced models—quite frankly, however, we suggest that the best models will be those that integrate across these levels (e.g., Meehl, 1990; see also Meehl, 1972). The importance of genetic factors in both normative and pathological development is indisputable (Rowe, 1994; Rutter, 1991) and the essential role of neurobiological factors in temperament (e.g., Kagan, 1994), emotion (Ekman & Davidson, 1994), personality development (e.g., Depue & Collins, in press), and the emergence of psychopathology (e.g., Breslin & Weinberger, 1990; Cocarro & Murphy, 1990; Grace, 1991) is axiomatic, some would even say confirmed. The meaningful integration of brain, emotion, behavior, and environmental influences currently represents an exceptionally active research area in various areas of psychological science, especially cognition and personality. In short, developmental psychopathology cannot afford not to heed these advances and emerging research strategies.

We believe this is a particularly opportune time to look forward from within the developmental psychopathology approach. It is indeed a time to take stock and consolidate earlier research findings, but it is particularly a ripe time to walk to the frontiers of this exciting new area to see the territory and challenges ahead for developmental psychopathology. In order to accomplish this mission, we invited several leading scholars to Cornell University to present their views on various severe and complex psychopathologies within a developmental psychopathology framework and to articulate their models with an eye toward the future. Indeed, as Sir Michael Rutter points out in his chapter (Chapter 7), developmental psychopathology *"in no way constitutes a separate discipline"*; rather, it is a vantage point. We urged our contributors to stand at that vantage point and show us what they see as being genuinely at the frontier of developmental psychopathology. Our contributors were encouraged to take risks, to be generative, and when necessary, provocative. All of the papers presented at the Cornell meeting were subsequently transformed into the chapters contained in this volume, and we are particularly pleased with the result. We are especially pleased to draw attention to the concluding chapter that rounds out this volume—namely, Sir Michael Rutter's chapter. Whether one works within the specific substantive area addressed by any of the authors in this volume or is, perhaps, more interested in the general *form* of the models presented herein, we think the reader will find each of these chapters stimulating and heuristic.

Moreover, we are pleased to present this volume, *Frontiers of Developmental Psychopathology,* as the second in the continuing Cornell University *Series in Developmental Psychological Science.* The first volume in the *Series* was an outgrowth of the *festschrift* held in honor of Professor Henry Ricciuti and was titled *Future Directions in Infant Development Research* (Suci & Robertson, 1992).

Finally, we should like to take this opportunity to express our gratitude to those individuals whose assistance has greatly facilitated the undertaking and completion of this project. We are especially indebted to Sir Michael Rutter who served so very generously as our consultant at all phases of this project, provided incisive commentary on all presentations at the symposium in Ithaca, and contributed a comprehensive overview and critique chapter included in this volume. Professors George Suci and Henry Ricciuti, both of Cornell, initially suggested that such a volume as this would fit well in the Cornell University *Series in Developmental Psychological Science* and have been most supportive of the endeavor for which we are grateful. Completion of this project was greatly facilitated by a sabbatical leave for one of us (M. F. L.) and a most productive sabbatical environment provided by Professor Philip S. Holzman at Harvard University and the Psychology Laboratory at McLean Hospital. Invaluable guidance and support were provided by our editor, Joan Bossert, at Oxford University Press; additional expert production assistance was delivered faithfully by Ellen Fuchs and Stanley George (late), both of Oxford as well. Finally, we thank Dean Firebaugh at Cornell for her generous financial support of the original symposium held at Cornell University in Ithaca, New York.

Let us now proceed to the frontiers of developmental psychopathology.

March, 1995   M. F. L.
Ithaca, NY   J. J. H.

References

Achenbach, T. M. (1974). *Developmental psychopathology*. New York: Wiley.

Breslin, N. A., & Weinberger, D. R. (1990). Schizophrenia and the normal functional development of the prefrontal cortex. *Developmental and Psychopathology, 2*, 409–424.

Cicchetti, D., & Cohen, D. J. (Eds.). (1995a). *Developmental psychopathology: Volume I. Theory and method*. New York: Wiley.

Cicchetti, D., & Cohen, D. J. (Eds.). (1995b). *Developmental psychopathology: Volume II. Risk, disorder, and adaptation*. New York: Wiley.

Coccarro, E. F., & Murphy, D. L. (Eds.). (1990). *Serotonin in major psychiatric disorders*. Washington, DC: American Psychiatric Press.

Depue, R. A., & Collins, P. (in press). *Neurobehavioral systems, personality, and psychopathology*. New York: Springer-Verlag.

Ekman, P., & Davidson, R. J. (1994). *The nature of emotion: Fundamental questions*. New York: Oxford University Press.

Grace, A. A. (1991). Phasic versus tonic dopamine release and the modulation of dopamine system responsivity: A hypothesis for the etiology of schizophrenia. *Neuroscience, 41*, 1–24.

Kagan, J. (1994). *Galen's prophecy: Temperament in human nature*. New York: Basic Books.

Lewis, M., & Miller, S. (Eds.). (1990). *Handbook of developmental psychopathology*. New York: Plenum.

Meehl, P. E. (1972). Specific genetic etiology, psychodynamics, and therapeutic nihilism. *International Journal of Mental Health, 1*, 10–27.

Meehl, P. E. (1990). Toward an integrated theory of schizotaxia, schizotypy, and schizophrenia. *Journal of Personality Disorders, 4*, 1–99.

Rutter, M. (1991). Nature, nurture, and psychopathology: A new look at an old topic. *Development and Psychopathology, 3*, 125–136.

Rowe, D. C. (1994). *The limits of family influence: Genes, Experience, and behavior*. New York: Guilford.

Suci, G. J., & Robertson, S. S. (Eds.). (1992). *Future directions in infant development research*. New York: Springer-Verlag.

Contents

Contributors xi

I Psychobiological Models in Developmental Psychopathology

1. Heritable Variability and Variable Heritability in Developmental Psychopathology, *5*
   H. Hill Goldsmith and Irving I. Gottesman

2. A Model of Neurobiology–Environment Interaction in Developmental Psychopathology, *44*
   Richard A. Depue, Paul F. Collins, and Monica Luciana

II Developmental Models of Complex Psychopathologies

3. Some Characteristics of a Developmental Theory for Early Onset Delinquency, *81*
   Gerald R. Patterson

4. Markers, Developmental Processes, and Schizophrenia, *125*
   Barbara A. Cornblatt, Robert H. Dworkin, Lorraine E. Wolf, and L. Erlenmeyer-Kimling

5. Developmental Psychopathology in the Context of Adolescence, *148*
   Jeanne Brooks-Gunn and Ilana Attie

6. Behavioral Research in Childhood Autism, *190*
   Marian Sigman

III Developmental Psychopathology

7. Developmental Psychopathology: Concepts and Prospects, *209*
   Michael L. Rutter

Index, 239

Contributors

Editors

Mark F. Lenzenweger   Cornell University, Ithaca, N.Y.

Jeffrey J. Haugaard   Cornell University, Ithaca, N.Y.

Contributors

Ilana Attie   St. Lukes-Roosevelt Hospital Center, New York

Jeanne Brooks-Gunn   Columbia University, Teachers College, New York

Paul F. Collins   University of Oregon at Eugene, Eugene, Ore.

Barbara A. Cornblatt   Mount Sinai School of Medicine and Elmhurst Hospital Center, Elmhurst, N.Y.

Richard A. Depue   Cornell University, Ithaca, N.Y.

Robert H. Dworkin   Columbia University College of Physicians and Surgeons, New York

L. Erlenmeyer-Kimling   Columbia University College of Physicians and Surgeons, New York; New York State Psychiatric Institute, New York

H. Hill Goldsmith   University of Wisconsin–Madison, Madison, Wisc.

Irving I. Gottesman   University of Virginia, Charlottesville, Va.

Monica Luciana   University of Minnesota, Minneapolis

Gerald R. Patterson   Oregon Social Learning Center, Eugene, Ore.

Michael Rutter   MRC Child Psychiatry Unit, Institute of Psychiatry, De Crespigny Park, London

Marian Sigman   University of California at Los Angeles, Los Angeles

Lorraine E. Wolf   Mount Sinai School of Medicine, Elmhurst Hospital Center, Elmhurst, N.Y.

Frontiers of Developmental Psychopathology

I

Psychobiological Models in Developmental Psychopathology

1

Heritable Variability and Variable Heritability in Developmental Psychopathology

H. HILL GOLDSMITH AND IRVING I. GOTTESMAN

Genetic Orientations to Antisocial Behavior

Genes are among the acknowledged potential risk factors relevant to developmental psychopathology. In the areas of developmental psychopathology related to antisocial behavior, the roles of genetics are complex and controversial. The reader's receptivity to the notion that genetic and other biological factors must be given their due as credible risk factors for various problematic outcomes in adolescence and adulthood involving antisocial behaviors will probably depend upon the reader's professional discipline and past exposure to purveyors of this idea. Even enlightened advocates for giving genes a chance to explain some of the variance observed within a population must acknowledge the misguided, naive, and sometimes inhumane efforts to misapply biological concepts in order to guarantee "law and order" (Proctor, 1988; Reilly, 1991). Readers whose immediate associations with the phrase "behavioral genetics" are the Holocaust, racism, or compulsory sterilization will probably wonder why we are promoting enlightened perspectives on the appropriate roles to be accorded genetic considerations. However, readers whose associations with the phrase "behavioral genetics" are amniocentesis, genetic counseling, dietary treatment for phenylketonuria, or gene replacement therapy are likely to view genetic hypotheses more favorably.

Attitudes toward the explanatory power of possible genetic factors for such traits or disorders as two of the "deadly sins" (lust and anger), aggression, disruptive behaviors, delinquency, criminality, and antisocial personality have varied greatly over the past five centuries, depending on which discipline had appointed itself as caretaker of the public order.

The pendulum swung far to the right with such early studies of "crime families" as the Jukes and the Kallikaks. Most readers will be familiar with the influential writings (1876) on the concept of "criminal man" by the Italian psychiatrist Cesare Lombroso (1835–1909). As a military physician Lombroso had been quite impressed with the differences in the amount of obscene tattooing on good and criminal soldiers and by one [sic] "pathological" brain autopsy on a notorious murderer; he also considered carnivorous plants to be criminal, thus indicating, to him, the universality of such behaviors.) Needless to say, such efforts have accelerated the ridicule of genetic and biological constructs up to the present day. The pendulum has swung back toward the middle in recent years, to a mulifactorial framework (Carey, 1992a; Walters, 1992). Researchers are aware of the many steps in gene-to-behavior pathways that give such global variables as individual differences in liability to antisocial behaviors, socio-ecological differences (nutrition, poverty, crowding), and parenting differences (abuse, divorce, discipline) a chance to improve or worsen the fit of causal models.

Contemporary researchers recognize that *different* explanatory factors are not always *competing* explanatory factors. This recognition is partly due to appreciation that effect sizes in the prediction of antisocial behavior are typically modest, and thus that there is ample room for multiple predictors from different domains. However, there is a more fundamental recognition that distal and proximal causes can be different in kind, and that factors that play a role in the origins of behavioral dispositions are different from those that elicit or maintain actual behavior. In this chapter, we shall make the case for genetic influences as one factor influencing individual variability in the strength of dispositions toward some classes of antisocial behavior. Nothing we have to say about genetics, however, negates the observation that, for instance, much human aggression is a crude attempt to control the behavior of others (Patterson, 1986) or that aggressive behavior patterns are often maintained by reinforcement from parents, peers, and victims (see Berkowitz, 1993, chap. 6, for review).

An important general principle is that genes have only a probabilistic effect on the development of normal or disordered behavior. However, the degree of probability ranges widely according to the particular genotype and phenotype being studied. The unfortunate individual who inherits a particular pair of recessive genes on chromosome pair 12 will surely exhibit the symptoms of phenylketonuria early in life. Only one copy of a stretch of a recently specified gene which contains a trinucleotide repeat (that is expanded and unstable in the mutant, disease-causing form; see report of The Huntington's Disease Collaborative Research Group, 1993) on chromosome 4 will also surely lead to Huntington's disease, although the affected person will live for 40 or 50 years before frank signs of the illness appear. Thus, the probability of a particular gene leading to a disorder can be 100%.

On the other hand, for many more common disorders, the probability that the bearer of a gene—or a set of genes—will ever experience the disorder is much less. For example, we can conclude from studies of identical twins that an individual with an "average" genotype for schizophrenia (average for schizophrenics, not for the general population) has only roughly a 50% chance of eventually developing enough symptoms to be diagnosed as schizophrenic. Thus, for complex, genetically influenced disorders (King, Rotter, & Motulsky, 1992) such as schizophrenia, the path from genotype to behavioral manifestation is indeed probabilistic, with the chances of developing schizophrenia ranging from zero to 55% (Gottesman, 1991), depending on ill-understood processes involving interactions, thresholds, and biopsychosocial contingencies. Thinking about genetic risk factors for other behavioral patterns, such as aggressiveness or antisocial behavior, becomes even more complex, especially in developmental perspective.

As a brief survey of some demographic and psychiatric epidemiological facts will reveal, antisocial behaviors are too important to be left to practitioners of any one discipline, such as criminologists, sociologists, lawyers, neuroscientists, or the builders of the Republican or Democratic political platforms. U. S. Bureau of the Census (1991) statistics tell us that 23.5 million households were "touched by crime" in one year (1989) as victims; 11.3 million citizens were arrested (1989) (82% males and 15.5% under age 18); 3.7 million adults were under correctional supervision (of whom 2.8 million were on parole or probation and 0.9 million in prison) and a further 344 thousand were in jails; 1.2 million (1986) delinquency cases were adjudicated by the courts; and 94,000 juveniles were in custody (1987).

We are concerned in this chapter with antisocial behavior, which is a much broader phenotype than those adjudicated by the criminal justice system. Thus, we turn to epidemiological studies of criteria-based and structured-interview-determined rates of DSM-III-R antisocial personality disorder (ASP) in the massive sample of 19,182 adults (93% in households, 7% in institutions) interviewed in the Epidemiologic Catchment Area (ECA) study reported by Robins and Regier (1991) and their colleagues. The ECA study contains a gold mine of information for the developmental psychopathologist. By the conventions of DSM-III-R, ASP requires a diagnosis of conduct disorder (CD) before age 15 as a "gateway" diagnosis to one of ASP. The CD diagnosis is met by any 3 of 12 criteria, and the adult diagnosis requires the presence of at least 4 of 10 problem areas. The childhood problems emphasize aggression, with 6 of the 12 criteria consisting of fighting, weapon use, cruelty to humans or animals, forced sex, and mugging/armed robbery. Many problems exist with the taxonomy and nosology of disruptive behaviors (Achenbach, 1993; Caron & Rutter, 1991; Lilienfeld & Waldman, 1990), and we shall return to these important problems of defining a useful phenotype for behavioral genetic analyses below. All of the subjects in the

ECA were age 18 or over, so that diagnoses of CD, and therefore of ASP, are necessarily retrospective. The best estimate for the lifetime prevalence (now or ever) of ASP was obtained by including extra questions about illegal activities for the St. Louis sample that were not allowed at the other sites; the estimate was 7.3% in males and 1.0% in females (rates that are 53% higher by using the information about illegal activities). Such rates, when projected against the adult population of this nation, give minimal estimates of the proportion of the adult population that engage in, or have engaged in, nontrivial and syndromic antisocial behaviors of 8.87 million males and 1.27 million females! It is noteworthy that there were no differences in the rates between African-Americans and Caucasians. The structure of the data gathered for ASP diagnoses (Robins, Tipp, & Przybeck, 1991) permits many additional analyses to inform the developmentalist interested in the correlates of antisocial behaviors. The average age of the first symptom reported for satisfying the CD step was between the eighth and ninth birthdays; of all males who ever had an ASP diagnosis, 53% reported no symptoms within the past year, as did 50% of the females, a quite unexpected result regarding the phenotypic plasticity of antisocial behaviors. Almost all of the ASPs apparently were in "remission" after they reached age 45; even then, the mean duration from first to last symptom in the ASP "career" was 19 years.

With this documentation of the magnitude of ASP and related problems, it should be clear why behavioral scientists are motivated to understand the causes. In seeking some tentative understandings, we begin with two complications. First, antisocial or aggressive behavior can have many developmental roots, each with its own set of genetic and environmental underpinnings. Among the psychological dispositional roots might be such features as a robust constitution, a typically high energy level, a tendency to be a sensation seeker, low anxiety under conditions that typically evoke inhibition, and other such tendencies or predispositions. Second, each of these tendencies can have multiple—and divergent—outcomes. For example, the energetic mesomorph who is unafraid to enter dark alleys might be a successful mugger or a decorated patrolman, depending on neighborhood heroes/heroines in childhood, attitudinal, cultural, and other factors—including luck—that are easily imagined.

The behavior-genetic principles embodied in these two complications are (1) genetic heterogeneity and (2) pleiotropy. A behavioral pattern can have different genetic roots in different individuals (and no genetic roots at all in some—phenocopies), and a single genotype can have different behavioral manifestations in different individuals. When genetic heterogeneity and pleiotropy are the rule rather than the exception, as they surely must be for antisocial behavior, the genetic analysis of behavior becomes a daunting task.

The concept of proximal versus distal causes is also pertinent to this issue. Notions such as "genes for crime" are nonsense, but the following notion is reasonable: There may be *partially* genetically influenced *predispositions* for basic behavioral tendencies, such as impulsivity, that in certain experiential contexts make the *probability* of committing certain crimes higher than for individuals who possess lesser degrees of such behavioral tendencies. The most proximal causal factor in the spiral of influences leading to commission of a sanctioned act is the situational context surrounding the act—who said or did what to whom for which reason before the act. The next most proximal cause is perhaps the reinforcement histories and coercive cycles emphasized by social learning theorists. But more distal factors concern who enters into these cycles and what helps maintain them. Genes might influence these more distal factors probabilistically.

Genetic heterogeneity, pleiotropy, and distal versus proximal causes are not the only complications we face in conceptualizing how genes might influence antisocial behavior. For instance, some aggressive acts are influenced by genes common to all members of our species; these include actions required to survive or to guarantee survival of kin or others under extreme conditions. In these cases, individual differences in genetic constitution might have no impact. In addition, there are surely some individuals with no genetic risk factors at all who commit crimes of all sorts. Crimes such as civil disobedience immediately come to mind; consider the folk heroine seamstress Rosa Parks refusing to relinquish her seat at the front of the bus during the early days of the American civil rights movement.

It should not be necessary to emphasize that when the *norm* in a community is for an adolescent to join a criminal gang, genetic factors become trivially important in predicting who will get into trouble. Nor should it be necessary to mention that the behavior-genetic considerations we are treating apply to *individual* variability rather than intergroup differences. But in these times of high tension among ethnic groups across the earth, both of these obvious qualifications do need to be stated explicitly and emphasized to our policy makers.

Defining Phenotypes for Genetic Analysis

Thus far, we have discussed and differentiated criminality and the diagnosis of ASP. Most epidemiologic data pertain to one of these operational definitions. However, we do not imply that either sanctioned crime or the DSM diagnosis of ASP is the optimal phenotype for genetic analysis.

Meaningful distinctions among antisocial behavioral patterns have emerged from experimental psychopathology. For example, Harpur, Hare, and Hakstian (1989) summarized evidence for two correlated but distinguishable psychopathy-related factors in groups of incarcerated males. The first factor included items such as glibness, grandiose sense of self-worth, lying, conning, and lack of remorse and empathy. This factor encompasses key features of the psychopathic personality described by Cleckley (1976). The second factor was more similar to the DSM-III-R diagnosis of ASP in that it described a chronically unstable and antisocial lifestyle, with impulsive, irresponsible behaviors and relationships. More important than the psychometric distinctiveness of these two factors are their different correlates. The Harpur et al. review indicates that the first factor correlated with higher narcissism ratings and lower self-report of anxiety, whereas the second factor correlated with personality scales more commonly associated with antisocial behavior (self-report on the Minnesota Multiphasic Personality Inventory [MMPI] Psychopathic deviate [Pd], California Psychological Inventory [CPI] Socialization [So], and sensation-seeking scales). Despite these and other "life-history" differential correlates of the two factors, Harpur et al. view psychopathy as a valid unitary syndrome. Clearly, genetic analysis with samples extending outside the incarcerated population could help validate the distinction between the constellation of Cleckley personality features and the constellation of chronic antisocial behaviors.

Another key distinction among individuals who exhibit antisocial behavior is developmental. DiLalla and Gottesman (1990), drawing on behavior-genetic considerations, suggest that adult criminality and juvenile delinquency have some different roots. Moffitt's (1993) review summarizes evidence that antisocial behavior in some individuals is essentially limited to adolescence, whereas in others the behavior persists throughout the life span. The relatively large group of individuals (by some estimates, a clear majority of adolescents) who exhibit the adolescence-limited pattern of antisocial behavior do so, in part, because of secular trends that have created a gap between biological maturation and the assumption of adult privileges and responsibilities. In a sense elaborated by Moffitt, this antisocial behavior can be considered adaptive as well as normative. On the other hand, the life-course-persistent group is characterized by neuropsychological risk, which in turn is often correlated with nonoptimal contexts for development. Although the distinction between the roughly 5% of the male population belonging to the life-course-persistent group and the larger adolescence-limited group would be difficult to make on the basis of data from the adolescent period alone, the distinction would be clear in developmental perspective. (See Moffitt, 1993, for other data and hypotheses concerning these two groups, including hypothesized mechanisms of entry and exit in antisocial behavior for the adolescence-limited group). Of primary concern to us here is that behavior-genetic data support this distinction, with childhood conduct problems and adult criminality and ASP showing heritable variation, in contrast to juvenile delinquency, as we shall see later in this chapter.

Aggression researchers have drawn our attention to the different roots of aggressive behavior. The most widely accepted distinction is between instrumental and emotional aggression (Berkowitz, 1993). People who engage in instrumental aggression seek to control or dominate others or to gain resources, whereas those who engage in emotional aggression tend to interpret others' actions as hostile and make hostile attributions.

It is important to emphasize that the three dichotomies just mentioned are based on different sources of data. Harpur et al.'s distinction between Cleckley- and DSM-III-R ASP-type psychopaths is based on adult criminals; the distinction concerning developmental course is based on adolescents who engage in risky and illegal behaviors, many of which are never punished, and the distinction between different types of aggressiveness is based more on analysis of the immediate motivation underlying the behavior than on individuals' enduring dispositions. Thus, it is unsurprising that the overlap among the various sets of dichotomies is incompletely understood. It is also crucial to relate these distinctions to basic personality dispositions, such as inhibitory control and anger proneness. These issues will prove difficult to resolve on a phenotypic basis alone, partly because—as researchers surely realize—the rather clear-cut distinctions that we have portrayed are probably much more fuzzy in reality. Genetics can provide a tool to sharpen these distinctions and test their validity.

Appreciating the Molecular Level of Genetic Analysis

Ideally, both statistical and biological evidence is gathered to render a genetic hypothesis tenable. The statistical evidence involves documentation of the heritability of behavioral tendencies such as aggressiveness or impulsiveness. Evidence must also be adduced that the behavioral tendencies predict antisocial behavior and that antisocial patterns of behavior are heritable. Then demonstration is needed that the genetic influences on the behavioral tendencies and antisocial behavioral patterns overlap. Such evidence—to the extent that it is available—will be reviewed later in this chapter.

The other line of genetic evidence is biological; identification of specific stretches of DNA associated with antisocial behavioral patterns. Of course, the genetic evidence is only one aspect of the biological evidence. Other aspects, such as reactivity of the autonomic nervous system, are not considered in this chapter. As we consider biological processes, our examples will stray far from antisocial behavior. However, these processes need to be appreciated by future-oriented behavioral developmentalists, partly because they represent a complementary approach to understanding dynamic development and partly because of their heuristic value.

Perhaps because of the ambiguity of our subject matter, we developmentalists search for metaphors with heuristic value to guide our understanding. For instance, Rene Spitz looked to descriptive embryology as a metaphor for behavioral development. Waddington's epigenetic landscape is another such metaphor (Gottesman, 1974). More recently the chaotic behavior of, say, weather systems has been attractive to some developmentalists as a metaphor for the nonlinearity of development. In trying to move beyond metaphor to actual process, developmentalists have only recently begun to identify bodies of knowledge that are instructive for studying human behavior (Smith & Thelen, 1994). Genetic regulatory systems are processes that embody instructive dynamic principles for developmentalists. For genetically influenced development to occur, it seems likely that the pattern of gene expression would change via regulatory processes. The existence of these regulatory processes is an underlying basis for the claim, made above, that genetic influences should be viewed as dynamic rather than static.

Twenty-five years ago, the only reasonably well-understood examples of gene regulation involved bacteria. Classic examples were regulation of genes controlling production of enzymes involved in metabolic systems in bacteria. In a typical system, a product of the metabolic pathway interacted with the product of a regulatory gene, and the resulting complex then interacted with a section of the DNA that "shut down" transcription of genes controlling production of enzymes in the metabolic pathway.

Many scientists suspected that this and similar systems would prove prototypic for regulation of eukaryotic gene expression, including that of mammals. However, a mammalian cell has about 800 times the amount of DNA that a bacterium contains (but not so many times the number of proteins), and the mechanisms of gene expression and regulation proved to be much more complex. Part of the reason for the greater complexity of regulatory systems lies in differences in the structure of DNA—not in the genetic code itself but in features such as the greater prevalence of split genes. Split genes contain both introns (*in*tervening sequences of DNA that do not code for protein) and exons (sequences that are *ex*pressed in messenger RNA [mRNA]). Another structural difference is that DNA in higher organisms contains extensive repeated segments of identical or nearly identical DNA. Yet another difference is the chromosomal structure of eukaryotic (organisms higher than bacteria) DNA.

Studies of the physical structure of chromosomes have clarified some mechanisms of gene activation and inactivation. Inactivation can be short-term or long-term. The best-known example of long-term inactivation is that of one of the two X chromosomes in females—the so-called Lyon effect or lyonization (after Mary Lyon, the discoverer). The finding that an entire chromosome can be inactivated for most of an individual's life suggests that similar processes might also occur for briefer periods for shorter chromosomal segments.

Genetic regulation occurs at *hierarchical* levels, as outlined in Table 1.1. Long-term gene inactivation is apparently accomplished by changes

Table 1.1. Stages of Gene Expression and Levels of Regulation of Eukaryotic Gene Expression

Stages of Gene Expression	Type of Regulation[a]
1. Chromatin configuration	Regulation of chromatin structure DNA methylation
2. Initiation of transcription	Promotor utilization Activation or repression by various transcription factors
3. Transcript elongation and polyadenylation	Rate of transcription Premature termination Regulated polyadenylation
4. Splicing of pre-mRNA and transport out of the nucleus	Splicing at alternative sites Different forms of splicing Sequestering of mRNA from ribosomes
5. Translation	Availability of factors required for initiation of protein synthesis Translational blocks and reversal of blocks

[a]The types of regulation listed are illustrative rather than comprehensive.

in the way DNA is associated with proteins in the three-dimensional structure of chromosomes. Heterochromatin is a form of chromosomal structure, involving principally DNA and various histone proteins, that is so dense that it can be seen under a light microscope when the cell is not dividing. Highly compacted heterochromatin is apparently not transcribed, whereas euchromatin, with a much more open structure, is transcribed. Thus, heterochromatin is a visible marker of inactive genes. Two observations important for understanding development have been made: First, there are regions of the genome that appear completely heterochromatic in later life but that were euchromatic at earlier stages. The notion, of course, is that these regions contain genes that are programmed to function at only one developmental period. Of even more interest is the finding (confirmed in both fruit flies and mammals) that a stretch of genes can be inactivated by *insertion* into a heterochromatic region.

The second observation is that longer-term regulation of gene expression can involve DNA methylation. In the DNA of most animal species, about 5% of the cytosine residues are methylated (cytosine is one of four bases that carry the genetic code). Several lines of evidence suggest that methylated DNA is usually not transcribed; thus methylation in regulatory regions is perhaps a feature of longer-term inhibition of gene expression. Interestingly, patterns of DNA methylation can be retained through inheritance across multiple generations (Holliday, 1987).

Of course, some genes are active only for limited periods, and there is substantial knowledge about how genes are activated and deactivated.

Estimates are that about 1% of our genes are being transcribed at any given time. Of course, this is a different 1% of the genes in various cells. And the proportion of genes being expressed at a given time may vary according to tissue type, with the nervous system being more physiologically active. Genes referred to as *constitutive* or *housekeeping* genes are expressed more or less continually, whereas *regulated* genes are expressed in stage- and tissue-specific ways. Studies of DNA and protein chemistry are revealing the molecular processes that facilitate or inhibit transcription of various types of genes by RNA polymerases. These processes include the action of DNA elements called *promoters* and *enhancers*, as well as other factors. Promoters are regions near the coding segment of a gene where proteins called *basal factors* attach to the DNA. One of these basal factors, the enzyme RNA polymerase, actually catalyzes the transcription. Transcriptional enhancers, or *activator proteins*, attach to another regulatory site in the DNA sequence and interact with the basal factors to maximize the rate of transcription. Enhancers may also facilitate binding of RNA polymerase enzymes to initiation regions of the DNA, and recent models suggest that histone proteins play a role in this process (Grunstein, 1992). After the gene (both introns and exons) is transcribed, the pre-mRNA is packaged with specific nuclear proteins and then processed further.

Let us return to Table 1.1 and summarize the stages once again, realizing that any attempt to enumerate the molecular control mechanisms for gene expression must be incomplete. First are the mechanisms that determine whether the region of a chromosome on which a particular gene resides is physically amenable to transcription. Assuming that it is, there are many steps that can potentially be regulated before an mRNA is produced. There is the transcriptional stage, where, for example, steroid hormones act. Aspects of transcription that can be regulated include, for example, promoter utilization. Posttranscriptional steps that can be regulated include splicing of mRNA, addition of certain chemical "tags" to the mRNA, and transport of the mRNA from the nucleus. Steroid hormones also act at this posttranscriptional stage by stabilizing the hormone-induced mRNAs against degradation in the cytoplasm. Then there are translational controls that regulate whether, or at what rate, mRNA and associated cellular machinery in the ribosomes actually produce protein. After the steps outlined in Table 1.1, there are other processes that are also subject to regulatory control, such as sorting of proteins and transport of proteins across membranes.

Our brief description of regulatory mechanisms should not imply that these processes are fully understood. The myriad developmental genetic mechanisms in mammals will likely defy complete explanation for some time. However, as each mechanism is elucidated, we gain insight into another possible source of variability among individuals. Thus, the sources of genetically based individuality are not confined to polymorphic structural genes (genes that vary in some bases of the DNA sequence across individuals). Even if all structural genes were the same, as in identical twins, cascades of interacting regulatory genes controlling molecular developmental pathways would still result in functional genetic differences among individuals.

We have barely scratched the surface of molecular genetic research that holds relevance for the study of behavioral development. For instance, the investigation of the nature of "developmental switches" and how they function at the molecular level seems fundamental to the understanding of the timing of development. It is thought that sex determination may be initiated by a molecular switch on the Y chromosome, and other major developmental transitions might also be influenced by such switches. Another relevant topic is growth hormone's mechanism of action. In fact, much immunology and cancer research is leading to fundamental insights into the molecular-genetic nature of development and regulation.

Now that we have some appreciation for genetic regulatory mechanisms and understand that it is not simply an abstract possibility that genes can be *both* a source of *flexibility and* a source of *constancy* in development, let us return to the behavioral level. The notion that genes act developmentally alerts us to study such features as the *age of onset* and the *course* of disorders. Thus, in the complex area of antisocial behavior, researchers are led to investigate the determinants of early- versus late-onset juvenile delinquency rather than grosser measures such as criminality unqualified by developmental considerations. Recognizing that genetic effects must be considered in developmental perspective, we consider in some detail a conceptual aid—the reaction range—that helps us illustrate the complexity of the issues involved.

Explicating the Reaction Range for Antisocial Behavior

As long as we avoid interpreting them too literally, some heuristic concepts can hint at the complexities of development while we await more process-oriented understandings at levels ranging from the molecular to the social. The concept that we want to emphasize is the *norm of reaction*, which was introduced into genetics by Dobzhansky and into psychology by Gottesman (1963) as the *reaction range* of behavior. One virtue of the reaction range is that it can be given quantitative meaning. For instance, the largest differences observed between identical twins with varying experiences would be a lower-bound estimate of the reaction range for a given genotype. Figure 1.1 shows the latest incarnation of this heuristic concept—the *reaction surface* of a behavior (Turkheimer & Gottesman, 1991).

The hypothetical reaction surface in the lower left portion of Figure 1.1 shows risk of antisocial behavior on the vertical axis. The other two axes are the relevant genotype and the environment. The diagram does

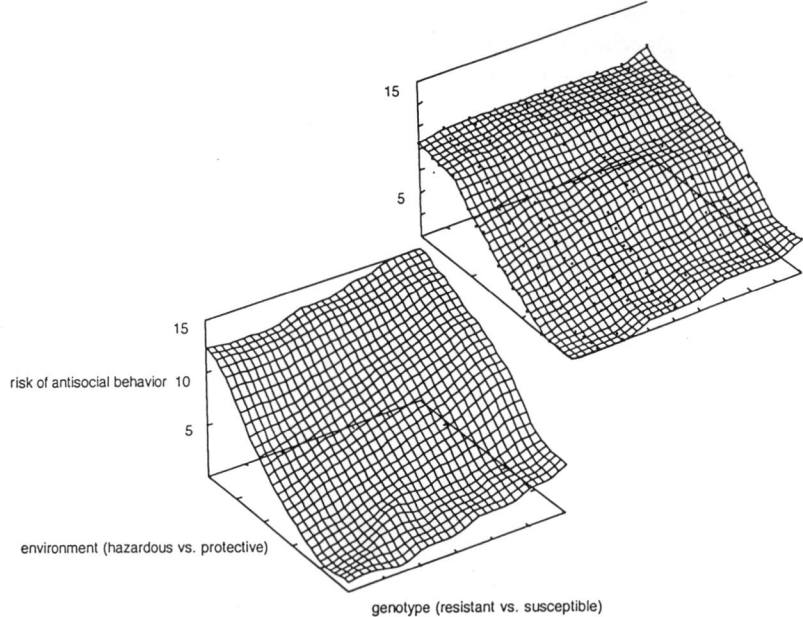

Figure 1.1 Hypothetical reaction surface for antisocial behavior.

not embody assumptions about the frequency distributions of either genotypes or environments. The shape of the surface suggests nonlinear effects, which are meant to hint at the complexity of underlying processes. The left side of the environmental axis represents experiences conducive to the development of antisocial behavior; these experiences are designated "hazardous" in the figure. The right side of the environmental axis is labeled "protective." The shape of the surface implies that very hazardous environments—perhaps approached in some inner-city areas—result in a very high probability of antisocial behavior in most young males, regardless of genotype. Also, the low level (with resistant

Table 1.2. Candidates for Components of the Reaction Range: Behavioral Tendencies Reflective of Genotype and Social Processes Reflective of Environment

Behavioral Tendencies That May Be Genetically Influenced	Social Processes That May Facilitate Development of Various Forms of Undercontrolled Behavioral Patterns
Impulse control	Processes that retard moral development
Need for stimulation	Processes that hinder perspective taking and empathy
Activity level	Processes that lead to overattribution of hostility
Anxiety proneness	Escalating cycles of coercive family interaction
Frustration tolerance	Peer group processes

genotypes) and gradual rise (with increasing genetic susceptibility) of antisocial behavior in protective environments (seen along the front edge of the surface) suggest that the predisposing effects of susceptible genotypes can be countered by experience. The effect of genotype is apparent at all levels of environment, but there is a multiplicative effect when both genotype and environment are high. This interaction can be discerned in the steeper slope of the surface as the environment becomes more hazardous and the genotype becomes more susceptible. Of course, the shape of the reaction surface is simply illustrative, supported by some data but largely hypothetical. Even a diagram as complex as the lower left portion of Figure 1.1 is inadequate to portray all the processes involved. One inadequacy of the diagram is the incomplete representation of individual development. Individual possibilities are represented in the sense that there is a wide—but variable—range of phenotypic outcomes for each genotype (Gottesman, 1974). However, the lower left portion of the diagram only represents those outcomes at one time, and we have already reviewed evidence that genotypic effects on antisocial behavior can change with age. Thus, a second reaction surface—a developmental transformation of the first—is depicted in the upper right portion of Figure 1.1. This second surface is reduced in elevation, an effect that is clearest at the highest levels of the antisocial behavior axis. Optimally, we would show reaction surfaces like those in Figure 1.1 for all developmental periods, with different shapes depending on the age when antisocial behavior is assessed.

Another complication of our depiction of the reaction surface is that the causes of antisocial behavior are undoubtedly heterogeneous, and the single axis for genotype does not capture this heterogeneity. The same is true for environmental causes of antisocial behavior. We can be more concrete by hypothesizing that two relevant genotypes might be, for example, those for frustration tolerance or delay of gratification. One relevant environment might be, for example, processes that lead to overattribution of hostility to others—a kind of paranoid ethnocentrism. When we begin to specify the processes more concretely, we see immediately that a multivariate family of reaction surfaces that incorporates genetically independent, risk-increasing traits and potentially independent environmental risk factors is needed. Table 1.2 outlines some specific traits and social factors that are implicated in the genesis of antisocial behavior. How these traits and social factors interact developmentally is a task for the next stage of developmental behavioral genetic research.

The potential fruitfulness of this next stage of research is suggested by recent research in Oregon. Patterson, Crosby, and Vuchinich (1992), committed to a social learning approach, tried to predict early police arrest (by age 16) using multiple regression models that focused on three sets of variables: societal, parenting, and individual differences in an "antisocial trait" (a latent disposition and therefore of great interest to geneticists). Their sample included 206 boys from high-delinquency neighborhoods followed from age 10. Family interactional variables were posited to be indirectly related to early arrests, whereas trait scores at age 10 were directly related. Indicators for the variables were carefully selected with the trait score derived from information from parent, peer, teacher, and target child. A couple of boys had been arrested by age 6, but the rate grew to 39% by age 16 and these boys became the focus of attention. The model tested by these social learning theorists showed that the parenting practices related to discipline and monitoring were unrelated to age at first arrest; that social disadvantage was virtually unrelated; but that the antisocial trait score was an impressive predictor—an increase of one standard deviation for this construct measured at age 10 increased the risk of early arrest by 20%. The investigators did not raise questions about the antecedents of the individual differences in the trait; we would not have been surprised to have poor parenting or bad peers be significant predictors, but we would then press such results with the same kinds of questions—what are the antecedents of poor parenting, and what are the antecedents of susceptibility to peer aggression modeling? These findings lend themselves to interpretation within the multivariate, reaction surface framework outlined above.

Returning to Table 1.2, we could expand the conceptualization by adding putative biological markers of genotypes related to antisocial behavior. An overview of the field (Reiss & Roth, 1993) suggests some candidates: steroid hormones (testosterone and glucocorticoids) and their receptors; some functions of the neurotransmitters dopamine, norepinephrine, serotonin, acetylcholine, GABA, and various neuropeptides; and neurophysiological measures such as measures of EEG abnormalities and limbic system dysfunction (see also Raine & Venables, 1988). In a study of 29 children and adolescents with disruptive behavior disorders (attention deficit hyperactivity disorder, CD, and oppositional defiant disorder), lower levels of a serotonin metabolite (5-hydroxyindoleacetic acid) were detected in cerebrospinal fluid, as compared to children with obsessive-compulsive disorder (Kruesi et al., 1990). In a follow-up of the same sample, the same lower 5-hydroxyindoleacetic acid concentration levels predicted more physical aggression (Kruesi et al., 1992). The genetic aspects of these and other candidate markers should be studied with the tools of behavioral genetics in both probands and their relatives and in the general population at all age levels.

Unfortunately, as psychologists working with human behavior, we cannot observe reaction surfaces directly. So we turn to the reflection of genetic processes in the similarity of kin. The disciplines that encompass the tools and concepts for such investigation are quantitative genetics and genetic epidemiology. In this chapter, we shall not explicate the logic, assumptions, and validity evidence for family, twin, and adoption studies, nor shall we discuss the virtues and liabilities of concepts such as heritability (the proportion of observed variation associated with genetic differences), genetic variance, shared and nonshared environment, and gene–environment covariance (see standard texts such as Falconer, 1990, or Plomin, DeFries, & McClearn, 1989; the developmental behavior-genetic text by Plomin (1986); or review chapters written for developmentalists such as Goldsmith, 1988; Gottesman, 1974; and Simonoff, McGuffin, & Gottesman, 1994).

Statistical Genetic Evidence Concerning Childhood Antisocial Behaviors and Their Possible Antecedents

We shall review some of the statistical evidence in a way that is intended to be sensitive to both developmental and clinical concerns. Much of our discussion depends on results from studies of identical and fraternal twins. The logic and assumptions of the classic twin method have been reviewed and researched extensively. The most important assumptions are that twins are representative of the general population and that identical twins are not treated more similarly than fraternals in ways that make them more alike for the behavioral pattern under investigation. Various caveats related to these assumptions are covered in standard references (e.g., Plomin, DeFries, & McClearn, 1989). Heritability, the proportion of observed variation associated with variation in genetic effects, can be simply estimated as twice the difference between identical and fraternal twins. Although the possibility threatens the validity of our assumptions in the twin method, even identical twins without somatic mutations can vary in the temporal pattern of expression of their genotypes, as mentioned above. Thus, some differences between identical twins could be due to differential gene activation. It is unclear—and perhaps irrelevant—whether this should be considered an environmental or a genetic effect. Of course, we must also avoid the tendency to attribute any change in behavior or any new behavioral pattern to the activation of genes. One tenet of systems theory is that systems, once functioning, can undergo state changes in the absence of external forces (Gunnar & Thelen, 1989).

Misunderstandings

Before reviewing the results of relevant twin studies, we must discuss some common misunderstandings about genetics. The major fallacy that characterizes many psychologists' views of genetic risk factors is thinking of genetics as a static rather than a dynamic influence on development. This basic fallacy is manifest in several ways. For instance, we often read that genetic factors influencing some feature of antisocial behavior are "already in place at the time of birth." Of course, millions of copies of all genes are already in place at birth and there is one copy at conception, but the genetic factors that influence antisocial behavior are perhaps no more "in place" at birth than are one's parents or social class—that is, they exist as potential influences, but most of their manifestation lies in the future. Another aspect of the basic fallacy is that we tend to think of gene action as a process that occurs early in life, with subsequent changes due to experience. The behavior-genetic data—as well as our knowledge of molecular genetics—indicate otherwise. Consider some results from twin studies of temperament (see Goldsmith, 1989, for a more extensive review of the genetics of temperament). Systematically testing the behavior of neonates in the Louisville Twin Study, Riese (1990) observed that the similarity of identical and fraternal twins was quite comparable. Motoric activity, irritability, resistance to soothing, reactivity, and other objectively observed variables were no more similar for identical than fraternal twins, and thus *no* genetic effects on individual variability were implicated. This null finding does not mean that genes are unimportant for neonatal behavioral reactions because the genes that operate during the neonatal period might be invariant in the species. Analyses of older infants and young children in the Louisville Twin Study and in other studies suggest moderate heritability of the dimensions of activity and negative affectivity that are not heritable in the neonatal period. For example, Matheny (1989) rated emotional reactivity in a series of laboratory tasks at ages 9, 12, 18, 24, and 30 months. Fraternal twin similarity was indexed by correlations of about .30 throughout this time span, while identical twin correlations rose from the .50's during the first year of life to the .80's later. The influence of genetic factors is apparent.

Several interpretations of the difference between the neonatal and late infancy findings are possible, but the findings at least demonstrate that genetic *effects* are not a given at the beginning of life. Surely genes can act early in life to create some structures, such as receptors for transmitters in a particular tissue, and the functioning of these structures can later be involved in behavioral dispositions such as poor impulse control in emotionally laden situations. However, just as surely, gene action at any point in the life span can modify a physical structure or set in motion a physiological process that affects behavioral dispositions. It is clear that heritability established at one developmental period does not necessarily generalize to earlier or later periods.

Genetics of Development

Let us consider a more complex question. How are developmental processes represented in quantitative genetics? The approach has been empirical: collect longitudinal data and fit models. We ask if observed longitudinal data, structured by degree of genetic kinship and rearing family, will fit various models for initial status, change, stability, and outcome. The approach can be illustrated by Goldsmith and McArdle's (1995) structural modeling analyses of temperamental reactivity and persistence. In brief, composite measures of reactivity and persistence were formed from psychologists' ratings in the context of mental testing at ages 4 and 7 years. Both temperamental composites were moderately heritable at both ages. Of more interest to developmentalists, practically all the stability, in both reactivity and persistence, was associated with stable genetic differences. For reactivity, there was evidence that some new genetic variance at age 7 had arisen since age 4; in contrast, all the genetic variance in persistence at age 7 had been captured by the age 4 analysis. Thus, a statistical picture consistent with dynamic genetic action over time emerges from this analysis. This dynamic view of twin development is being implemented more fully in an ongoing twin study of emotional development that involves assessments spaced by weeks and months rather than years (Goldsmith, Winebarger, Losoya, & Bowden, 1992). This approach has yielded developmental functions (McCall, 1979) for twins over the first 3 years of life for various emotion systems. Thus, it is possible to study the effect of genetic variation on times of onset, rates of acceleration of growth, and other temporal qualities of behavior.

Let us now return to infant and childhood temperament and consider some components that might be related to later antisocial behavior. Findings of moderate genetic influence are common, as shown by data in Table 1.3 on temperament reported by parents (Goldsmith, 1993a, plus additional data).

The upper portion of Table 1.3 shows twin similarity for Activity Level and Distress to Limitations (Anger) scales of Rothbart's (1981) Infant Behavior Questionnaire (IBQ). These two correlated IBQ scales seem most closely related to undercontrolled behavior. Greater identical than fraternal twin similarity for the Activity Level and Anger scales is apparent for these maternal ratings. Other twin studies tend to support this finding of moderate heritability for parental report temperament questionnaire scales (e.g., Buss & Plomin, 1984; Cohen, Dibble, & Grawe, 1977; Cyphers, Phillips, Fulker, & Mrazek, 1990).

Temperament shows some interesting patterns of twin resemblance after infancy. In the lower portion of Table 1.3, we provide parental report twin data on toddler temperament assessed via maternal report on Goldsmith's (in press) Toddler Temperament Assessment Questionnaire (TBAQ) for the same two dimensions as in the infant data. The results for same-sex twins imply heritabilities in the .40's. We note that opposite-sex similarity is somewhat lower than same-sex fraternal similarity for Activity Level, as it was for IBQ Distress to Limitations (Anger) in the infant data. Because the activity and anger scales are correlated in both questionnaires, these two sex differences might represent the same underlying phenomenon. Preliminary data on preschooler-age twins

Table 1.3. Twin Similarity for Normal Range Variation in Temperamental Dimensions Possibly Relevant to the Risk of Externalizing Behavioral Problems[a]

Questionnaire Scales	Identical R	Same-sex Fraternal R	Opposite-sex Fraternal R	Pooled Fraternal R
I Twin Similarity for Selected Scales of Rothbart's Infant Behavior Questionnaire[b]				
Activity level	.55	.37	.33	.35
Distress to limitations (anger proneness)	.65	.39	.12	.25
II Twin Similarity for Selected Scales of Goldsmith's Toddler Behavior Assessment Questionnaire[c]				
Activity level	.72	.51	.14	.40
Anger Proneness	.72	.49	.55	.53

[a] The correlations are adjusted for the effects of age within each of the two groups defined by assessment with the IBQ or TBAQ. Such adjustments typically showed minor differences from the raw correlations.

[b] The number of twin pairs in each group was as follows: identical (80), same-sex fraternal (65), opposite-sex fraternal (66), pooled fraternal (131).

[c] The number of twin pairs in each group was as follows: identical (88), same-sex fraternal (62), opposite-sex fraternal (34), pooled fraternal (96).

suggest that these two characteristics remain heritable in maternal report data, and that potentially relevant features of personality not easily measured in infants and toddlers, such as impulsivity and inhibitory control, are heritable as well (Gottesman & Goldsmith, 1994).

The data suggesting moderate heritability are not limited to parental report. Let us consider only three examples of objective measures of temperament/emotionality in twin research. Consider infant activity level: Using motion recorders, Saudino and Eaton (1991) observed an identical R of .76, which was significantly higher than the fraternal R of .56 for a composite actometer score. Consider infant fearfulness: Goldsmith and Campos (1986) showed a similar moderate genetic effect on the tendency to express fearful facial and vocal affect during the standardized approach of a stranger and on the visual cliff, both in the laboratory. Consider the domain of empathy: Zahn-Waxler, Robinson, and Emde (1992) recorded twins' reactions to stimulated distress by the mother and an experimenter during home visits at ages 14 and 20 months. They found evidence for modest genetic input to the emotional facets of empathetic responses (empathic concern and being unresponsive or indifferent). Positive, but sometimes equivocal, genetic evidence has emerged for laboratory and observational measures of temperament in other studies as well (e.g., Braungart, Plomin, DeFries, & Fulker, 1992; Emde et al., 1992; Goldsmith & Gottesman, 1981; Matheny, 1989).

Our developing knowledge of gene regulation suggests a couple of caveats about twin studies. Positive evidence of heritability does not necessarily imply that gene action underlies the physiology directly relevant to a temperamental behavioral pattern (Goldsmith, 1988; Tooby & Cosmides, 1990). Direct evidence for this must await molecular genetic studies of temperament. A second caveat is that although identical twins have identical *structural* genotypes (with the exception of somatic mutations), the active set of genes can differ. That is, identical twins can have different *functional* or *effective* genotypes in some cases (Gottesman & Bertelsen, 1989). The point is made well by the five known cases of identical female twins (and one case of identical female triplets) who are *discordant* for X chromosome traits (red-green color blindness, Duchenne muscular dystrophy, and fragile X syndrome), due to the normal twins having most of the mutation-bearing X chromosomes inactivated and the affected twin having the opposite pattern (Jorgensen et al., 1992).

The study of identical twins is also uniquely capable of revealing genetic effects due to interaction of nonallelic genes (epistasis) or to behavioral characteristics that emerge from particular constellations of heritable traits in certain individuals. Lykken, McGue, Tellegen, and Bouchard (1992) refer to this process as *emergenesis* and suggest that it is widespread. Note that an emergenic characteristic requires a configuration of genetic elements that will typically break apart during transmission to offspring; thus emergenic characteristics will characterize identical twins but will not be seen to run in families, as additive genetic traits do. Unfortunately, detecting epistasis is difficult, partly due to power considerations and partly because psychometric scaling effects can mimic epistasis.

Genetic Architecture of Childhood Behavioral Disorders Related to Antisocial Behavior

We consider next two behavioral disorders of childhood that involve an externalizing or disruptive quality. One is CD and the other is hyperactivity, often diagnosed as attention deficit hyperactivity disorder (ADHD), which we consider first. Of course, changing diagnostic issues cloud any review of the literature. The diagnostic progression in this country was from minimal brain dysfunction to hyperactivity to attention deficit disorder (ADD), the latter not always distinguished from ADHD. The mix of impulsivity, motoric activity, and inattention probably differs from one sample to another. Other complications are frequent comorbidity with CD or oppositional defiant disorder (ODD) in children (Caron & Rutter, 1991) and a different set of diagnostic entities for older persons (e.g., ASP), including sanctioned behavior (criminality) and sometimes sanctioned behavior (alcoholism). The best twin study of hyperactivity is Goodman and Stevenson's (1989) examination of a large sample of English 13-year-olds. Among many analyses, they examined twin concordance for a broad but clinically relevant definition of hyperactivity that identified a subsample of 39 identical and 54 same-sex fraternal probands. The identical concordance rate was 51% and the fraternal rate was 33%. Derived heritability was 64%, but this figure may be somewhat inflated by rating biases. In this sample, adverse family factors were only weakly related to hyperactivity.

Several earlier studies suggested that ASP is overrepresented in parents of hyperactive children (Cantwell, 1972; Morrison, 1980; Weiss, Hechtman, Milroy, & Perlman, 1985). For example, Morrison (1980) found that 11% of hyperactive children had at least one parent with ASP or Briquet's syndrome compared to 2% in a group of matched psychiatric controls. Hyperactivity or ADD was also overrepresented in the brothers of probands in two family studies (Biederman et al., 1986; Welner, Welner, Stewart, Palkes, & Wish, 1977). Another study showed full sibling concordance to be greater than half-sibling concordance (Safer, 1973).

Data supporting genetic hypotheses have also emerged from adoption designs, including studies of hyperactivity and ASP in male biological relatives of hyperactive adoptees (Cantwell, 1975; Morrison & Stewart, 1973). A recent adoption study in Toronto revealed greater ADD symptomatology in the biological parents and siblings of adopted ADD probands than in the adoptive families or biological families of normal controls (Deutsch & Swanson, 1985). A complication of adoption studies is the replicated finding that adoptees per se are at higher risk than base rate for ADD. This finding perhaps partially reflects transmission of genetic liability from unwed mothers who give up their children for adoption (or from their sexual partners); these mothers often show excessive sociopathic tendencies (Horn, Green, Carney, & Erickson, 1975).

Studies have not always distinguished between the purely activity-related aspects of the syndrome and problematic conduct (Lilienfeld & Waldman, 1990). In fact, Stewart, deBlois & Cummings (1980) studied the families of ADHD children without CD, CD children, and a control group. The excess of ASP and alcoholism was confined to fathers in the CD group. Lahey, Piacentini, McBurnett, Stone, Hartdagen, and Hynd (1988), using updated diagnostic criteria and assessment instruments, determined the prevalences of ASP in the parents of outpatients with only CD, with only ADHD, and with both disorders. Their data show that the association with parental ASP is limited to the presence of CD in the offspring: For example, 38% of fathers of CD children were diagnosed with ASP (8% had a prison sentence), as were 52% (50% with prison sentences) of the fathers of CD+ADHD children, while only 6% of the fathers of ADHD-only children and 17% of the control fathers were diagnosed with ASP; parallel findings were reported for the mothers. Thus, the only excess disorder in parents of ADHD children may be ADHD itself.

Another recent family study (Biederman et al., 1986; 1987) also suggests that aggressive behavior in ADHD is an important variable that predicts familial aggregation of antisocial psychopathology. Taxonomy and familiality were clarified further when Faraone, Biederman, Keenan, and Tsuang (1991) stratified their 73 ADD probands as a function of comorbid diagnoses of CD, OPD (oppositional defiant), and no antisocial diagnoses before studying the parents and siblings (psychiatric and normal control families were also studied). ADD appeared to be transmitted separately from the antisocial behaviors. ASP and childhood OPD were observed in excess only among the parents and sibs of ADD probands with comorbid antisocial patterns.

Twin studies of childhood externalizing problems are important for interpretation of the family studies. Unfortunately, systematic studies of twin probands diagnosed with CD are difficult to undertake. However, two studies have employed Achenbach's Child Behavior Checklist (CBCL) with samples of relatively unselected twins. Ghodsian-Carpey and Baker (1987), studying 3- to 7-year olds, observed identical and fraternal correlations of .78 and .31, respectively, for the CBCL Aggression scale. Studying somewhat older children (mean age = 11 years), Edelbrock, Rende, Plomin, and Thompson (1992) estimated identical twin intraclass correlations of .72 and .75 for the Delinquent and Aggressive Behavior Problem scales, respectively; the corresponding fraternal correlations were .55 and .45. Thus, both studies suggest substantial heritability of early antisocial behavior, viewed as a continuous trait. A series of model-fitting analyses on these same CBCL Delinquent and Aggression scales for 10- to 15-year-old international adoptees in the Netherlands also showed moderate to high genetic effects and modest shared environmental effects, with a tendency for heritability to be higher in males (Van den Oord, Boomsma, & Verhulst, 1994). These same Dutch investigators also analyzed CBCL scores in a large sample (about 1,200 pairs) of 3-year-old twins. The Delinquency scale was obviously not employed for these young subjects, but the parental ratings on the CBCL Aggression scale again showed moderate heritabilities (Van Den Oord, Verhulst, Boomsma, & Orlebeke, 1994). Other behavior-genetic studies of aggression were reviewed by Plomin, Nitz, and Rowe (1990). Thus, a very recent body of diverse evidence converges to suggest that genetic differences contribute importantly to variation in externalizing behaviors in childhood, at least as perceived by caregivers.

Prediction of Childhood Externalizing and Conduct Problems from Early Temperament

The general issue of forecasting childhood behavioral problems from infant temperament has not been the subject of many extensive or systematic studies, perhaps because the methodological problems are daunting. Bates (1989) reviewed the available evidence. Here we review studies that focus on prediction of externalizing behavior. In Bates' longitudinal study in Indiana (Bates, Bayles, Bennett, Ridge, & Brown, 1991), parental reports of frequent and intense displays of negative affect, even from age 6 months, predicted more negative control interactions at age 2 years; that is, these children elicited (or were subjected to) more prohibitions, warnings, and physical restraint than other children. Sequences of the child engaging in a troubling behavior, the mother seeking to control it, the child resisting the attempt at control, and so on were more common than for other children. This description reminds us of Patterson's description of the coercive interaction styles that characterize older aggressive children's interactions. Bates followed up his normal sample at ages 3, 5, 6, 7, and 8 years, with difficult temperament consistently predicting externalizing behavior problems. As in many studies of this issue, interpretation must be tempered because temperament was primarily assessed via parental informants and the sample was essentially a normal range group, opening the possibility that some putative predictions from temperament to disorder are simply manifestations of temperament at different ages in different contexts.

When the interval between temperament assessment and assessment of disorder is lengthy, inferences become somewhat more secure. A recent report concerning over 800 children from New Zealand is instructive. Caspi, Henry, McGee, Moffitt, and Silva [in press] assessed children at 3, 5, 7, 9, 11, 13, and 15 years of age, with fascinating predictions from temperament rated by examiners during a testing session at ages 3 and 5 to behavior problems rated by parents and teachers at ages 9 and 11 and by parents only at ages 13 and 15. A temperamental factor at ages 3 and 5 called Lack of Control loaded on ratings of impulsivity, inattention, and negativity. It predicted antisocial behavior ratings at 9 and 11, with average correlations of .25 for boys and .15 for girls. The same Lack of Control factor also predicted conduct disorder rated (using a different instrument) at 13 and 15; boys' correlations averaged .16 and girls' .12. Although these correlations are not high, they are noteworthy given the large and representative sample, the methodologically independent nature of the assessment of early temperament and later behavioral problems, and the obvious consideration that influences other than temperament affect the development of behavioral problems.

Continuity and Persistence of Antisocial Behavioral Patterns

At least since the time of Olweus's (1979) review, we have known that aggressive behavior in boys, variously measured, is quite stable across the childhood and adolescent years. Subsequent studies confirm the finding, with correlations of about .50 over various 3-year intervals (Moscowitz, Schwartzman, & Ledingham, 1985). A fatalistic view is certainly not encouraged, however, because the plasticity of aggressive behaviors is also demonstrable in studies involving early intervention (Pepler & Rubin, 1991), and there is evidence that aggressive behavior can be inhibited in a variety of ways (Lore & Schultz, 1993).

It is important to determine the extent to which infant and early childhood patterns of aggression or "aggressive equivalents" and childhood patterns of attention deficit, hyperactivity, and CD actually are risk factors for adolescent and adult antisocial behaviors, partially indexed by diagnoses or categories from the criminal justice system. The taxonomic systems we use to select our index cases and to classify their biological and adoptive relatives are riddled with so much heterogeneity at each stage of ontogeny that this problem seriously compromises our ability to assess the strength of the roles, if any, to be accorded genetic factors as risk factors. Although we do not treat taxonomic problems here, we do note the important differences between *ICD* 10 (World Health Organization, 1992) and both DSM-III-R and the options proposed for "disruptive behavior and attention deficit disorders" in DSM-IV. The latter reminds one of Babel, where the inhabitants lost the ability to speak intelligibly to one another as punishment for their presumptuous effort to build a tower reaching to heaven: Clinicians and researchers are praying for a return of intelligibility via field trials and empiricism. Let us return briefly to the lessons from the ECA work with ASP. It is clear that CD is not a good predictor of who will get a diagnosis of ASP; only 27% of boys and 21% of girls with three or more CD symptoms by age 15 go on to fulfill the criteria for ASP. The results suggest, though, that CD should be treated dimensionally rather than categorically, as six or more CD behaviors lead to 49% of boys and 33% girls going on to develop ASP. It was also shown that in this large representative population, delinquency before age 15, defined as arrested or sent to juvenile court, forecast ASP in only 29% of white males and 19% of black males and in only 13% of young females. Looking back from adulthood to adolescence reveals that, just as delinquency is not isomorphic with either CD or ASP, criminality (841 felons or persons arrested twice or more for other than traffic offenses were in the ECA sample) is not isomorphic with ASP, thereby confirming less rigorous studies in the literature. Only 40% of male criminals and 18% of female criminals qualified for an ASP diagnosis, and only 55% of male ASPs and 17% of female ASPs were now or ever criminals (628 ECA diagnoses of ASP were detected). Farrington, Loeber, and Van Kammen (1990) shed further light on these issues by their follow-up to age 25 of the 411 8- or 9-year-old boys in the study of delinquent development in working-class London. They used multi-informant indicators of hyperactivity impulsivity-attention deficit (HIA) and conduct problems (CP) by age 10 to predict juvenile and adult convictions. Other variables examined included socioeconomic status, parenting, and having a criminal parent. Some 20% of boys were convicted by age 17, and a further 13% were convicted by age 25; 23 males (5.6%) were termed "chronics" with six or more convictions, and they accounted for half of all convictions by the 136 offenders. High HIA and high CP each predicted juvenile convictions (with phi values of .23 and .29); having a criminal parent predicted just as well (phi, .23). Within the group of all offenders, HIA and CP predicted chronic cases (phi values of .16 each); however, HIA did not predict adult convictions, while CP did, with a phi of .14.

It is likely that insofar as genetic risk factors may be important, they are most relevant to a subset of individuals manifesting chronic antisocial behaviors with nonacute onsets. That such a subgroup exists has been repeatedly shown in the literature (Farrington et al., 1990). In both of the Philadelphia cohorts studied by Wolfgang and colleagues (Tracy, Wolfgang, & Figlio, 1990), chronic recidivists stood out from the crowd, as did the fact that 46% of delinquents stopped after their first offense and a further 35% desisted after a second offense. In the 1945 birth cohort, 6% overall and 18% of the broad category of delinquents perpetrated 61% of the UCR Index crimes (71% of homicides, 73% of rapes, 82% of robberies, and 69% of aggravated assaults). In the 1958 birth cohort of boys, 8% were qualified as chronic recidivists, again defined as five or more offenses before their 18th birthday. By race, the chronic recidivists comprised 3% of whites and 11% of blacks, and together they perpetrated 68% of the Index crimes. Two caveats are recorded at this point: The race difference mentioned here is merely descriptive and cannot be taken as an indicator of the relevance of any kind of genetic explanation; and questions about between-group differences in this area cannot be answered with available methods. Violence per se is an area of inquiry that is separable to a large degree from the broader concern with antisocial behaviors, especially if divided into acute and chronic violence; it is only the latter aspect that interests us in this chapter (Carey, 1992a; Elliott, 1992; Reiss & Roth, 1993).

Genetic Considerations in Juvenile and Adult Antisocial Behaviors

The stage has now been set for a review of evidence that bears on the question of the degree to which the observed familiality of adolescent and adult antisocial behaviors merits a partial genetic explanation. We will divide the evidence into traits assessed with psychometric devices such as personality questionnaires with twins and with adoptive families. We will concentrate on those scales that are associated with valid indicators of aggression, such as the Pd scale of the MMPI and the Aggression scale of the Multidimensional Personality Questionnaire

(MPQ). The Pd scale of the MMPI comprises items that reliably distinguish psychopaths from various comparison groups. The Aggression scale of the MPQ comprises rationally selected and factor analytically verified items concerning physical acts of aggression, retaliation, and vengefulness. We will also consider evidence from twin and adoption studies of antisocial personality, criminality, and adjudicated delinquency. Table 1.4 shows the correlational patterns for MMPI Pd and MPQ Aggression in various samples of identical (MZ) and fraternal (DZ) twins reared together (T) and apart (A). The consistent, replicable results should convince even the skeptical that the psychometric indicators of behavioral traits related to antisocial behavior are familial and that the familiality is under important genetic influence. Various estimates of the heritability derived from doubling the difference between MZ and DZ correlations or from MZA correlations alone are substantial. The McGue, Bacon, and Lykken (1993) study of normal twins at both ages 20 and 30, reported in Table 1.4, adds the information that the level of MPQ Aggression decreases with maturity and that the genetic effect on individual differences decreases with maturity, but that the heritability values are substantial at both ages ($>.60$).

Table 1.5 shows that the adoption strategy applied to MMPI Pd scale scores confirms the picture from twin strategies and defends against the possible criticism of twin studies that similarity within pairs is due to modeling or imitation. In the Texas Adoption Project (Willerman, Loehlin, & Horn, 1992), MMPIs were available at similar ages for both the birth mothers and their adoptees. For the MMPI Pd scale, adoptees showed virtually no resemblance to their genetically unrelated siblings, fathers, or mothers. However, significant correlational similarity to the birth mothers was apparent. Doubling this correlation of .27 between birth mothers and adoptees generates a heritability of .54, quite close to those of .64 that we calculated from the MZA results and of .60 that we calculated from twice the difference between MZA and the small sample of DZA.

An extension of these results for antisocial traits is provided by clever analogizing to selection studies for quantitative traits in mammalian behavioral genetics. Willerman et al. (1992) divided the Texas Adoption Project adoptees into groups selected for high ($N = 21$) versus low ($N = 51$) Pd scale scores (≥ 70 vs. ≤ 55). The high-Pd adoptees had more elevated profiles in general, with particularly notable peaks on the Sc (schizophrenia) and Ma (hypomania) scales. Then these authors calculated the mean MMPI profiles of the two groups of biological mothers (at roughly the same age) of these selected adoptees. The biological mothers of the high-Pd adoptees had significantly higher elevations on all except two of the clinical scales than did the biological mothers of the low-Pd adoptees. The difference between the two groups for mothers was particularly salient for high Pd scores, and the biological mothers of the high-Pd adoptees showed secondary elevations on the Sc and Pa

Table 1.4. Quantitative Genetic Evidence for Self-reported Antisocial Traits: Twins Reared Together and Apart

I. Studies of Twins on a Single Occasion

Study	Measure	R_{MZ}	R_{DZ}	N pairs (MZ, DZ)
Gottesman (1963), Minnesota	MMPI Pd	.57	.18	34, 34
Gottesman (1965), Boston	MMPI Pd	.46	.25	80, 68
Rose (1988)[a] Indiana	MMPI Pd	.47	.23	228, 182
Gottesman, Carey, and Bouchard (1984), Minnesota Reared apart	MMPI Pd	.64	.34	51, 25
McCartney, Harris, and Bernieri (1990) (meta-analysis)	8 aggression scales	.49	.28	
Tellegen, Lykken, Bouchard, Wilcox, Segal, and Rich (1988), Minnesota				
Reared apart	MPQ Aggression	.46	.06	44, 27
Reared together	MPQ Aggression	.43	.14	217, 114

II. McGue et al. (1993) Twin Correlations for MPQ Personality Traits Conceptually Related to Antisocial Behavior: Longitudinal Analyses

	MPQ Traits		
	Agression	Control	Alienation
MZ similarity at age 20	.61	.53	.54
DZ similarity at age 20	−.09	.01	.39
MZ similarity at age 30	.58	.44	.41
DZ similarity at age 30	−.14	.19	.30
Individual stability from age 20 to 30	.54	.55	.40
MZ cross-twin, cross-time similarity	.43	.45	.27
DZ cross-twin, cross-time similarity	−.11	.01	.06

[a]These MMPI Pd data were provided by personal communication from R. J. Rose, based on the same sample and assessment procedure described in Rose (1988).

(paranoia) scales. The authors interpret this profile as suggesting "antisocial characteristics, including failure to internalize societal standards of conduct, immaturity, narcissism, and self-indulgence. Such individuals tend to deny serious psychological problems, attributing blame to others . . . [and there is also a suggestion of] anger, sullenness, a tendency to deny responsibility, and a moderate degree of confusion"

Table 1.5. Quantitative Genetic Evidence for Self-reported Antisocial Traits: An Adoption Study

Relatives	Measure	Correlation	N (pairs)
Birth mother X Adopted child (similar ages)	MMPI Pd	.27	133
Adopted sib X Adopted child	MMPI Pd	.02	44
Adoptive father X Adoptive child	MMPI Pd	.07	180
Adoptive mother X Adoptive child	MMPI Pd	.01	177

Source: Adapted from Loehlin, Willerman, and Horn (1985).

(Willerman et al., 1992, p. 522). The similarity of the high-Pd adoptee profiles to those of their biological mothers, and the similarity of both to the numerous textbook and folk wisdom descriptions of sociopathic persons, support the notion that some kind of antisocial trait configuration (perhaps involving the Sc scale) is transmitted. The same inference was suggested by data in Tables 1.4 and 1.5. To counter any inclination to attribute the proband adoptees' antisocial profiles to the rearing effects of their adoptive families, Willerman et al. (1992) provided MMPI profiles for the mothers who reared them. These profiles were remarkably similar for rearing mothers of both high- and low-Pd adoptees, and they suggested normal and healthy functioning, thus confirming the wisdom of the adoption agencies in selecting these mothers for child rearing.

A further suggestion that the Pd, Sc-configured MMPI profile may indicate a personological risk factor for antisocial behaviors comes from work still in progress (Gottesman and Hanson) involving the long-term follow-up of the Hathaway-Monachesi sample of Minnesota ninth graders to determine who among them became mentally disordered (Hanson, Gottesman, & Heston, 1990), or alcoholic, or who got in trouble with the criminal justice system in Minnesota. We were able to find 29 boys tested at age 15 who went on to become relatively serious offenders, with stays at Redwing Training School and often at St. Cloud Reformatory by their mid-20s. We selected classroom controls with clean records, thereby matching on many other variables. Our initial impression is that the profiles at age 15 of these two groups suggest that the "sociopathic" configuration distinguishes the actual antisocial persons from their controls, at least quantitatively. In this form, the information is not useful for making individual predictions of future ASP from the age 15 MMPIs, but it does suggest that there is some signal despite the noise in these data.

With the foregoing as a bridge to the clinically relevant evidence that implicates genetic factors in the liability to develop antisocial behaviors, we can examine the twin studies of so-called juvenile delinquency that have been conducted with varying degrees of sophistication (Walters, 1992; Walters & White, 1989) since 1941 in North America, Japan, and England, concentrating on males. The upper portion of Table 1.6 shows little to support a genetic interpretation of the results of the four available delinquency studies: The pairwise concordance rates for MZ and DZ twins are both very high and resemble the results obtained from studying such infectious diseases as measles or mumps. Consider also that the base rates of delinquency, variously defined, are 33% or so (in Philadelphia) and in some neighborhoods are close to 100%. Rowe (1983) conducted a twin study with normal adolescent twins who were asked to self-report antisocial acts. This methodology clearly addresses a somewhat different question from the studies in Table 1.6, which began with delinquent probands. Both identical and fraternal twins showed substantial similarity, with reasonable evidence for both additive genetic and shared environmental factors. Twins in this study reported that they engaged jointly in antisocial acts, a phenomenon that is perhaps biasing in some analyses (see Carey, 1992b, for a detailed treatment of this issue). Note that, according to Moffitt's (1993) distinction—discussed above—life course persistent antisocial individuals should have heritable input to their behavior. However, their small number in the pool of juvenile delinquents means that any genetic effect might not be discernible. Not only would the number of genetically rooted cases be dwarfed by the nongenetic ones, but the fraternal twin of a life-course-persistent individual might well be an adolescent-limited case.

A contrasting picture from the delinquency data is obtained from the

Table 1.6. Clinical Genetic Evidence for Antisocial Behaviors: Twin Concordance[a]

I Twin Studies of Juvenile Delinquency: Four Studies Pooled from North America, Japan and England

Twin Groups	Pairwise Concordance Rate
Identical (55 pairs)	90.9% (s.e. = 3.9%)
Fraternal (30 pairs)	73.3% (s.e. = 8.1%)

II Twin Studies of Adult Criminality: Seven Studies Pooled from Germany, North America, Japan, Norway, and Denmark

Twin Groups	Pairwise Concordance Rate
Identical (229 pairs)	51.5% (s.e. = 3.3%)
Fraternal (316 pairs)	23.1% (s.e. = 2.4%)

[a]Data from male twins only.

pooled studies of criminality, largely felony offenses, from seven studies conducted in North America, Germany, Japan, Norway, and Denmark since 1931, again concentrating on males (female twin felons are rare; see Gottesman, Carey, & Hanson, 1983; see also the lower portion of Table 1.6). Differences in concordance rates such as those shown in the lower portion of Table 1.6 when contrasted to base rates of 10% or so in the general adult male population, generate heritabilities of the liability to the antisocial behaviors embodied in the penal codes of these countries that are quite close to those generated by the personality trait scores for the MMPI Pd and MPQ Aggression scales.

Details of the largest twin study of criminality in the literature are provided in Table 1.7 for both sexes and for all three kinds of twin pairs. The more appropriate probandwise rates can be reported (McGue, 1992), as well as the tetrachoric correlation coefficients of liability (Cloninger & Gottesman, 1987); the liability to felony offenses in these Danish twins born around the turn of the century and followed to 1980 through various national registers is equally heritable in the two sexes, about .54, with substantial shared environmental influences, $c^2 = .20$ (see Baker, Mack, Moffitt, & Mednick, 1989, for an elegant analysis of this issue in Danish adoptees). In this country, with very few crimes of violence compared with the United States, we calculated the heritability separately for recidivist property crime only versus violent crimes against persons: The former was .76 and the latter was .50, a nonsignificant difference that is nevertheless in the expected direction for environmentally triggered assaults (Carey, 1992a).

Twin data on criminality, absent adoption data, are on thin ice. Fortunately, the Danish adoption studies of criminality were being conducted simultaneously, and with the same data registers, as the twin studies (Hutchings & Mednick, 1975; Mednick, Gabrielli, & Hutchings, 1984). The highlights of the important findings are shown in Table 1.8 as a cross-fostering design. The base rate for felony offenses to keep in mind in evaluating the results is about 9% in the general male population. It is clear that adoptees and their biological parents are a higher than average offending population. The adopted-away sons of biological fathers who have violated the penal code commit such offenses at twice the rate of their controls and at almost three times the rate of the general population. There is little ceiling left for any interaction effect for the sons of criminals reared by criminal adoptive fathers.

A more telling analysis of the relationship between recidivistic crime in biological fathers and the risk of recidivistic crime in their adopted-away sons is shown in Table 1.9 as a link to the data reviewed earlier on the role of chronicity and severity as an indicator of genetic liability to antisocial behaviors. When the biological fathers (adoptive fathers are removed in this analysis) have no convictions, 3 percent of their adopted-away sons become chronic offenders with three or more convictions; when the fathers are themselves chronic offenders, 9 percent

Table 1.7. Details of Concordance and Correlation for Registered Criminality in Christiansen's Danish Twin Sample

Zygosity Groups	Pairing Proband-twin	N of Pairs	N of Affected	N Concordant Pairs	Probandwise rates Freq./N	%	Tetrachoric Correlation
MZ	Male–male	365	73	25	50/98	51.0	.74±.07
MZ	Female–female	347	15	3	6/18	33.3	.74±.12
DZ	Male–male	700	146	26	52/172	30.2	.47±.06
DZ	Female–male	2,073	30	7	7/30	23.3	.23±.10
DZ	Male–female	2,073	198	7	7/198	3.5	.23±.10
DZ	Female–female	690	28	2	4/30	13.3	.46±.11

Source: After Cloninger and Gottesman (1987).

Table 1.8. Cross-Fostering Analysis: Percentage of Adoptive Sons Registered for Criminal Law Offenses

Have Adoptive Parents Been Registered	Have Biological Parents Been Registered	
	Yes	No
Yes	24.5 (of 143)	14.7 (of 204)
No	20.0 (of 1,226)	13.5 (of 2,492)

Source: After Mednick et al. (1987).

of the sons are chronic offenders. Such an analysis maximizes the possibility of detecting a genetic signal, as did the MMPI Pd scale analysis in the Texas Adoption Project discussed above.

Implications and Future Directions

The general implications of the concepts and data that we have presented can be stated very simply: The evidence for genetic influences on antisocial behavior outside the adolescent period is strong enough to convince developmentalists that they should make room for genetic concepts not only in their broad theorizing but also in their research programs. Surely the twin fallacies of thinking of genetic effects as deterministic and as being only an early influence on behavior should be put to rest. And the concept of *genetic risk* should be appreciated as much broader than *family history*. On the other hand, the complexity of behavioral transitions, the ubiquity of genetic heterogeneity, and the difficulty of specifying the ways in which genotypes and experiences covary and interact demand that behavioral geneticists be modest in stating the

Table 1.9. Percentage of Chronic Penal Code Offenders, Other Offenders, and Nonregistered among Male Adoptees as a Function of Convictions of Biological Parents

Number of Male Adoptee Convictions	Number of Biological Parent Convictions			
	0	1	2	3 or more
Nonoffenders (no convictions)	.87	.84	.80	.75
Other offenders (one or two convictions)	.10	.12	.15	.17
Chronic offenders (three or more convictions)	.03	.04	.05	.09
Number of adoptees	2,492	547	233	419

Source: After Mednick et al. (1987).

implications of their findings and circumspect in drawing implications for development more generally. We cannot state the causal steps that link genes to dispositions toward antisocial behavior or the causal steps that link these dispositions to actual behavior. However, some initial understandings about these steps have been reviewed in this chapter, and the lack of more complete understandings is, unfortunately, not limited to the role of genetics.

With regard to antisocial behavior more specifically, we must realize that evidence from many quarters needs to be collected and weighed before the taxonomy and etiology are clarified. Consider simply the adult psychiatric disorders that are implicated in discussions of antisocial behavior; antisocial personality disorder, substance abuse disorders of various sorts, various impulse control and adjustment disorders, and somatization disorder (in females). In developmental perspective, we must add CD and oppositional defiant disorder in children and delinquency in its many forms in adolescents. In this chapter, we have only considered a subset of these disorders, but the complexity is nevertheless apparent. It is important to emphasize here that such concepts as age of onset, type of onset (acute vs. insidious), severity, and chronicity are worth importing to the area of antisocial behaviors (DiLalla & Gottesman, 1990, 1991) from the broader field of psychopathology (Gottesman, Shields, & Hanson, 1982) as an aid in clarifying taxonomy and etiological risk factors.

Antisocial behavior is, unfortunately, not the sole province of psychopathology. To varying degrees, antisocial acts also pervade normal behavior; thus a full understanding requires integration of the fields of personality development and psychopathology. This will involve assessing the various relevant dimensions of personality, such as those listed in Table 1.2, in genetic epidemiological studies. Recognition of the need for this integration is now widespread (Nigg & Goldsmith, 1994), and some of the statistical tools needed to execute it are in place (Eaves et al., 1993). Success will require sustained collaborative efforts.

Notes

1. Abridged and adapted from Gottesman, I. I., & Goldsmith, H. H. (1994). Developmental psychopathology of antisocial behavior: Inserting genes into its ontogenesis and epigenesis. In C. A. Nelson (Ed.), *Threats to Optimal Development: Integrating Biological, Psychological, and Social Risk Factors*. Hillsdale, NJ: Lawrence Erlbaum Associates.

2. The information in this section might be considered textbook knowledge of molecular genetics, based on accumulated findings. References to the original empirical reports are not given, with a few exceptions. Texts used in the preparation of this section included the fourth edition of *Molecular Biology of the Gene*, Vols. I and II (Watson, Hopkins, Roberts, Steitz, & Weiner, 1987) and *An Introduction to Molecular Neurobiology* (Zall, 1992).

References

Achenbach, T. M. (1993). Taxonomy and comorbidity of conduct problems: Evidence from empirically based approaches. *Development and Psychopathology, 5*, 51–64.

Baker, L. A., Mack, W., Moffitt, T. E., & Mednick, S. A. (1989). Sex differences in property crime in a Danish adoption cohort. *Behavior Genetics, 19*, 355–370.

Bates, J. E. (1989). Applications of temperament concepts. In G. A. Kohnstamm, J. E. Bates, & M. K. Rothbart (Eds.), *Temperament in childhood* (pp. 111–132). Chichester, U.K.: Wiley.

Bates, J. E., Bayles, K., Bennett, D. S., Ridge, B., & Brown, M. M. (1991). Origins of externalizing behavior problems at eight years of age. In D. J. Pepler & K. H. Rubin (Eds.), *The development and treatment of childhood aggression* (pp. 93–120). Hillsdale, NJ: Erlbaum.

Berkowitz, L. (1993). *Aggression: Its causes, consequences, and control*. Philadelphia: Temple University Press.

Biederman, J., Munir, K., Knee, D., Armentano, M., Autor, S., Waternaux, C., & Tsuang, M. (1987). High rate of affective disorders in probands with attention deficit disorder and in their relatives: A controlled family study. *American Journal of Psychiatry, 144*, 330–333.

Biederman, J., Munir, K., Knee, D., Habelow, W., Armentano, M., Autor, S., Hoge, S. K., & Waternaux, C. (1986). A family study of patients with attention deficit disorder and normal controls. *Journal of Psychiatric Research, 20*, 263–284.

Braungart, J. M., Plomin, R., DeFries, J. C., & Fulker, D. W. (1992). Genetic influence on tester rated infant temperament as assessed by Bayley's Infant Behavior Record: Nonadoptive and adoptive siblings and twins. *Developmental Psychology, 28*, 40–47.

Buss, A. H., & Plomin, R. (1984). *Temperament: Early developing personality traits*. Hillsdale, NJ: Erlbaum.

Cantwell, D. P. (1972). Psychiatric illness in the families of hyperactive children. *Archives of General Psychiatry, 27*, 414–417.

Cantwell, D. P. (1975). Genetic studies of hyperactive children: Psychiatric illness in biologic and adopting parents. In R. R. Fieve, D. Rosenthal, & H. Brill (Eds.), *Genetic research in psychiatry* (pp. 273–280). Baltimore: John Hopkins University Press.

Carey, G. (1992a). *Genetics and violence*. A commissioned paper for the Panel for the Understanding and Control of Violent Behavior. National Academy of Sciences/National Research Council.

Carey, G. (1992b). Twin imitation for antisocial behavior: Implications for genetic and family environment research. *Journal of Abnormal Psychology, 101*, 18–25.

Caron, C., & Rutter, M. (1991). Comorbidity in child psychopathology: Concepts, issues and research strategies. *Journal of Child Psychology and Psychiatry, 32*, 1063–1080.

Caspi, A., Henry, B., McGee, R. O., Moffitt, T. E., & Silva, P. A. (in press). Temperamental origins of child and adolescent behavior problems: From age 3 to age 15. *Child Development*.

Cleckley, H. (1976). *The mask of sanity* (5th ed.). St. Louis: Mosby.

Cloninger, C. R., & Gottesman, I. I. (1987). Genetic and environmental factors in antisocial behavior disorders. In S. A. Mednick, T. E. Moffitt, & S. A. Stack (Eds.), *The causes of crime: New biological approaches* (pp. 92–109). New York: Cambridge University Press.

Cohen, D. J., Dibble, E., & Grawe, J. M. (1977). Fathers' and mothers' perceptions of children's personality. *Archives of General Psychiatry, 34,* 480–487.

Cyphers, L. H., Phillips, K., Fulker, D. W., & Mrazek, D. A. (1990). Twin temperament during the transition from infancy to early childhood. *American Journal of Child and Adolescent Psychiatry, 29,* 392–397.

Deutsch, C. K., & Kinsborne, M. (1990). Genetics and biochemistry in attention deficit disorder. In M. Lewis & S. M. Miller (Eds.), *Handbook of developmental psychopathology* (pp. 93–107). New York: Plenum Press.

Deutsch, C. K., & Swanson, J. M. (1985). An adoptive parents and siblings study of attention deficit disorder (abstract). *Behavior Genetics, 15,* 590–591.

DiLalla, L. F., & Gottesman, I. I. (1990). Heterogeneity of causes for delinquency and criminality: Lifespan perspectives. *Development and Psychopathology 1,* 339–349.

DiLalla, L. F., & Gottesman, I. I. (1991). Biological and genetic contributors to violence: Widom's untold tale. *Psychological Bulletin, 109,* 125–129.

Eaves, L. J., Silberg, J. L., Hewitt, J. K., Rutter, M., Meyer, J. M., Neale, M. C., & Pickles, A. (1993). Analyzing twin resemblance in multi-symptom data: Genetic applications of a latent class model for symptoms of conduct disorder in juvenile boys. *Behavior Genetics, 23,* 5–19.

Edelbrock, C., Rende, R., Plomin, R., & Thompson, L. A. (1992). *Genetic and environmental effects on competence and problem behavior in childhood and early adolescence.* Manuscript under review.

Elliott, F. A. (1992). Violence. The neurologic contribution: An overview. *Archives of Neurology, 49,* 595–603.

Emde, R. N., Plomin, R., Robinson, J., Corley, R., DeFries, J., Fulker, D. W., Reznick, J. S., Campos, J., Kagan, J., & Zahn-Waxler, C. (1992). Temperament, emotion, and cognition at fourteen months: The MacArthur Longitudinal Twin Study. *Child Development, 63,* 1437–1455.

Falconer, D. S. (1990). *Introduction to quantitative genetics* (3rd ed.). New York: Longman.

Faraone, S. V., Biederman, J., Keenan, K., & Tsuang, M. T. (1991). Separation of DSM-III attention deficit disorder and conduct disorder: Evidence from a family-genetic study of American child psychiatric patients. *Psychological Medicine, 21,* 109–121.

Farrington, D., Loeber, R. & Van Kammen, W. B. (1990). Long-term criminal outcomes of hyperactivity-impulsivity-attention deficit and conduct problems in childhood. In L. N. Robins & M. Rutter (Eds.), *Straight and devious pathways from childhood to adulthood* (pp. 62–81). New York: Cambridge University Press.

Ghodsian-Carpey, J., & Baker, L. A. (1987). Genetic and environmental influences on aggression in 4- to 7-year-old twins. *Aggressive Behavior, 13,* 173–186.

Goldsmith, H. H. (1988). Human developmental behavioral genetics: Mapping the effects of genes and environments. *Annals of Child Development, 5,* 187–227.

Goldsmith, H. H. (1989). Behavior-genetic approaches to temperament. In G. A. Kohnstamm, J. E. Bates, & M. K. Rothbart (Eds.), *Temperament in childhood* (pp. 111–132). Chichester, U.K.: Wiley.

Goldsmith, H. H. (1993a). Temperament: Variability in developing emotion systems. In M. Lewis & J. M. Haviland, (Eds.), *Handbook of emotion*. New York: Guilford Press.

Goldsmith, H. H. (in press). Studying temperament via construction of the Toddler Behavior Assessment Questionnaire. *Child Development*.

Goldsmith, H. H., & Campos, J. J. (1986). Fundamental issues in the study of early temperament: The Denver Twin Temperament Study. In M. E. Lamb, A. L. Brown, & B. Rogoff (Eds.), *Advances in developmental psychology* (Vol. 4, pp. 231–283). Hillsdale, NJ: Erlbaum.

Goldsmith, H. H., & Gottesman, I. I. (1981). Origins of variation in behavioral style: A longitudinal study of temperament in young twins. *Child Development*, 52, 91–103.

Goldsmith, H. H., & McArdle, J. J. (1995). *Longitudinal biometric models for twin analyses: The case of childhood temperament*. Manuscript under review.

Goldsmith, H. H., Jaco, K. L., & Elliott, T. K. (1986). Genetic analyses of infant and early childhood temperament characteristics (abstract). *Behavior Genetics*, 16, 620.

Goldsmith, H. H. & Rothbart, M. K. (1991). Contemporary instruments for assessing early temperament by questionnaire and in the laboratory. In J. Strelau & A. Angleitner (Eds.), *Explorations in temperament* (pp. 249–272). New York: Plenum Press.

Goldsmith, H. H., Winebarger, A., Losoya, S., & Bowden, L. (1992). The Genetics of Emotional Ontogeny Project (abstract). *Infant Behavior and Development*, 15, 429.

Goodman, R., & Stevenson, J. (1989). A twin study of hyperactivity—II. The aetiological role of genes, family relationships and perinatal adversity. *Journal of Child Psychology and Psychiatry*, 30 691–709.

Gottesman, I. I. (1963). Heritability of personality: A demonstration. *Psychological Monographs*, 77, 1–21.

Gottesman, I. I. (1965). Personality and natural selection. In S. G. Vandenberg (Ed.), *Methods and goals in human behavior genetics* (pp. 63–80). New York: Academic Press.

Gottesman, I. I. (1974). Developmental genetics and ontogenetic psychology: Overdue detente and propositions from a matchmaker. In A. D. Pick (Ed.), *Minnesota symposia on child psychology* (pp. 55–80). Minneapolis: University of Minnesota Press.

Gottesman, I. I. (1991). *Schizophrenia genesis: The origins of madness*. New York: Freeman.

Gottesman, I. I., & Bertelsen, A. (1989). Confirming unexpressed genotypes for schizophrenia: Risks in the offspring of Fischer's Danish identical and fraternal discordant twins. *Archives of General Psychiatry*, 46, 867–872.

Gottesman, I. I., Carey, G., & Bouchard, T. J. (1984, June). *The Minnesota Multiphasic Personality Inventory of identical twins reared apart*. Paper presented at the Behavior Genetics Association meeting, Bloomington, IN.

Gottesman, I. I., Carey, G., & Hanson, D. R. (1983). Pearls and perils in epigenetic psychopathology. In S. B. Guze, E. J. Earls, & J. E. Barrett (Eds.), *Childhood psychopathology and development* (pp. 286–299). New York: Raven Press.

Gottesman, I. I., & Goldsmith, H. H. (1994). Developmental psychopathology of antisocial behavior: Inserting genes into its ontogenesis and epigenesis. In C. A. Nelson (Ed.), *Threats to optimal development: Integrating biological, psychological, and social risk factors* (pp. 69–104). Hillsdale, NJ: Erlbaum.

Gottesman, I. I., & Shields, J. (with the assistance of Hanson, D. R.). (1982). *Schizophrenia: The epigenetic puzzle.* Cambridge: Cambridge University Press.

Grunstein, M. (1992). Histones as regulators of genes. *Scientific American, 267,* 68–74B.

Gunnar, M. R., & Thelen, E. (1989). (Eds.). *Systems and development* (Vol. 22). *Minnesota symposium on child psychology.* Hillsdale, NJ: Erlbaum.

Hanson, D. R., Gottesman, I. I., & Heston, L. L. (1990). Long range schizophrenia forecasting: Many a slip twixt cup and lip. In J. Rolf, K. Neuchterlein, A. Masten, & D. Cicchetti (Eds.), *Risk and protective factors in the development of psychopathology* (pp. 224–244). New York: Cambridge University Press.

Harpur, T. J., Hare, R. D., & Hakstian, A. R. (1989). Two-factor conceptualization of psychopathy: Construct validity and assessment implications. *Psychological Assessment, 1,* 6–17.

Holliday, R. (1987). The inheritance of epigenetic defects. *Science, 238,* 163–170.

Horn, J. M., Green, M., Carney, R., & Erickson, M. T. (1975). Bias against genetic hypotheses in adoption studies. *Archives of General Psychiatry, 32,* 1365–1367.

Hutchings, B., & Mednick, S. A. (1975). Registered criminality in the adoptive and biological parents of registered male criminal adoptees. In R. R. Fieve, D. Rosenthal, & H. Brill (Eds.), *Genetic research in psychiatry,* (pp. 105–116). Baltimore: Johns Hopkins University Press.

Jorgensen, A. L., Philip, J., Raskind, W. H., Matsushita, M., Christensen, B., Dreyer, V., & Motulsky, A. G. (1992). Different patterns of X inactivation in MZ twins discordant for red-green color-vision deficiency. *American Journal of Human Genetics, 51,* 291–298.

King, R. A., Rotter, J. I., & Motulsky, A. G. (Eds.). (1992). *The genetics of common diseases.* London: Oxford University Press.

Kruesi, M. J. P., Hibbs, E. D., Zahn, Z. P., Keysor, C. S., Hamburger, S., Bartko, J. J., & Rapoport, J. L. (1992). A 2-year prospective follow-up study of children and adolescents with disruptive behavior disorders. *Archives of General Psychiatry, 49,* 429–435.

Kruesi, M. J. P., Rapoport, J. L., Hamburger, S., Hibbs, E., Potter, W. Z., Lenane, M., & Brown, G. L. (1990). Cerebrospinal fluid monoamine metabolites, aggression and impulsivity in disruptive behavior disorders of children and adolescents. *Archives of General Psychiatry, 47,* 419–426.

Lahey, B. B., Piacentini, J. C., McBurnett, K., Stone, P., Hartdage, S., & Hynd, G. (1988). Psychopathology in the parents of children with conduct disorder and hyperactivity. *Journal of the American Academy of Child and Adolescent Psychiatry, 27,* 163–170.

Lilienfield, S. O., & Waldman, I. D. (1990). The relation between childhood attention-deficit hyperactivity disorder and adult antisocial behavior reexamined: The problem of heterogeneity. *Clinical Psychology Review, 10,* 699–725.

Loeber, R. (1982). The stability of antisocial and delinquent child behavior: A review. *Child Development, 53,* 1431–1446.

Loehlin, J. C., Willerman, L., & Horn, J. M. (1985). Personality resemblances in adoptive families when the children are late adolescent or adult. *Journal of Personality and Social Psychology, 48,* 376–392.

Lombroso, C. (1876). *L'uomo delinquante* (cited in S. Hurwitz & K. O. Christiansen (1983). *Criminology.* London: Allen & Unwin).

Lore, R. K., & Schultz, L. A. (1993). Control of human aggression: A comparative perspective. *American Psychologist, 48,* 16–25.

Lykken, D. T., McGue, M., Tellegen, A., & Bouchard, T. J., Jr. (1992). Emergenesis: Genetic traits that may not run in families. *American Psychologist, 47,* 1565–1577.

Matheny, A. P. (1989). Children's behavioral inhibition over age and across situations: Genetic similarity for a trait during change. *Journal of Personality, 57,* 215–226.

McCall, R. B. (1979). Qualitative transitions in behavioral development in the first two years of life. In M. H. Bornstein & W. Kessen (Eds.), *Psychological development in infancy: Image and intention* (pp. 183–224). Hillsdale, NJ: Erlbaum.

McCartney, K., Harris, M. J., & Bernieri, F. (1990). Growing up and growing apart: A developmental meta-analysis of twin studies. *Psychological Bulletin, 107,* 226–237.

McGue, M. (1992). When assessing twin concordance, use the probandwise not the pairwise rate. *Schizophrenia Bulletin, 18,* 171–176.

McGue, M., Bacon, S., & Lykken, D. T. (1993). Personality stability and change in early childhood: A behavioral genetic analysis. *Developmental Psychology, 29,* 96–109.

Mednick, S. A., Gabrielli, W. F., & Hutchings, B. (1984). Genetic influence in criminal convictions: Evidence from an adoption cohort. *Science, 224,* 891–894.

Moffitt, T. E. (1993). Adolescence-limited and life-course-persistent antisocial behavior: A developmental taxonomy. *Psychological Review, 100,* 674–701.

Morrison, J. R. (1980). Adult psychiatric disorders in parents of hyperactive children. *American Journal of Psychiatry, 137,* 825–827.

Morrison, J. R., & Stewart, M. A. (1973). The psychiatric status of the legal families of adopted hyperactive children. *Archives of General Psychiatry, 28,* 888–891.

Moscowitz, D. S., Schwartzman, A. E., & Ledingham, J. E. (1985). Stability and change in aggression and withdrawal in middle childhood and early adolescence. *Journal of Abnormal Psychology, 94,* 30–41.

Nigg, J. T., & Goldsmith, H. H. (1994). Genetics of personality disorders: A joint perspective from personality and psychopathology research. *Psychological Bulletin, 115,* 346–380.

Olweus, D. (1979). Stability of aggressive reaction patterns in males: A review. *Psychological Bulletin, 86,* 852–875.

Patterson, G. R. (1986). Performance models for antisocial boys. *American Psychologist, 41,* 432–444.

Patterson, G. R., Crosby, L., & Vuchinich, S. (1992). Predicting risk for early police arrest. *Journal of Quantitative Criminology, 8,* 335–355.

Pepler, D. J., & Rubin, K. H. (Eds.). (1991). *The development and treatment of childhood aggression.* Hillsdale, NJ: Erlbaum.

Plomin, R. (1986). *Development, genetics, and psychology.* Hillsdale, NJ: Erlbaum.

Plomin, R., DeFries, J. C., & McClearn, G. E. (1989). *Behavioral genetics: A primer* (2nd ed.). New York: Freeman.

Plomin, R, Nitz, K., & Rowe, D. C. (1990). Behavioral genetics and aggressive behavior in childhood. In M. Lewis & S. M. Miller (Eds.), *Handbook of developmental psychopathology* (pp. 119–133). New York: Plenum Press.

Proctor, R. N. (1988). *Racial hygiene: Medicine under the Nazis.* Cambridge, MA: Harvard University Press.

Raine, A., & Venables, P. H. (1988). Antisocial behaviour: Evolution, genetics, neurophysiology, and psychophysiology. In A. Gale & M. Eysenck (Eds.), *Handbook of individual differences: Biological perspectives.* (pp. 287–321). Chichester, UK: Wiley.

Reilly, P. R. (1991). *The surgical solution: A history of involuntary sterilization in the United States.* Baltimore: Johns Hopkins University Press.

Reiss, A. J., & Roth, J. A. (1993). *Understanding and preventing violence.* Washington, DC: National Academy Press.

Resnick, S. M., Gottesman, I. I., & McGue, M. (1993). Sensation seeking in opposite-sex twins: an effect of prenatal hormones? *Behavior Genetics, 23,* 323–329.

Riese, M. L. (1990). Neonatal temperament in monozygotic and dizygotic twin pairs. *Child Development, 61,* 1230–1237.

Robins, L. N., & Regier, D. A. (1991). *Psychiatric disorders in America.* New York: Free Press.

Robins, L. N., Tipp, J., & Przybeck, T. (1991). Antisocial personality. In L. N. Robins & D. A. Regier (Eds.), *Psychiatric disorders in America* (pp. 258–290). New York: Free Press.

Rose, R. J. (1988). Genetic and environmental variance in content dimensions of the MMPI. *Journal of Personality and Social Psychology, 55,* 302–311.

Rothbart, M. K. (1981). Measurement of temperament in infancy. *Child Development, 52,* 569–578.

Rothbart, M. K., Ahadi, S. A., & Hershey, K. L. (1994). Temperament and social behavior in childhood. *Merrill-Palmer Quarterly, 40,* 21–39.

Rowe, D. (1983). Biometrical genetic models of self-reported delinquent behavior: A twin study. *Behavior Genetics, 13,* 473–489.

Safer, D. J. (1973). A familial factor in minimal brain dysfunction. *Behavior Genetics, 3,* 175–186.

Saudino, K. J., & Eaton, W. O. (1991). Infant temperament and genetics: An objective twin study of motor activity level. *Child Development, 62,* 1167–1174.

Scarr, S., & Kidd, K. K. (1983). Developmental behavioral genetics. In M. M. Haith & J. J. Campos (Eds.), *Infancy and developmental psychobiology* (Vol. 2). In P. H. Mussen (Series Ed.), *Handbook of child psychology* (4th ed., pp. 345–433). New York: Wiley.

Smith, L. B., & Thelen, E. (Eds.). (1994). *Dynamic systems in development: Applications.* Cambridge, MA: MIT Press.

Simonoff, E., McGuffin, P., & Gottesman, I. I. (1994). Genetic influences on normal and abnormal development. In M. Rutter, E. Taylor, & L. Hersov (Eds.), *Child and adolescent psychiatry* (3rd ed., pp. 129–151). Oxford: Blackwell.

Stewart, M. A., de Blois, C. S., & Cummings, C. (1980). Psychiatric disorder in the parents of hyperactive boys and those with conduct disorder. *Journal of Child Psychology and Psychiatry, 21,* 283–292.

Tellegen, A., Lykken, D. T., Bouchard, T. J., Jr., Wilcox, K. J., Segal, E. L., & Rich, S. (1988). Personality similarity in twins reared apart and together. *Journal of Personality and Social Psychology, 54,* 1031–1039.

The Huntington's Disease Collaborative Research Group (1993). A novel gene containing a trinucleotide repeat that is expanded and unstable on Huntington's disease chromosomes. *Cell, 72,* 971–983.

Tooby, J., & Cosmides, L. (1990). On the universality of human nature and the uniqueness of the individual: The role of genetics and adaption. *Journal of Personality, 58,* 17–68.

Tracy, P. E., Wolfgang, M. E., & Figlio, R. M. (1990). *Delinquency careers in two birth cohorts.* New York: Plenum Press.

Turkheimer, E., & Gottesman, I. I. (1991). Individual differences and the canalization of behavior. *Developmental Psychology, 27,* 18–22.

U.S. Bureau of the Census (1991). *Statistical abstract of the United States: 1991* (111th ed.). Washington, DC: U.S. Governmental Printing Office.

Van Den Oord, E. J. C. G., Boomsma, D. I., & Verhulst, F. C. (1994). A study of problem behaviors in 10- to 15-year-old biologically related and unrelated international adoptees. *Behavior Genetics, 24,* 193–205.

Van Den Oord, E. J. C. G., Verhulst, F. C., Boomsma, D. I., & Orlebeke, J. F. (1994). A genetic study of maternal and paternal ratings of problem behaviors in three-year-old twins. In E. van den Oord, *A genetic study of problem behaviors in children* (pp. 69–85). Doctoral dissertation, Erasmus Universiteit, Rotterdam.

Walters, G. D. (1992). A meta-analysis of the gene–crime relationship. *Criminology, 30,* 595–613.

Walters, G. D., & White, T. W. (1989). Heredity and crime: Bad genes or bad research? *Criminology, 27,* 455–485.

Watson, J. D., Hopkins, N. H., Roberts, J. W., Steitz, J. A., & Weiner, A. M. (1987). *Molecular biology of the gene* (Vols. I and II) (4th ed.). Menlo Park, CA: Benjamin/Cummings.

Weiss, G., Hechtman, L., Milroy, T., & Perlman, T. (1985). Psychiatric status of hyperactives as adults: A controlled prospective 15-year follow-up of 63 hyperactive children. *Journal of the American Academy of Child Psychiatry, 24,* 211–220.

Welner, Z., Welner, A., Stewart, M., Palkes, H., & Wish, E. (1977). A controlled study of siblings of hyperactive children. *Journal of Mental and Nervous Disease, 165,* 110–117.

White, J. L., Moffitt, T. E., Earls, F., Robins, L., & Silva, P. A. (1990). How early can we tell?: Predictors of childhood conduct disorder and adolescent delinquency. *Criminology, 28,* 507–533.

Willerman, L., Loehlin, J. C., & Horn, J. M. (1992). An adoption and a cross-fostering study of the Minnesota Multiphasic Personality Inventory (MMPI) Psychopathic Deviate scale. *Behavior Genetics, 22,* 515–529.

World Health Organization (1992). *ICD 10.* Geneva: WHO.

Zahn-Waxler, C., Robinson, J. L., & Emde, R. N. (1992). The development of empathy in twins. *Developmental Psychology, 28,* 1038–1047.

Zall, Z. W. (1992). *An introduction to molecular neurobiology.* Sunderland, MA: Sinauer.

2

A Model of Neurobiology–Environment Interaction in Developmental Psychopathology

RICHARD A. DEPUE, PAUL F. COLLINS,
AND MONICA LUCIANA

Although our research background is in psychopathology and, more recently, in the neurobiology of personality (Depue & Collins, in press; Depue, Luciana, Arbisi, Collins, & Leon, 1994; Luciana, Depue, Arbisi, & Leon, 1992) and its implications for personality disorders and for psychopathology (Depue & Collins, in press; Depue & Luciana, in press; Depue & Zald, 1993), we have only recently become interested in developmental psychopathology per se (Collins & Depue, 1992). Our novice status in the area may represent a deficit and a benefit simultaneously. On the negative side, we are no doubt less aware of the complexities and literature in the area of developmental psychopathology than other colleagues contributing to this volume. On the positive side, however, we are relatively free of the constraints always associated with the conceptual frameworks and established "truths" that exist in any area of scientific study. This being the case, we will capitalize on the latter strength in approaching the task laid before us by the editors of this volume: to attempt to define what developmental psychopathology is from our own perspective and research investigations. The editors strongly encouraged us to be critical of current approaches in the area and to be as theoretical as possible where data or methods are lacking, so we have felt free to do both throughout this chapter. Portions of the discussion in this chapter are available in more detailed form in other papers (Collins & Depue, 1992; Depue & Iacono, 1989; Depue & Zald, 1993), so we will focus here particularly on developing a model of neurobiology–environment interaction that is relevant to developmental psychopathology.

The Concept of Developmental Psychopathology

In our experience, there is little agreement on what constitutes a precise definition of developmental psychopathology, that is, what constitutes its unique focus relative to, and its delimitation from, other approaches to psychopathology. Perusal of texts and attendance of conferences in the area seldom lead to an appreciation of what is unique to the content area or methods of developmental psychopathology. One of us (R. A. D.) recalls that several years ago a colleague at the University of Minnesota, Bill Iacono, and I, in the midst of a job search for a developmental psychopathologist, discussed at length our definitional confusion with one of our colleagues, and one of the primary founders of developmental psychopathology as an area, Norman Garmezy. We were never able to arrive at more than a vague notion. All of this is to say that we are not aware of a consistent view of what developmental psychopathology entails. Therefore, we will express our perspective on what we believe it should entail if it is to contribute uniquely to an understanding of psychopathology.

We presume that the descriptor *developmental* constitutes the uniqueness of this approach to psychopathology, so it is the implications of the concept of development that seem critical. For us, the concept of development implies, at the most abstract level, a focus on a *dynamic process* across time and/or developmental periods, rather than on a state or static perspective of a phenomenon. This means that developmental psychopathology, for us, would not be limited to the study of children or adolescents, as is so often assumed. Investigations of the development of an episode or the course of a disorder in adults could be viewed more appropriately, in our opinion, as developmental psychopathology rather than as static studies of, for instance, the clinical picture or pathophysiology of childhood depression.

With the growing awareness of the plasticity of the central nervous system, it is likely that a dynamic process in development reflects the influence of both genetic-biological and environmental factors as they interact over time. It is, of course, just this notion that is inherent in the construct of diathesis-stress as a theoretical framework for understanding psychopathology, and it could be reasonably argued that diathesis-stress theory comprises the intellectual foundation for developmental psychopathology. We would suggest that diathesis-stress notions, while helpful when introduced 30 years ago, are much too limited for current conceptions of developmental psychopathology. Perhaps more useful today is to enhance the limited and poorly defined term *stress* by incorporating the notions of neural plasticity and experience-dependent neural modifications (Greenough, Black, & Wallace, 1987) into the framework. A renaming of this framework would then yield something like a *diathesis–experience-dependent process* model. We will attempt to develop features of this model throughout this chapter.

The difficulties inherent in studying a dynamic process are many, so there may be unique methodological and theoretical considerations in developmental psychopathology. To begin with, the researcher will not simply need to select reliable, valid dependent measures; she or he will first be required to identify the nature of a *process*. This process must encompass the dynamic interplay between variables that contribute to the phenotypic expression of that process. Once such a candidate process has been identified, the types of variables to be studied and the experimental design employed must be sensitive to dynamic variation and temporal influences. Thus, in addition to magnitude as a variable, sensitivity to rate of onset, slope of ascending and descending limbs, and recovery functions will be important response variables of the process. Complexities in studying a dynamic process also arise in relation to two major factors:

1. The relative contribution to phenotype of biological and environmental factors probably varies over time and across developmental periods. This complexity may require (a) a theoretical framework for predicting if and when changes in the relative contributions of variables to the process may occur and (b) finely graded measures with a broad range of measurement that will be sensitive to high variation in a variable over time.
2. The second complexity relates to the possibility that the phenotypic expression of this process may also vary across time and development. This complexity is exemplified by the qualitative change of phenotype across childhood and adolescence that may be observed in temporal lobe epilepsy and perhaps schizophrenia (Weinberger, 1987). In temporal lobe epilepsy, for instance, minor motor irregularities, learning disorders, and bouts of severe headaches may occur early in development, followed by behavioral manifestations accompanying seizures at puberty. A changing phenotype is a major problem in studying normal dynamic processes over several developmental periods, and presumably the complexities are greater in pathological dynamic processes studied over time and development.

At the least, these various complexities require thought as to the basic elements of, or basic functional principles underlying, the psychobiological system in which a dynamic process is being studied. Identification of basic elements or functional principles may allow the derivation of phenotypic measures that, even though varying operationally, are conceptually equivalent across different developmental periods. For instance, the different phenotypic manifestations of the biological diathesis for temporal lobe epilepsy may reflect a basic principle of a low threshold for stimulus elicitation of neural activation in certain temporal lobe structures. This basic principle (a stimulus-intensity–neural activation trade-off function) could then be used as a guide to derive conceptually equivalent operational measures of the principle at different developmental periods. Thus, although the overt clinical picture of temporal lobe epilepsy may appear qualitatively different in different developmental periods, the underlying dynamic process would be assessed in a conceptually equivalent manner over time.

Finally, we do not agree that developmental psychopathology research must be longitudinal in nature, that is, extend beyond more than one developmental period, in order to be informative. Laboratory measurement during one developmental period, or at a specific time during a particular period of disorder, seems a meaningful part of developmental psychopathology. But this is with the stipulation that a dynamic process, which is believed to be relevant to the development of disorder, is being studied. That is, the dynamic process studied is believed to represent a process that is a central feature of the disorder throughout many developmental periods. Hence, a pharmacological challenge protocol may provide substantive information on the integrity of dynamic processes during an episode of disorder, or even during intermorbid periods of disorder, that has implications for the manner in which biological processes react to activation from naturally occurring, environmental sources.

We will attempt to illustrate the above issues and complexities by focusing on one neurobehavioral system described in animals that may underly an important human emotional system (Depue et al., 1994). We will emphasize a dynamic process of the effects of experience on the biology underlying this system, and how this dynamic process may *contribute* to the development of several forms of psychopathology. Although the discussion is based on a substantial animal literature, most of the implications for human psychopathology are speculative. Therefore, the purpose of the discussion is to stimulate a new line of research in developmental psychopathology rather than to integrate what has already been investigated.

Neurobehavioral Systems as Emotional Systems

Neurobehavioral systems represent a newly emerging approach to the study of human behavior. This approach involves an integration of the rapidly expanding database in behavioral neuroscience within the behavioral system framework of ethology. Accordingly, neurobehavioral systems organize a coherent domain of behavior, an underlying circuit of neuroanatomical and neurochemical pathways, and a set of neurobehavioral functions that account for brain–behavior relations within the system. From an evolutionary biology perspective, such systems represent neurobehavioral mechanisms that have evolved as a means of adapting to stimuli that are critical to the organism's survival and to the preservation of the species (Gray, 1973, 1982; MacLean, 1986; Panksepp, 1986; Rolls, 1986). For instance, defensive aggression serves as an adaptive neurobehavioral response to pain and potential destruction, whereas in the case of appetitive behaviors such as sex and feeding, specific olfactory cues serve as critical stimuli in signaling a suitable mate or appropriate food. As is evident in these examples, a system is defined by the class of stimuli that engages it, as well as by the response patterns expressed by it. The importance of delineating such systems at the behavioral level is that they provide a framework for discovering the neurobiological systems that mediate the interface between classes of stimuli and specific response patterns.

Because their development has been closely tied to critical stimulus conditions, behavioral systems may be tightly linked with brain structures responsible for recognition of stimulus significance, on the one hand, and for subsequent activation of effector systems, on the other. Collectively, this group of interrelated brain functions has been referred to as *emotion* or as *emotional evaluation* and *emotional expression*, respectively (LeDoux, 1987). Thus, adaptive behavioral systems, in the broadest sense, are really emotional systems that motivate and, in a general way, guide behavior in response to critical stimuli. Indeed, the term *emotion* derives from the latin verb *emovere:* to move, to push. Emotional systems, then, not only elicit certain patterns of behavior in response to particular stimuli, but also provide a motivational state and a subjective emotional experience that is concordant with the affective nature or reinforcement qualities of critical stimuli (Gray, 1973, 1982; MacLean, 1986; Rolls, 1986). Thus, a particular class of stimuli, the emotion generated, and the behavior patterns expressed all form integral components of a coherent emotional system.

Phenomenology of the Behavioral Facilitation System

The focus of the current discussion concerns an emotional system that has been consistently described in all animals across phylogeny (Hebb, 1949; Schneirla, 1959). It has been described variously as a search system (MacLean, 1986), a foraging-expectancy system (Panksepp, 1986), and an approach system (Fowles, 1980; Gray, 1973; Schneirla, 1959), but we integrate these terms into the *behavioral facilitation system* (*BFS*) (Collins & Depue, 1992; Depue & Collins, in press; Depue & Iacono, 1989; Depue & Zald, 1993). All of these descriptions converge on the same basic theme: The BFS is an emotional system that has evolved to motivate forward locomotion and search behavior as a means of approaching and acquiring rewarding goals.

There is general agreement on the class of stimuli that elicit activity in the BFS. Stimuli that elicit consummatory responses are primary positive reinforcers. These same stimuli, when perceived at a distance, are referred to as *primary incentive stimuli* (Beninger, 1983) because they facilitate forward locomotion, alertness, and a goal-directed approach to the primary positive reinforcer. The occurrence of the latter behavior suggests the existence of an internal state of incentive motivation (an intervening variable), and indeed, activation of this internal state is inherently rewarding in and of itself, as indicated by the occurrence of facilitated behavior in sated animals in the presence of incentive stimuli (Blackburn, Phillips, Jakubovic, & Fibiger, 1989; Stewart, de Wit, & Eikelboom, 1984). The fact that neutral stimuli can become conditioned incentive stimuli is important (Beninger, 1983; Panksepp, 1986; Stewart et al., 1984): The role of the BFS in determining an enduring emotional disposition in humans is most relevant in relation to conditioned stimuli because of the generally predominant influence of symbolic processes in guiding human behavior in the absence of unconditioned stimuli. Conditioned incentive stimuli may also be established by association with cues occurring in close proximity to the *termination* of a primary negative reinforcer, as in active avoidance learning where the conditioned incentive stimuli may be conceived of as cues denoting the reward of safety (Gray, 1973, 1982). Finally, the BFS facilitates (but does not mediate) affective aggression, in which the opportunity to engage serves as a reward (Depue & Spoont, 1986). Under conditions in which reward acquisition is blocked, the BFS may facilitate aggression whose goal is removal of stimuli associated with frustrative nonreward (Depue & Spoont, 1986). It may be that the BFS is elicited in this latter case by expectations of the reward acquisition that will result from removal of the obstacle to reward. Thus, whereas the BFS is activated by a broad array of stimulus contexts, these contexts share in common an incentive-reward component.

All of these stimulus conditions could be viewed as initiating at least three core BFS processes: (1) incentive-reward motivation, (2) forward locomotion as a means of supporting goal acquisition, and (3) cognitive processes, since active goal seeking facilitated by the BFS will increase interaction with, and hence the need to evaluate, the environment.

Dopamine and the Behavioral Facilitation System

These core processes are mediated by activity in two major ascending dopamine (DA) projection systems (Collins & Depue, 1992; Depue & Collins, in press; Depue & Iacono, 1989; Depue et al., 1994): the mesolimbic system, arising from A-10 DA cells in the ventral tegmental area (VTA) of the midbrain and projecting to limbic structures such as the amygdala, hippocampus, and nucleus accumbens (NAS, included here as part of the limbic striatum; Oades & Halladay, 1987); and b) the mesocortical system, also originating in the VTA and projecting to all areas of the cerebral cortex.

A Motivational/Emotional Role for the Mesolimbic System

A vast literature on the behavioral effects of DA manipulations indicates that mesolimbic DA projections play a critical role in motivational and emotional aspects of the BFS (Depue & Collins, in press; Depue et al., 1994; Le Moal & Simon, 1991; Louilot, Taghzouti, Deminiere, Simon, & Le Moal, 1987; Oades, 1985).

Incentive-reward Motivation

Several recent reviews have concluded that DA is integral to rewarding stimulation of mes- and diencephalic loci (Bozarth, 1987; Fibiger & Phillips, 1987; Mason, 1984). Fibiger and Phillips (1987) reported increased DA metabolism during VTA-intracranial self-stimulation (ICSS) confined to the structures of the ventral striatum (NAS, olfactory tubercle, ventromedial caudate) ipsilateral to the stimulating electrode. Furthermore, direct pharmacological evidence for specific DA involvement in VTA-ICSS was obtained in a study employing unilateral microinjections of the DA receptor antagonist spiroperidol into the NAS (Fibiger & Phillips, 1987). In contrast to early studies, microinjections into either the ipsilateral or contralateral prefrontal cortex did not affect VTA-ICSS, suggesting that DA mediation of rewarding VTA stimulation does not require activation of telencephalic DA receptors (Bozarth, 1987; Fibiger & Phillips, 1987).

In a related line of research, psychomotor stimulants, such as amphetamine and cocaine (Koob & Bloom, 1988), have been shown to enhance responding during ICSS (Bozarth, 1987). Moreover, humans, other primates, and rats readily perform operant responses to receive intravenous administrations or microinjections of these drugs (stimulant self-administration or SSA). It has been proposed that the VTA-NAS pathway is activated by all forms of rewarding stimuli, and DA lesioning studies have indicated that an intact VTA-NAS pathway is necessary for the rewarding effects of stimulants. In contrast, lesions of other DA terminal fields or of norepinephrine (NE) projections do not affect SSA (Roberts & Zito, 1987). Furthermore, studies using both ICSS and SSA have revealed an overlapping pattern of regional alterations in subcortical DA metabolism, leading Porrino (1987) to conclude that rewarding self-administration of electrical stimulation and psychomotor stimulants produce converging activation of VTA mesolimbic DA pathways. On the basis of these findings, Stein (1983) concluded that DA activity mediates the incentive type of reward that activates goal acquisition, rather than the gratifying type of reward that terminates behavior.

Initiation of Locomotor Activity (LA)

Processes involved specifically in the *initiation* of LA relate to the facilitation of emotion, because the initiation process is closely tied to affective-motivational input to the motor system (Mogenson, Jones, & Yim, 1980). There is a vast literature demonstrating that DA (but not NE) is the primary neurotransmitter in the initiation of LA (see reviews by Fishman, Feigenbaum, Yanaiz, & Klawans, 1983; Oades, 1985). Importantly, LA initiation occurs via the action of DA and its agonists in the mesolimbic DA system, in general, and in the VTA A10 DA projection to the NAS, in particular (Fishman, et al., 1983). Moreover, the quantity of spontaneous exploratory LA and the magnitude of amphetamine-induced LA are both positively related to the number of DA neurons (including those of the VTA cell group), to the relative density of innervation of DA terminals in target fields, and to DA content in the NAS in inbred mouse strains, effects perhaps related to the proportionately greater synthesis and release of DA in high-DA neuron strains (Fink & Reis, 1981; Oades, 1985; Sved, Baker, & Reis, 1984, 1985). Mesolimbic DA projections to the amygdala and olfactory tubercle do not account in a significant way for initiation of LA (Oades, 1985; Oades, Taghzouti, Rivet, Simon, & Le Moal, 1986).

Threshold of Emotional Responding

DA appears to play a generalized role in facilitating emotional behavior. Mesolimbic DA, in particular, serves to modulate the expression of emotional responding (Depue & Iacono, 1989), particularly under conditions in which a rewarding cue is either present or expected. A relationship also exists between mesolimbic DA activity and, most consistently, affective forms of aggression (for reviews, see Depue & Spoont, 1986; Mason, 1984), the goal of which is removal of sources of frustrative nonreward and other aversive stimuli. Intra-amygdala DA injection has strong facilitatory effects on affective aggression in male rats and shows the habituation of aggressive attacks. Furthermore, DA, but not NE, receptor agonists greatly increase foot shock-induced aggressive attacks in unrestrained male rats and naturally occurring aggressive behavior in rats and monkeys, although large variations exist among animals in relation to social dominance positions. Finally, sensitization for eliciting apomorphine (a DA agonist)-induced aggressiveness in male rats was shown following the supersensitization of DA receptors following withdrawal of chronic neuroleptics. Conversely, acute neuroleptics (DA antagonists), but not NE antagonists, counteract apomorphine and amphetamine (a DA agonist) -elicited aggressive behavior in male rats.

DA projections to the central and medial amygdaloid nuclei, which are particularly dense (Oades & Halladay, 1987), may have significance for facilitation of emotional behavior, since these nuclei serve as the amygdala output centers to brain stem and hypothalamic areas involved in the activation of vocal, gross motor, facial, hormonal, autonomic aspects of emotional behavior (Aggleton & Mishkin, 1986; LeDoux, 1987; MacLean, 1986). DA apparently influences the threshold of output from the amygdala, since increased DA activity specifically in the central nuclei, for instance, facilitates remarkably the expression of aggressive behavior (Depue & Iacono, 1989). Thus, DA activity appears to lower momentarily the threshold for initiation of emotional responding.

Cognitive Processes and the Mesocortical System

To ensure that approach behavior is adaptively related to stimulus events, there will be an increased need to construct maps of extrapersonal space, to identify objects in space, to organize behavioral strategies, and to evaluate the emotional significance of objects and the outcome of those behavioral strategies. These are complex cognitive functions. Their functional integrity requires the passage of information among distinct brain regions that serve as processing nodes in neural networks devoted to cognitive functions (Goldman-Rakic, 1987, 1988; Kosslyn, 1988; Mesulam, 1990; Posner, Petersen, Fox, & Raichle, 1988). Although a role for the BFS in cognitive processes has not been emphasized previously, Plutchik (1980) and Luciana et al. (1992) have argued compellingly that cognitive systems evolved for the purpose of increasing the adaptability of emotional behavior in complex environments.

Mesocortical DA projections, like mesolimbic DA projections, appear to facilitate goal-directed activity, but they facilitate neocortical, rather than limbic, processes that underly cognitive functions necessary for behavioral flexibility. This evidence is reviewed elsewhere (Depue et al., 1994; Luciana et al., 1992; Oades, 1985) but can be summarized briefly. First, behavioral responses to changing environmental contingencies, as in alternation, reversal, and extinction paradigms, and to tasks requiring changes in cognitive behavioral strategies are markedly influenced by DA activity (see reviews by Louilot et al., 1987; Oades, 1985). DA agonists increase and neurochemical DA lesions of the VTA, dorsolateral PFC, and even the NAS reduce or completely abolish alternation, reversal, or extinction behavior. Moreover, VTA treatment with DA agonists and antagonists increases or reduces, respectively, the number of cognitive behavioral strategies used in response to environmental challenges or modifications. These findings provide *indirect* support for the notion that the facilitation of higher-order cognitive functions is dependent on mesocortical DA activity. Second, mesocortical-prefrontal, compared to mesolimbic, neurons also show markedly enhanced DA utilization to perturbations of environmental conditions that require adaptive responding (such as in a range of mild stressors; Thierry, Tassin, & Glowinski, 1984). This effect is particularly strong in the BALB/cj inbred mouse stain, which is characterized by a high VTA DA cell number. From an evolutionary biology perspective, the relatively higher reactivity to variation in environmental challenge by the prefrontal mesocortical, compared to the mesolimbic, DA system seems beneficial: It would be appropriate to encode environmental conditions through cognitive processing *prior* to the facilitation of overt emotional responding. And, third, mesocortical DA projections play a critical role in spatial working memory processes of the principal sulcal (PS) region of the dorsolateral convexity of the prefrontal cortex (DLPFC) (Goldman-Rakic, 1987, 1988). Neurochemical DA lesioning of the DLPFC has produced impaired spatial delayed alternation performance in rhesus monkeys that was almost as severe as that caused by surgical ablation of the same cortical region (Brozoski, Brown, Rosvold, & Goldman, 1979). Furthermore, the impairment was reversed by the DA precursor L-dopa and by the DA receptor agonist apomorphine. Also, pharmacological blockade of D_1 receptors in the PS region of monkeys has been shown to cause a reversible decrement in accuracy and latency on an oculomotor spatial delayed-response (DR) task (Sawaguchi & Goldman-Rakic, 1991), whereas D_2 receptor agonists facilitate a visuospatial DR task (Luciana et al., 1992). Finally DA enhances the activity of PS neurons of monkeys that show activity associated with mnemonic processes, including the spatial visual cue, the delay, and/or the response during DR tasks (Sawaguchi, Matsumura, & Kubota, 1988; 1990a, b).

Conclusion

In general, the BFS, via its underlying VTA DA ascending projection systems, a) facilitates cognitive processes required in the construction and evaluation of the environment, b) provides an interface between neural structures communicating the emotional state of incentive motivation and the initiatory structures of the motor system (Depue & Collins, in press; Mogenson, et al., 1980; Panksepp, 1986), and c) initiates emotional response patterns that support goal acquisition. This is readily seen at the behavioral level (see reviews by Louilot et al., 1987; Oades, 1985), where bilateral neurotoxic lesions of the VTA resulting in DA reductions of 90% or more result in major behavioral deficits associated with incentive motivation, including social interaction, sexual behavior, food hoarding, maternal nursing behavior, acquisition and performance of approach and active avoidance responses (Beninger, 1983), and exploratory activity (Fink & Reis, 1981). These deficits are not simply the result of motor impairment, since these animals can be helped to start moving, after which their motor behavior is relatively normal (Oades, 1985). Moreover, 24-hour spontaneous activity in lesioned animals has often been found not to differ from that of control animals, but these same lesioned animals have a distinctly impaired ability to *initiate* exploratory responses to novelty in the environment (Louilot et al., 1987; Oades, 1985). Taken together, *VTA DA activity facilitates a broad range of emotional and cognitive processes that support goal-directed behavior.*

A Functional Model of VTA Dopamine Response Facilitation

Models of behavioral facilitation, developed for both substantia nigra (SN) DA and VTA DA facilitatory processes, typically define the minimum threshold for response facilitation as being a joint function of two main variables: level of DA postsynaptic receptor activation and amplitude of stimulation (Blackburn et al., 1989; Oades, 1985; Schultz, 1986; White, 1986). Because the two variables determining the minimum threshold for response facilitation are interactive, independent variation in either variable not only modifies the probability of response facilitation, but also simultaneously modifies the value of the other variable that is required to reach a minimum threshold for facilitation. The relationship between these two variables is represented in Figure 2.1 as a trade-off function (White, 1986), whereby the set of values of the two input variables (DA receptor activation and stimulus amplitude) required to produce a minimum threshold value for response facilitation is described. The trade-off function can be thought of as a central nervous system weighting of the external and internal factors that contribute to response facilitation (White, 1986).

There is a large body of evidence demonstrating that modulation of VTA DA projection systems markedly influences the probability of response facilitation. The data reviewed above on the significant influence of DA agonists and antagonists on facilitation of forward locomotion and emotional expression, and on the response-eliciting properties of incentive-reward motivation, clearly demonstrate the effect of VTA DA influence on the threshold for response facilitation. Moreover, enduring alterations of VTA DA functioning, particularly in DA release in the NAS, are associated with long-term or permanent changes in the threshold for response facilitation. For instance, the number of DA neurons in the VTA cell group, the relative density of innervation of DA terminals in target fields, and the DA content in the NAS in inbred mouse strains are positively related to the degree of facilitation of spontaneous exploratory and amphetamine-induced locomotion, effects perhaps related to the proportionately greater synthesis and release of DA in high-DA neuron strains (Fink & Reiss, 1981; Oades, 1985; Sved et al., 1984, 1985). Also, studies on behavioral sensitization, a phenomenon that appears to be dependent on activation of mesolimbic DA systems (e.g., Robinson, Jurson, Bennett, & Bentgen, 1988), are concordant with DA modulation of a response facilitation threshold. That is, repeated, intermittent exposure to DA agonists results in an enduring enhancement of DA release in the NAS that is associated with increased facilitation of locomotor activity and intraspecific aggression to subsequent test doses of DA agonists (Piazza, Deminiere, Le Moal, & Simon, 1989; Robinson et al., 1988).

It also appears to be the case that the effective value of stimulation with respect to the threshold for response facilitation is modified by

[Figure: A model of behavioral facilitation by DA. Axes: Magnitude of Incentive Stimulus (strong to weak) vs Trait Dopamine Receptor Activation (low to high); right axis: Range of Effective Incentive Stimuli (low to high). Diagonal line labeled "Facilitation Threshold" with points A and B, and a serotonin arrow (high/low).]

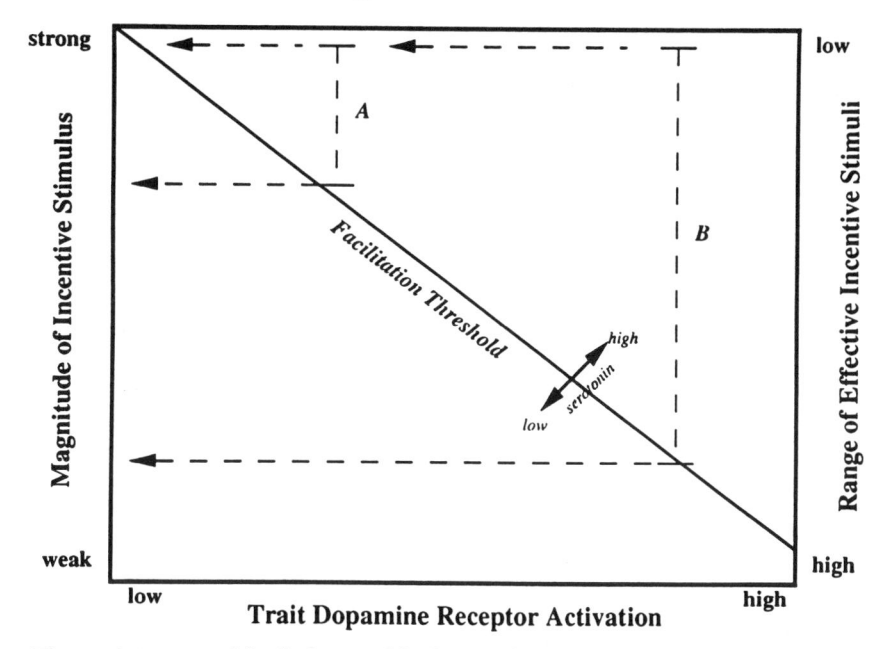

Figure 2.1 A model of behavioral facilitation by DA, represented as a trade-off function between magnitude of incentive stimulation and of trait levels of DA receptor activation. Various combinations of these two variables lead to facilitation of behavior. The differential range of effective (behaviorally facilitating) stimuli for two individuals, one low (A) and one high (B) in DA trait level, is shown on the right vertical axis.

alterations in DA activity. Increased DA activity has been found to enhance responding to conditioned reinforcers (Beninger, 1983; Robbins, 1975), and, in several studies, the facilitatory effects of conditioned stimuli on motor activity have been increased by sensitization-induced enhancement of DA responsiveness to apomorphine and amphetamine. Similarly, the potency of novel stimuli to facilitate locomotor activity appears to be increased in rats and inbred mice strains that have high numbers of VTA DA neurons (Fink & Reiss, 1981; Oades, 1985; Sved et al., 1984, 1985) or high levels of locomotor reactivity to amphetamine (Piazza et al., 1989). Conversely, DA receptor antagonists reduce the effective facilitatory value of conditioned incentive stimuli at doses that do not decrease subsequent consummatory motor patterns (Blackburn et al., 1987, 1989), suggesting that response facilitation under such conditions is achieved by only the most efficacious stimuli.

Thus, it appears that VTA DA activity plays a significant role in determining the probability and magnitude of motor responses in relation to the salience of the eliciting stimuli (Fibiger & Phillips, 1987; White, 1986). As illustrated in Figure 2.1, with increasing levels of VTA DA postsynaptic receptor activation, the effective facilitatory value of stimuli also increases in that an increasing number of weaker stimuli, which may even be normally of subthreshold facilitatory efficacy, now have the capacity to facilitate responses.

A similar trade-off function emerges when the stimulus amplitude component of the model is considered. *Amplitude* is a general construct that incorporates a number of different factors that contribute to the facilitatory efficacy of a stimulus. A large body of data indicates that primary and conditioned incentive stimuli facilitate emotional behavior via elicitation of DA activity and, hence have a strong impact on the minimum threshold for response facilitation. Probably the main determinant of the facilitatory efficacy of incentive stimuli is the magnitude of reward, which by itself appears to show a trade-off function with DA activation. Response facilitation in sated animals is strongly related to sucrose or saccharine concentration in water or food (Blackburn et al., 1989), to the numeric quantity and quality of reward (Nishino, Taketoshi, Muramoto, Fukuda, & Sasaki, 1987; Schultz, 1986), and to the level of enhancement (vs. degradation) of the conditioned stimulus complex (Schultz, 1986). Importantly, magnitude of reward is strongly inversely related (in a trade-off function manner) to the level of DA stimulation required to facilitate a response (Nishino et al., 1987; Schultz, 1986; White, 1986). Other stimulus–reward variables that influence DA neuronal activity are less well researched, but clearly the availability and effort required to obtain the reward are important factors (Nishino et al., 1987; Schultz, 1986).

The trade-off function between amplitude of stimulation and DA postsynaptic receptor activation may be further clarified through an analysis of the manner in which stimulus amplitude is expressed in DA activation patterns. Such an analysis may provide a framework for exploring the dynamic interaction of stimulus characteristics and DA functioning, a point emphasized in our introductory discussion. First, a basic effect of a conditioned incentive stimulus is to increase DA release, an increase that is largest in the NAS and less marked, but clearly evident, in the dorsal striatum of rats (Blackburn et al, 1989). DA release in the NAS is thought to underly the experience of incentive–reward motivation, thus raising the possibility that the magnitude of incentive–reward stimuli is expressed, in part, by the quantity of DA release in the NAS, as indeed was found in monkeys (Nishino et al., 1987). In the latter study, magnitude of reward was expressed by VTA DA neurons as a graded increase in the frequency and duration of neuronal reactivity, a reactivity that was well correlated with behavioral velocity. It is likely, therefore, that DA reactivity was important in motor initiation, and that it was also involved in modulatory regulation of motor acts, such as setting velocity and amplitude (Nishino et al., 1987).

Taken together, the findings of Blackburn et al. on DA activity in the NAS and of Nishino et al. and Schultz on increased neuronal impulse rate appear to converge on a similar response pattern for midbrain DA neurons: that conditioned incentive stimuli, via activation of VTA and SN DA neurons, generate a rapid increase in DA release. This convergence stems from the fact that impulse rate may affect release. As noted by Schultz (1986), when activated by pharmacological or physiological means, the continuous discharge activity of DA neurons rarely exceeds 10–15 impulses/second. However, impulses to conditioned incentive stimuli may be discharged at much higher instantaneous frequencies, as in Schultz's (1986) findings. Since impulse-dependent DA release in the striatum is exponentially related to the frequency of discharges (Schultz, 1986; White, 1986), a rapid onset of bursts of impulses of DA neurons may result in particularly high DA release within a very short time course. Schultz (1986) has suggested that this mechanism for producing phasic increases in DA release may be important in environmental situations requiring rapid reactions to significant stimuli.

A Dynamic Perspective on Response Facilitation

Thus far, we have considered behavioral facilitation within a static temporal framework, that is, an incentive stimulus activates VTA DA neuron firing and, hence, incentive–reward motivation and initiation of forward locomotion via DA release in the NAS and elsewhere. A more ecologically valid perspective on behavioral facilitation is to view the facilitation process not only as a phasic response system to incentive stimuli, but also as a dynamic process that influences the *emotional evaluation* of incentive stimuli. The latter would involve a focus on the interactive dynamics between stimuli and DA activity throughout an episode of environmental engagement.

The incentive–reward motivation hypothesis proposes that incentive stimuli influence the activity of DA neurons, which then facilitate the initiation and vigor of goal-directed approach behavior; the above discussion supports this hypothesis. The trade-off function illustrated in Figure 2.1 would predict, in addition, that as an incentive stimulus enhances DA release in the NAS, the facilitatory efficacy of subsequently encountered incentive stimuli will be increased in relation to the degree of the previous DA enhancement. Thus, after an initial encounter with an incentive stimulus, the facilitatory efficacy of all subsequent incentive stimuli may be altered, and under conditions of strong DA enhancement, perhaps even previously subthreshold, weak conditioned incentive stimuli may facilitate behavior for some period of time. Indeed, there is evidence suggesting that response facilitation by incentive stimuli is dependent on the current state of DA activity (Beninger, 1983; Beninger, Hanson, & Phillips, 1980; Blackburn et al., 1989; Panksepp, 1986; Robbins, 1975). This means that the subjective emotional evaluation of stimuli as incentives may be enhanced and dynamically changing during environmental engagements. An implication of this perspective is that excessively altered states of DA activity, such as extremely high DA activity due to psychomotor stimulant drugs (Depue & Iacono, 1989; Koob & Bloom, 1988), may markedly influence the emotional evaluation (or perceived intensity) of and responsiveness to normally subthreshold, ineffective stimuli and weak incentive stimuli associated with novelty. To the extent that the incentive values of these stimuli are then encoded in an enduring manner in memory, thus becoming valenced central affective representations of the stimulus (Mishkin, 1982), the learning of incentive value may represent one form of state-dependent learning. If this is an accurate view, then state factors, through these mechanisms, may have more enduring influences on the dynamic interaction of stimuli and DA activity than has been previously considered.

The Role of Individual Differences in Response Facilitation Processes

As an emotional system, the BFS is likely subject to sources of variation that ultimately produce stable individual differences in levels of BFS responsivity. Whether genetic or environmental, these influences will converge within the adaptive neural circuitry of the BFS to produce functional variations, such as individual differences in DA responsivity, that correspond to variations in behavioral trait levels. Thus, one approach to understanding the origins of individual differences within the BFS is to examine genetic and environmental processes that shape its underlying neural system.

The trade-off function between stimulus amplitude and DA activation would predict that individual differences in DA reactivity to incentive stimuli may have marked effects on the level of behavioral facilitation. It is surprising, therefore, that with rare exceptions, individual difference factors are seldom considered in theoretical discussions of response facilitation processes (e.g., Piazza et al., 1989, Robinson et al., 1988). Yet their influence would seem to be particularly important when considered together with the above discussion on dynamic aspects of behavioral facilitation. From a dynamic perspective, individual differences in DA responsivity may strongly influence (1) the initial DA response to an incentive stimulus; (2) and, in turn, the facilitatory efficacy of subsequently encountered incentive stimuli during, and the affective experience derived from, environmental engagement; (3) and, thus, the incentive value encoded in central affective representations of incentive stimuli; (4) and, hence, enduring individual differences in the emotional evaluation of incentive stimuli and in the level of behavioral facilitation expressed across reward-related situations.

There are several lines of evidence in animal work that support the importance of individual difference in DA responsiveness for behavioral facilitation processes. Interestingly, the source of the individual variation has been both genetic and experiential, but the effects on behavioral facilitation are qualitatively similar. In terms of genetic sources of variation, an inbred mouse strain that has a significantly increased number of neurons in all DA cell groups examined (including the VTA DA cell group) reliably shows markedly facilitated behavior, including higher levels of spontaneous exploratory locomotion in novel but not frightening environments, and a greater locomotor activity response to amphetamine challenge (Fink & Reiss, 1981; Oades, 1985; Sved et al., 1984, 1985). That this increased behavioral facilitation in high-DA neuron strains is due to DA activation is suggested by a greater density of innervation of DA terminals in target fields, proportionately greater synthesis and release of DA, greater inhibition of prolactin secretion by a DA agonist, and, importantly in terms of locomotor facilitation, an increased DA content in the NAS. Similarly, Piazza et al. (1989) found that rats selected for highly facilitated locomotor activity in novel environments also showed a significantly greater locomotor activity response to a DA agonist (amphetamine) challenge, as well as a more rapid acquisition and a higher final level of self-administration of amphetamine than rats selected for low locomotor responses to novelty.

Experiential factors have also been analyzed in sensitization studies as a between-group source of variation in DA functioning in animals. This work arises from the observations that a) addicts of psychomotor stimulant drugs exhibit marked individual differences in response to their first dose, a response that appears to correlate positively with addiction rate (Piazza et al., 1989); and b) animals exhibit significant individual variation in initial response to amphetamine and, in correlated fashion, in the rate of acquiring self-administration of DA agonists (Piazza et al., 1989; Robinson et al., 1988). Sensitization is most commonly induced by repeated, intermittent doses of a DA agonist, such as amphetamine, but it may also be induced by repeated, intermittent experience of stressful stimuli, although stress has mainly been employed as an effective challenge for demonstrating prior sensitization experience (Robinson et al., 1988). Sensitization is most reliably reflected in enduring increases (over a month or more) in the phasic responses of locomotor activity or DA utilization in the NAS to the experiential factors of amphetamine or stress challenge. Sensitized behavioral facilitation is also observed in response to conditioned incentive stimuli associated with the sensitization environment (Robinson et al., 1988). The fact that sensitization is manifested most strongly in phasic, rather than tonic, reactivity is consistent with a predominant view of the process underlying the phenomenon: that sensitization is related to an increased stimulated *release,* as opposed to receptor, reuptake, or metabolic processes, of DA in the NAS and striatum (Robinson et al., 1988). Thus, sensitization "may represent a type of neuronal plasticity common to other forms of behavioral adaptation" (Robinson et al., 1988, p. 220). Important for our discussion is the finding in rats by Piazza et al. (1989) that individual differences in the acquisition of sensitization and self-administration of DA agonists, and in the response to amphetamine challenge, appear to be linearly related to presensitization variation in locomotor activation by novelty, which is itself strongly related to individual variation in DA release in the NAS (Fink & Reiss, 1981; Oades, 1985; Sved et al., 1984, 1985).

The interaction of genetic and experiential sources of individual differences in BFS processes can be placed within a larger explanatory framework (Collins & Depue, 1992). Within the neurobiology literature, Greenough and colleagues (e.g., Black & Greenough, 1986; Greenough & Black, in press; Greenough, Black, & Wallace, 1987) have proposed a framework in which three basic sources of input to the brain induce functional specialization across a variety of information processing pathways. One of theses sources focuses on *genotype-driven* processes. Such processes influence the basic structure and function of neuron populations in a manner that is largely insensitive to experiential input. One outcome of genotype-driven development is of obvious importance to individual differences in BFS responsivity: variation across individuals in DA neuron number produced during prenatal development. In a 33-year-old man, there are approximately 650,000 cells in the VTA–SN complex, but this number may vary across individuals by as much as ±20,000 cells (Oades & Halliday, 1987). Importantly, as discussed above, variation in DA cell number does correlate with the quantitative expression of DA-dependent behaviors.

A dynamic perspective on BFS processes raises the possibility that genotype-driven variation in DA neuron number may interact with subsequent incentive experiences during development. Greenough and colleagues have described two processes that may be important. First, *experience-expectant* processes involve widespread cortical synapse overproduction, which defines sensitive periods in brain development (O'Kusky & Colonnier, 1982; Rakic, Bourgeois, Eckenhoff, Zecevic, & Goldman-Rakic, 1986). Following overproduction, excess cortical synapses are "pruned back" gradually in response to stimulation provided by the environment. The timing and regional location of experience-expectant synaptic overproduction are determined by genotypic influences, but the functional relations encoded by the preserved synapses vary in response to environmental experience. The basic implication of experience-expectant processes for the development of individual differences in neural system functioning is that the degree of stimulation-rich environment will be encoded in the number of functional synaptic connections within relevant neural system pathways. In relation to the BFS, if experience-expectant development occurs, an individual exposed to a reward-rich environment may establish functional synaptic relations that provide an enhanced capacity to respond to conditioned signals of reward in the future. Interaction between genotype-driven and experience-expectant processes might lead to the prediction that variation in the number of VTA DA neurons will significantly influence the seeking of and responsiveness to potentially rewarding stimuli, and thereby contribute to the variation in development of synaptic connectivity among BFS structures during an experience-expectant sensitive period (see Collins & Depue, 1992, for an application of this interaction to attachment behavior in childhood).

Second, *experience-dependent* processes modify neuronal cytoarchitecture to encode environmental experience that is unique to the individual and thus unpredictable on the basis of phylogeny. In contrast to experience-expectant development, experience-dependent processes involve localized synapse production that is initiated during the encoding of information arising from any significant form of experience, including mentation; thus, the timing and location of experience-dependent modifications are not influenced by genotype. These theoretical notions may be applied to the type of learning and memory that occurs in the BFS. Specifically, associative memories of positive behavioral engagements may be formed within the interconnected neural structures of the BFS (Collins & Depue, 1992), as they encode relations among the perceived incentive value of a stimulus, the incentive motivation experienced, and the rewarding consequences of the behavior expressed. Experience-dependent synaptic processes may mediate this ensemble encoding of emotional evaluation, experience, and expression, and thereby contribute over time to learning-related modifications in BFS responsivity. In this manner, experience-dependent processes may contribute substantially to individual differences in BFS responsivity, but unlike experience-expectant development, changes in neural system responsivity will accrue in a gradual, stepwise manner.

With respect to the role of DA in these processes, the specific patterns of neuronal cytoarchitecture produced by experience-expectant and experience-dependent processes appear to be regulated by local interactions with diffuse neurotransmitter projection systems. Through these mechanisms, activity in neurotransmitter projection systems may regulate patterns of functional synaptic connectivity within the distributed structures of a particular neural system; for example, the activity of VTA DA neurons during development may influence synaptic relations within critical neural pathways of the BFS. Concordant with this notion, recent work suggests that VTA DA activity provides a facilitatory modulation of dendritic branching in the NAS, hippocampus, and neocortex in rats. From this perspective, neurotransmitter projection systems may be viewed as modulators of synaptic structure as well as function, that is, as sources of influence over both cytoarchitectural and chemical encoding of information within neural pathways. In terms of the framework of Greenough and colleagues, neurotransmitter activity likely modulates dendritic outgrowth, synaptogenesis, and synaptic regression during both experience-expectant and experience-dependent development.

The regulation of neuroarchitecture by neurotransmitters may be one avenue for collaboration among all three forms of neurodevelopmental processes. As an illustration, consider the earlier suggestion that individual differences in the number of VTA DA neurons may be viewed as an outcome of genotype-driven processes. If the number of neurons is relatively large, an individual will possess the structural capacity to release high levels of DA at the terminals of VTA projections during experience-expectant sensitive periods. Such an individual would be predisposed to stabilize, and thereby retain, a large number of synaptic contacts within BFS structures, provided that a sufficient level of activity were maintained in the VTA source cells. Although this functional outcome would not occur if environmental experience were reward-impoverished, empirical findings in animal behavior genetics suggest that an individual with a rich genetic endowment of DA neurons would actively explore the environment in search of rewarding stimulation (Fink & Reis, 1981; Sved et al., 1984, 1985). Thus, the likely (but not inevitable) outcome of the sensitive period would be the emergence of a strong functional capacity in the VTA DA system to motivate and guide emotional responses to signals of reward, and this foundation for BFS responsivity would be resistant to large-scale modification in the future. As neural system development proceeds, experience-dependent processes would likely provide incremental increases in the synaptic connectivity within BFS structures, since an enduring predisposition to engage potentially rewarding stimuli would entail frequent demands for additional synapses in the terminal fields of VTA DA projections. By adulthood, the extensive synaptic arborization within BFS circuitry would consistently amplify responses of the VTA DA system to signals of reward, and the individual would exhibit a high and stable level of BFS responsivity.

To the extent that modulatory neurotransmitters form an integral component of neurobehavioral systems, they will incorporate these influences within basic parameters of neural functioning, such as synaptic connectivity, that underlie variations in neurobehavioral traits. With respect to the origins of individual differences in the BFS, trends in the level of BFS responsivity will emerge as individuals experience stimulus contexts that modify earlier neurodevelopmental outcomes involving the structural and functional capacities of the VTA DA projection system. In view of the potential for collaboration among neurodevelopmental processes, it is hypothetically probable that individuals will exhibit progressively discrepant outcome trajectories that ultimately stabilize as trait level variation in BFS responsivity.

Magnitude of Experience-Dependent Effects as a Function of Individual Differences in Dopamine Functional Activity

Whether the magnitude of effect of experience-dependent processes is linearly related to stable individual differences in DA receptor activation has not been fully assessed. Piazza et al. (1989) have clearly shown that animals with higher stable levels of locomotor reactivity to novelty and to amphetamine injection have a greater sensitization response to experiences of repeated pharmacological activation of DA activity than animals with lower stable locomotor levels. But it is not clear that the function relating stable individual differences in DA activity to magnitude of experience-dependent effects is linear. It is possible that the function is curvilinear, so that the greatest effect of experience on biological trait levels is greatest throughout the intermediate range of biological trait values and smallest at the extreme ends of the trait distribution. The reason for this possibility is that DA activation, by rewarding experience, may be diminished (1) at the low end of the activity distribution due to insensitivity of, and floor effects on, DA reactivity (i.e., DA reactivity may be so inherently weak that only the strongest but infrequent rewards will elicit experience-dependent activity, and reward-poor environments cannot reduce reactivity much further); and (2) at the high end of the activity distribution due to ceiling effects on DA reactivity (i.e., DA reactivity may be so inherently strong that a reward-rich environment cannot increase reactivity further). Thus, both extreme groups would be modified only toward the mean of the distribution but not in their respective extreme directions. Indeed, Piazza et al. (1989) demonstrated that an extremely high-trait group in terms of locomotor response to novelty acquired self-administration of amphetamine under typical dose conditions very quickly, as if they were naturally already sensitized, whereas an extremely low-trait group in terms of locomotor response to novelty failed to acquire self-administration of amphetamine under typical dose conditions, a result presumably due to the weak DA response to the normally effective amphetamine dose. Thus, the high-trait group demonstrated a ceiling effect in acquiring self-administration, whereas the low-trait group demonstrated a floor effect in DA reactivity to a typically effective stimulus. Indeed, the low-trait group was able to acquire self-administration only after undergoing sensitization of DA activity via repeated amphetamine injections (or, in terms of our argument, an increase in DA "functional" levels) (Piazza et al., 1989).

Relevance of the BFS Construct to the Structure of Personality

The importance of a neurobehavioral systems perspective for understanding the structure of *human* behavior has not been generally recognized. However, as Gray (1973) and others (Zuckerman, 1983) have cogently argued, behavioral systems that are closely linked to emotional mechanisms are largely unchanged along the pathway of mammalian evolution and, hence, are probably subject to strong genetic influence in our own species. Such systems are likely, therefore, to provide a foundation for individual differences in human emotional patterns (Plutchik, 1980). When viewed from a broad temporal perspective, emotional systems may be conceptualized not simply as phasic response patterns, but rather as emotional dispositions with respect to particular classes of stimuli (Gray, 1973). That is to say, humans may have individual differences in their sensitivity to particular classes of stimuli, and these differences may be evident as trait variation both in subjective emotional experience and in overt patterns of emotional expression. Thus, it is possible to view emotional systems as major structural components of stable patterns of human behavior—or, put simply, of personality (Fowles, 1980; Gray, 1973; Plutchik, 1980; Tellegen & Waller, 1992; Zuckerman, 1983).

It is unclear whether the structure of personality includes a trait that is analogous to the BFS defined in the animal literature. Almost every modern trait theory of personality, however, includes a dimension that encompasses positive affect, desire, incentive motivation, a sense of personal efficacy, and locomotor activity (Digman, 1990; Eysenck, 1981; Eysenck & Eysenck, 1985; Gray, 1973, 1982; Watson & Tellegen, 1985; Zuckerman, 1983). Of importance, desire, or one of its variant expressions, is cited as one of the primary emotions in most classificatory systems of emotion (MacLean, 1986; Plutchik, 1980; Plutchik & Kellerman, 1986), and is one of the few distinct emotional feelings that is reported with direct stimulation of the amygdala in conscious patients and by temporal lobe epileptics during the aura at the beginning of the epileptic storm (MacLean, 1986). Numerous labels have been used for this trait, including *extraversion,* but because of the emotional aspects of the trait as we have defined it, we prefer Tellegen's (1985) term, *positive emotionality* (*PEM*). Our hypothesis is that the PEM trait may represent an underlying dimension of sensitivity to signals of incentive reward, which is concordant with others' views (Fowles, 1980; Gray, 1973; Tellegen, 1985) and, thereby, may be analogous to the BFS construct.

The existence of an animal analog of PEM (i.e., the BFS construct), with a well-researched neurobiology and VTA DA foundation, may further our biological understanding of PEM in humans. The validity of drawing comparisons between the personality construct of PEM and the construct of the BFS developed from animal research may be addressed by assessing similarities in their neurobiology. To this end, we measured the effects of a specific DA D_2 receptor agonist (bromocriptine) on two indices of central DA activity in subjects widely distributed along the dimension of PEM (Depue et al., 1994). Two indices of DA response, prolactin secretion and spontaneous eye blinking, served as a within-study replication of a PEM–DA association, since they are innervated by separate DA projection systems. Findings clearly indicated that PEM (measured via Tellegen's Multidimensional Personality Questionnaire; Tellegen & Waller, 1992) is strongly and positively associated with reactivity of both DA indicators to the DA agonist challenge. Moreover, this correlation is specific to PEM, because the associations of DA indicator reactivity with the two other major superfactors of personality (Negative Emotionality or Neuroticism, and Constraint or Psychoticism) were minimal and nonsignificant.

Implications for Developmental Psychopathology

The typical approach to developmental psychopathology is to start with a disorder and study its developmental processes. The problem here is the same as in all investigations of psychopathology. Disordered samples defined on the basis of phenotype are always heterogeneous with respect to etiology (Depue & Monroe, 1986). Hence, results obtained from disordered individuals on any variable or process, including those with developmental implications, will apply to only certain subgroups of the phenotypically defined population. It is difficult to learn something robust about a disordered, complicated dynamic process when only unknown proportions of the sample have the disordered process in question. Moreover, to study this process in this way over time will only magnify the problem.

The discussion throughout this chapter suggests an alternative approach to thinking about developmental psychopathology that, while speculative at this time, offers a conceptual research strategy worth pursuing. This strategy is a *variant* of that applied to psychopathology by personality psychologists, whereby a normal trait running throughout the population is extended to psychopathological conditions. This has been particularly popular in the domain of personality disorders (Gray, 1973). The variation in this approach that we suggest is as follows: (1) start with a neurobehavioral-emotional system that may underlie major personality traits; (2) define the functional principle of this system; (3) consider the various ways in which this system may serve as the foundation for different forms of disordered behavior: that is, which types of variables of the system could, when reaching certain extreme values or having dysregulated features, result in psychopathology; and (4) consider the dynamic processes that may be involved in the development of disorder in each of these cases. We will apply this approach to the BFS, whose functional principle involves sensitivity to incentive–reward stimuli modulated through the VTA DA mesolimbic projections, and whose purpose is to facilitate engagement in goal-directed behavior.

Implications for the Development of Substance Abuse

Because the basic principle underlying the DA foundation of the BFS is sensitivity to incentive–reward stimuli, one way in which the BFS may serve as the foundation for psychopathology is as a susceptibility to self-administration behavior. That is, the BFS could serve as a liability factor to abuse of substances that are DA agonists. Such substances would naturally have incentive–reward effects, and individuals with extremely reactive DA systems could learn to self-administer the substance in order to create a strong subjective state of incentive reward. Substances that have been implicated as DA agonists that may lead to abuse, or excessive self-administration, include psychostimulant drugs (such as amphetamine and cocaine; Koob & Bloom, 1988); alcohol, whose initial excitatory effects involve the activation of DA release in the NAS (Depue & Iacono, 1989); and, most recently, certain sweet substances, such as chocolate, thereby contributing to obesity.

What is interesting about this class of disorders is that it is nicely congruent with a diathesis–experience-dependent process model: The diathesis in these cases is created by excessively high trait levels of DA reactivity, but this diathesis, by definition, is expressed only if self-administration behavior occurs. Self-administration behavior is a learned behavior that is subject to a process of sensitization with repeated experience, that is, where the self-administration behavior increases dramatically with repeated experience of the same dose of DA agonist. Thus, Piazza et al. (1989) demonstrated that rats could be inbred for extreme trait levels of locomotor reactivity to the incentive condition of novelty. Not only were these two extreme groups substantially different in their locomotor response to a single injection of the DA agonist amphetamine (the high locomotor group responded much more vigorously to amphetamine), but the groups also showed differential sensitization when the same dose of amphetamine was repeatedly injected once a day for several days. The high-locomotor group quickly sensitized, whereas the low-locomotor trait group sensitized much more slowly and achieved a less exaggerated level of sensitization. Moreover, the two groups differed with respect to their acquisition performance of self-administration of amphetamine: The high-locomotor group quickly learned to self-administer amphetamine and showed a sensitization effect over time, whereas the low-locomotor group *did not acquire* self-administration. Put differently, the high-trait group was more susceptible to acquiring self-administration of a DA agonist, whereas the low-trait group apparently experienced such low incentive–reward effects from the self-administration of amphetamine that they were resistant to acquiring this behavior.

Finally, the Piazza et al. study demonstrated the probabilistic nature of diathesis or liability, a probability that was modifiable with experience. After it was demonstrated that the low-locomotor group could not acquire self-administration of amphetamine, the low-trait group was first sensitized to amphetamine and then tested for acquisition of self-administration of amphetamine. Subsequent to the sensitization manipulation, the low-locomotor group was able to acquire self-administration of amphetamine at a comparable rate to the nonsensitized high-locomotor group. The liability or susceptibility to self-administration of a DA agonist had apparently been increased in the low-locomotor group as a function of the experience-dependent processes involved in sensitization of the mesolimbic DA projection system (Piazza et al., 1989).

Implications for the Development of Disorders of Affect

A natural extension of the BFS into the domain of psychopathology emerges on examination of the symptoms associated with disturbances of positive emotionality, that is, affective disorders. When core symptoms of affective disorders are considered, they fall primarily within locomotor, incentive–reward, and mood domains (Depue & Iacono, 1989), suggesting relevance of the BFS construct to affective disorders. Space limitations preclude a full discussion of this issue, and many of the points have been discussed elsewhere (Collins & Depue, 1992; Depue et al., 1987; Depue & Iacono, 1989; Depue & Zald, 1993). However, any BFS framework for disorders of affect probably needs to consider the following conditions.

Extreme BFS State Levels and Affective Disorders

Symptoms of bipolar depression and hypomania/mania appear to represent opposite extremes of normal behavioral dimensions (Depue & Iacono, 1989; Post & Uhde, 1982) that describe extreme states of engagement (and disengagement) with both interpersonal and achievement-related environments. The poles of the core behavioral dimensions may be viewed as the products of extreme variations of the probability that incentive stimuli of all forms—exteroceptive, interoceptive, and cognitive—will initiate or facilitate motor and affective responses. In these terms, the probability of initiating emotional behavior is excessively low in depression and excessively high in hypomania and mania. Both states, then, may be viewed along a single dimension representing the propensity to behavioral and affective reactivity to incentive stimuli. Thus, bipolar disorder may be modeled parsimoniously as an extreme statewise reduction (depression) or increase (hypomania/mania) in the effective value of rewarding stimuli to elicit the primary components of BFS activation: incentive–reward motivation, motor activation, and positive mood. That these extreme states may be related to a disordered aspect of DA functioning seems possible and has been reviewed elsewhere (Depue & Iacono, 1989).

BFS Regulatory Strength as a Trait and Disorders of Affect

Variation across these extreme affective states can occur rapidly within a single episode of bipolar disorder. This fact should be of great interest to developmental psychopathologists, because this natural feature of the course of an episode provides a dynamic process that appears to lie at the heart of the disorder (Depue & Iacono, 1989; Depue et al., 1987). In comparison to normal controls, bipolar patients demonstrate qualitatively similar but quantitatively exaggerated BFS responsivity when functional activity in their DA system is challenged by either enhancement or antagonism (Depue & Iacono, 1989). Together with their naturally occurring fluctuation in extreme states of affective symptomatology, this biological characteristic suggests that bipolar patients possess vulnerability to episodes of extreme engagement or disengagement (dysregulation) of DA-modulated processes within the BFS. This vulnerability suggests a dimension of BFS regulatory strength that may be conceptualized as independent of trait levels of BFS responsivity, since dysregulation of BFS activity may presumably occur at any trait level. With the introduction of a diathetic or dysregulation threshold at the extreme weak end of the regulatory strength dimension, a full neurobehavioral model of bipolar disorder emerges (see also Depue et al., 1987). A diathetic or dysregulation threshold is displayed schematically in Figure 2.2, which also illustrates the manner in which BFS regulatory strength can vary independently while the level of traitwise BFS responsivity remains fixed. It should be emphasized that the positions along the regulatory dimension in Figure 2.2 represent the range of variation across, not within, individuals, that is, the strength of BFS regulation is itself a stable, trait-like characteristic. As Tellegen and Waller (1992) noted, this model may be viewed as incorporating two basic parameters of interindividual measurement with respect to a dimensional personality trait, namely, the relative level and the relative consistency of trait expression (also referred to as *traitedness*). Accordingly, the model departs from the domain of normal personality only in that it includes a dysregulation threshold to account for distinctly pathological trait expression within the BFS system.

If trait level of regulatory strength is conceptualized as a diathesis or liability factor for bipolar disorder, experience-dependent processes may once again influence the probability of developing disorder. This raises the research question for developmental psychopathologists of whether certain types or magnitudes of experience can modify the regulatory strength of a neurobiological system for extended periods of time. If this is possible, then individuals may vary over time in their liability to their relative distance from the diathetic or dysregulation threshold demarcated in Figure 2.2. Post and Uhde (1982) raised a similar notion in reviewing course data in bipolar disorder: The frequency of episodes of both depression and mania increases over time as a function of the number of previous episodes, suggesting that the occurrence of an episode or dysregulation involves some form of experience-dependent process that modifies the functional properties of the neurobiological systems related to bipolar disorder. This might represent, conceptually at least, some form of sensitization of neurobiological systems. This opens

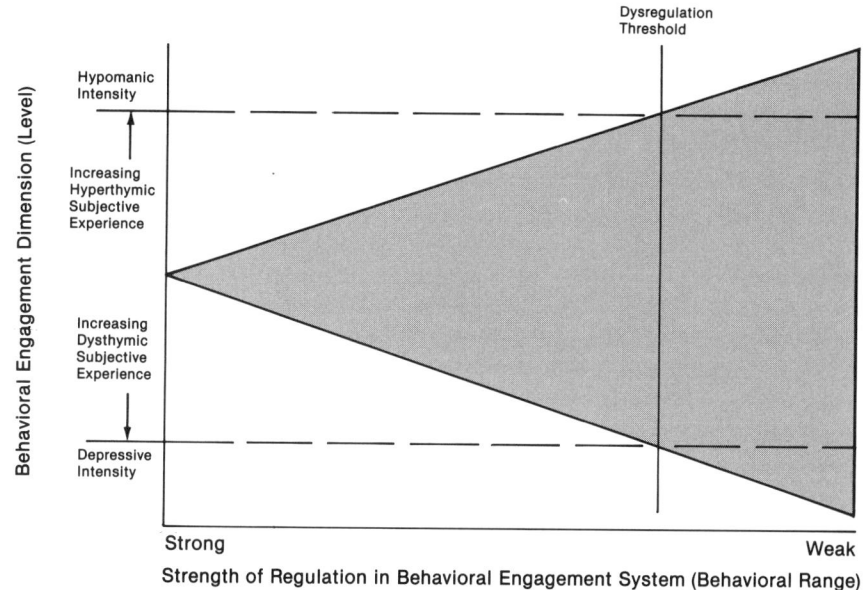

Figure 2.2 Schematic model of bipolar affective disorder. Bipolar disorder is hypothesized to occur at the weak end of a trait dimension of regulatory strength in the BFS. Disorder is hypothesized to occur when BFS regulatory strength is so weak that a dysregulation threshold is approached or surpassed. See text for details. (From Depue et al. 1987.)

the possibility that other forms of strong environmental experiences, such as separations, bereavements, extreme rewarding circumstances (including the use of DA agonists), and stressors, might modify the liability of an individual having the prerequisite diathesis for bipolar disorder.

Extreme BFS Trait *Level and Disorders of Affect*

A MODEL FOR GENE–ENVIRONMENT INTERACTION. Consistent with their classification as characterological entities, it is possible to view some forms of dysthymia and hyperthymia as reflecting levels of DA responsivity that constitute minimum and maximum values, respectively, along a trait dimension underlying positive emotionality in the normal population. One source of extreme BFS trait levels may be genotype driven in terms of the number of neurons per DA cell group formed during the prenatal period (Collins & Depue, 1992). As noted above, this variation can be substantial and strongly influences the range of functional expression of DA-modulated behaviors in rodents.

The possibility of genotypic variation in DA functioning raises the possibility of modeling a dynamic process of genotype–environment interaction, a process that should interest developmental psychopathologists. Consider low (vs. high) VTA DA cell number (which we will refer to as Person B vs. Person A, respectively) as an example that is most relevant to depressive conditions. In experience-expectant emotional periods, the condition of a reduced number of VTA DA cells (i.e., Genotype), and hence density of axon terminals in the NAS, would yield fewer possibilities for synaptogenesis in the NAS in Person B vs. Person A. Thus, even adequate environmental reward experiences at the *expected* time would have a reduced neurological substrate in Person B on which to reinforce synaptic connections in the NAS. In this way, the ontogenic development of sensitivity to reward in Person B may begin in a diminished way; or, put differently, VTA DA–NAS encoded incentive motivation would be less in Person B vs. Person A.

This differential sensitivity to reward could have at least two major effects. First, subsequent rewarding experiences would result in differential incentive motivation via VTA DA–NAS mechanisms and, hence, in a differential approach to or engagement with reward. This condition, in turn, would result in differential engagement-induced DA activation, with Person B experiencing much less DA activation than Person A. Accordingly, the resulting decrease in DA synapse maintenance in the NAS in Person B would exacerbate an already diminished sensitivity to reward. That is, a progressively weakened experience-dependent process of synaptic growth in the NAS might be expected in Person B relative to Person A. By adulthood, this experience-dependent process of diminished DA release to reward, and hence diminished synaptic growth in DA terminal areas, in Person B could result in significantly reduced synaptic arborization within BFS circuitry. Behaviorally, this might appear as a quantitatively low trait position on the dimension of positive emotionality—or, more simply, as a form of characterological depression we refer to here as *trait-related dysthymia*.

A second effect of reduced sensitivity to reward in Person B is that other traits that function *interactively* with DA in modulating emotional behavior would become dominant relative to BFS activity. For instance, a situation that presents signals of both reward and punishment may increasingly evoke constraint and behavioral inhibition rather than exploration and goal acquisition (Gray, 1973). Subjectively, the cumulative effect of reduced reward sensitivity and behavioral inhibition could be a sense of low self-efficacy in obtaining rewarding goals (a form of learned helplessness or passive avoidance?) and a persistent lack of positive affect or persistent dysphoria due to the low frequency of achieved rewards over time.

The above view of the ontogeny of some forms of characterological depression would be modified by the quality and quantity of environmental reward experience, and perhaps by the BFS trait level of caregivers, who are predominantly responsible in the early years for providing reward and for encouraging exploration and goal acquisition.

Importantly, however, the magnitude of effect of the interpersonal environment on the ontogenic development of BFS trait level may vary, depending on the individual's genotype-driven DA trait level (e.g., DA cell number). As discussed above, at extreme ends of a dimension of DA trait level, the effects of environmental reward are likely to be constrained in the direction of the extremity. For instance, in an individual at the low extreme of DA trait level, a reward-rich environment may increase DA function over time, but the effect of a rewarding stimulus will likely always be less in promoting experience-dependent plasticity in the DA system. Moreover, the effects of a reward-poor environment may be diminished due to the already low level of DA reactivity. The opposite effects would be predicted at the high extreme end of the DA trait level. It is in the midrange values of DA cell number that variations in environmental reward would be predicted to have complementary effects in experience-dependent synaptic growth, since rich and poor environments will have equally strong, but opposite, effects. This leads to the intriguing possibility that the effects of variation in rewarding environments on DA, and hence BFS, responsivity may be most powerfully demonstrated within less extreme or midrange values of DA or positive emotionality trait levels.

Implications for the Interaction of Neurobiological Systems in the Development of Psychopathology

It seems likely that any neurobiological system that naturally functions to modify strongly DA projection systems may come to influence substantially the various relations between DA and behavioral disorder proposed above. For instance, there is a large body of animal and human evidence that suggests that serotonin raises a threshold against facilitation of emotional behavior by DA processes (Depue & Spoont, 1986; Depue & Zald, 1993). Human disorders or impulsive and irritable aggression, impulsive suicidal behavior, unstable personality, certain types of alcohol abuse, pharmacological substance abuse, and impulse-related homicide have been repeatedly and strongly associated with indices of low serotonin functioning. The condition of low serotonin may be thought of as a lowering of the threshold for DA facilitation of emotional behavior (Depue & Zald, 1993). It may be that a condition of low serotonin interacts with variation in DA trait functioning, such that the phenotypic features of the low serotonin condition are modified by DA trait level. For example, perhaps variation in the phenotype of the unstable personality disorders associated with low serotonin functioning is, in part, related to variation in DA trait level: For example, antisocial and histrionic personalities may fall on the high end of DA trait functioning, whereas borderline personality with strong depressive features may fall lower on the DA trait dimension. Alternatively, low serotonin functioning may modify the regulatory strength of the BFS DA system: For instance, low serotonin has been associated with an increased frequency of depressive episodes or dysregulatory periods in bipolar disorder (Depue & Zald, 1993).

Future Directions in Developmental Psychopathology

To us, perhaps the main challenge to developmental psychopathologists is the complexities inherent in dynamic processes that represent an interaction between neurobiological systems and environmental influences. Not only do such processes require identification and conceptual elaboration, but they also will likely require a shift in our experimental designs, methods, and measurement variables and instruments. It is difficult enough to assess central nervous system functioning validly and reliably (Depue et al., 1994). This difficulty is exacerbated by the fact that in the area of developmental psychopathology we are also required to think about these biological variables within a temporal framework that incorporates the notions of plasticity and experience-dependent processes. The reward, nevertheless, seems worth the effort in that the developmental approach is likely to be extremely fruitful in illuminating, beyond the mere descriptive discussions of the past 30 years, a diathesis–experience-dependent process model of psychopathology.

Acknowledgment

This work was supported by NIMH Research Grants MH37195 and MH48114 and NIMH Research Training Grant MH 17069 awarded to R. A. Depue.

References

Aggleton, J. P., & Mishkin, M. (1986). The amygdala: Sensory gateway to the emotions. In E. Plutchik & H. Kellerman (Eds.), *Emotion: Theory, research, and experience: Vol. 3. Biological foundations of emotion* (pp. 281–299). New York: Academic Press.

Beninger, R. J. (1983). The role of dopamine in locomotor activity and learning. *Brain Research Reviews, 6,* 173–196.

Beninger, R. J., Hanson, D. R., & Phillips, A. G. (1980). The effects of pipradrol on the acquisition of responding with conditioned reinforcement: A role for sensory preconditioning. *Psychopharmacology, 69,* 235–242.

Black, J. E., & Greenough, W. T. (1986). Induction of pattern in neural structure by experience: Implications for cognitive development. In M. E. Lamb, A. L. Brown, & B. Rogoff (Eds.), *Advances in developmental psychology* (Vol. 4, pp. 1–50). Hillsdale, NJ: Erlbaum.

Blackburn, J. R., Phillips, A. G., & Fibiger, H. C. (1987). Dopamine and preparatory behavior: I. Effects of pimozide. *Behavioral Neuroscience, 101,* 352–360.

Blackburn, J. R., Phillips, A. G., Jakubovic, A., & Fibiger, H. C. (1989). Dopamine and preparatory behavior: II. A neurochemical analysis. *Behavioral Neuroscience. 103,* 15–23.

Bozarth, M. A. (1987). Ventral tegmental reward system. In J. Engel & L. Oreland (Eds.), *Brain Reward Systems and Abuse* (pp. 1–17). New York: Raven Press.

Brozoski, T. J., Brown, R. M., Rosvold, H. E., & Goldman, P. S. (1979). Cognitive deficit caused by regional depletion of dopamine in prefrontal cortex of rhesus monkey. *Science, 205,* 929–931.

Collins, P., & Depue, R. (1992). A neurobehavioral systems approach to developmental psychopathology: Implications for disorders of affect. In D. Cichetti & S. Toth (Eds.), *Developmental psychopathology* (Vol. 4, pp. 29–105). Rochester, NY: University of Rochester Press.

Depue, R. A., & Collins, P. F. (in press). *Neurobehavioral systems, personality, and psychopathology.* New York: Springer-Verlag.

Depue, R. A., & Iacono, W. G. (1989). Neurobehavioral aspects of affective disorders. *Annual Review of Psychology, 40,* 457–492.

Depue, R. A., Krauss, S., & Spoont, M. R. (1987). A two-dimensional threshold model of seasonal bipolar affective disorder. In D. Magnusson & A. Ohman (Eds.), *Psychopathology: An interactional perspective* (pp. 95–123). New York: Academic Press.

Depue, R. A., & Luciana, M. (in press). Neurochemistry of personality traits: Implications for personality disorders. In J. Clarkin (Ed.), *Personality disorders.* New York: Guilford Press.

Depue, R. A., Luciana, M., Arbisi, P., Collins, P. F., & Leon, A. (1994). Relation of agonist-induced dopamine activity to personality. *Journal of Personality & Social Psychology, 67,* 485–498.

Depue, R. A., & Monroe, S. M. (1986). Conceptualization and measurement of human disorders in life stress research: The problem of chronic disturbance. *Psychological Bulletin, 92,* 35–56.

Depue, R. A., & Spoont, M. R. (1986). Conceptualizing a serotonin trait: A behavioral dimension of constraint. *Annals of the New York Academy of Sciences, 487,* 47–62.

Depue, R. A., & Zald, D. (1993). Biological and environmental processes in nonpsychotic psychopathological disorders. In C. Costello (Ed.), *Basic issues in psychopathology.* New York: Guilford Press.

Digman, J. (1990). Personality structure: Emergence of the five-factor model. *Annual Review of Psychology 41,* 417–440.

Eysenck, H. J. (1981). *A model for personality.* New York: Springer-Verlag.

Eysenck, H. J., & Eysenck, M. W. (1985). *Personality and individual differences: A natural science approach.* New York: Plenum Press.

Fibiger, H. C., & Phillips, A. G. (1987). Role of catecholamine transmitters in brain reward systems: Implications for the neurobiology of affect. In J. Engel & L. Oreland (Eds.), *Brain reward systems and abuse* (pp. 61–74). New York: Raven Press.

Fink, J. S., & Reis, D. J. (1981). Genetic variations in midbrain dopamine cell number: Parallel with differences in responses to dopaminergic agonists and in naturalistic behaviors mediated by dopaminergic systems. *Brain Research, 222*, 335–349.

Fink, J. S., & Smith, G. P. (1980). Mesolimbic and mesocortical dopaminergic neurons are necessary for normal exploratory behavior in rats. *Neuroscience Letters, 17,* 61–65.

Fishman, R., Feigenbaum, J., Yanaiz, J., & Klawans, H. (1983). The relative importance of dopamine and norepinephrine in mediating locomotor activity. *Progress in Neurobiology, 20,* 55–88.

Fowles, D. C. (1980). The three arousal model: Implications of Gray's two-factor learning theory for heart rate, electrodermal activity, and psychopathy. *Psychophysiology, 17,* 87–104.

Goldman-Rakic, P. S. (1987). Circuitry of the prefrontal cortex and the regulation of behavior by representational memory. In J. Mountcastle (Ed.), *Handbook of physiology* (Vol, 5, Part 1, Ch. 9), pp. 373–417.

Goldman-Rakic, P. S. (1988). Topography of cognition: Parallel distributed networks in primate association cortex. *Annual Review of Neuroscience, 11,* 137–156.

Gray, J. A. (1973). Causal theories of personality and how to test them. In J. R. Royce (Ed.), *Multivariate analysis and psychological theory* (pp. 409–463). New York: Academic Press.

Gray, J. A. (1982). *The neuropsychology of anxiety.* New York: Oxford Press.

Greenough, W. T., & Black, J. E. (in press). Induction of brain structure by experience: Substrates for cognitive development. In M. R. Gunnar & C. A. Nelson (Eds.), *Minnesota Symposia on Child Psychology* (Vol. 24). Minneapolis: University of Minnesota Press.

Greenough, W. T., Black, J. E., & Wallace, C. S. (1987). Experience and brain development. *Child Development, 58,* 539–559.

Hebb, D. O. (1949). *The organization of behavior.* New York: Wiley.

Koob, G. F., & Bloom, F. E. (1988). Cellular and molecular mechanisms of drug dependence. *Science, 242* 715–723.

Kosslyn, S. M. (1988). Aspects of a cognitive neuroscience of mental imagery. *Science, 240,* 1621–1626.

LeDoux, J. E. (1987). Emotion. In J. Mountcastle (Ed.), *Handbook of physiology* (Vol. 5, Part 1, Ch. 10, pp. 419–429). Washington, DC: American Physiological Society.

Le Moal, M., & Simon, H. (1991). Mesocorticolimbic dopaminergic network: Functional and regulatory roles. *Physiological Reviews, 71,* 155–234.

Louilot, A., Taghzouti, K., Deminiere, J. M., Simon, H., & Le Moal, M. (1987). Dopamine and behavior: Functional and theoretical considerations. In M. Sandler (Ed.), *Neurotransmitter interactions in the basal ganglia* (pp. 193–204). New York: Raven Press.

Luciana, M., Depue, R. A., Arbisi, P., & Leon, A. (1992). Facilitation of working memory in humans by a D_2 dopamine receptor agonist. *Journal of Cognitive Neuroscience, 4,* 58–68.

MacLean, P. D. (1986). Ictal symptoms relating to the nature of affects and their cerebral substrate. In E. Plutchik & H. Kellerman (Eds.), *Emotion: Theory, research, and experience: Vol. 3: Biological foundations of emotion* (pp. 61–90). New York: Academic Press.

Mason, S. T. (1984). *Catecholamines and behavior.* New York: Cambridge University Press.

Mesulam, M. M. (1990). Large-scale neurocognitive networks and distributed processing for attention, language, and memory. *Annals of Neurology, 28,* 597–613.

Mishkin, M. (1982). A memory system in the monkey. *Philosophical Transactions of the Royal Society, B298,* 85–95.

Mogenson, G. J., Jones, D. L., & Yim, C. Y. (1980). From motivation to action: Functional interface between the limbic system and the motor system. *Progress in Neurobiology, 14,* 69–97.

Nishino, H., Taketoshi, O., Muramoto, K., Fukuda, M., & Sasaki, K. (1987). Neuronal activity in the ventral tegmental area (VTA) during motivated bar press feeding in the monkey. *Brain Research, 413,* 302–313.

Oades, R. D. (1985). The role of noradrenaline in tuning and dopamine in switching between signals in the CNS. *Neuroscience and Biobehavioral Reviews, 9,* 261–282.

Oades, R. D., & Halliday, G. M. (1987). Ventral tegmental (A10) system: Neurobiology. 1. Anatomy and connectivity. *Brain Research Reviews, 12,* 117–165.

Oades, R. D., Taghzouti, K., Rivet, J-M., Simon, H., & Le Moal, M. (1986). Locomotor activity in relation to dopamine and noradrenaline in the nucleus accumbens, septal and frontal areas: A 6-hydroxydopamine study. *Neuropsychobiology, 16,* 37–43.

O'Kusky, J., & Colonnier, M. (1982). Postnatal changes in the number of neurons and synapses in the visual cortex (A17) of the macaque monkey. *Journal of Comparative Neurology, 210,* 291–296.

Panksepp, J. (1986). The anatomy of emotions. In E. Plutchik & H. Kellerman (Eds.), *Emotion: Theory, research, and experience: Vol. 3. Biological foundations of emotion* (pp. 91–124). New York: Academic Press.

Piazza, P., Deminiere, Le Moal, M., & Simon, H. (1989). Factors that predict individual vulnerability to amphetamine self-administration. *Science, 245,* 1511–1513.

Plutchik, R. (1980). *Emotion: A psychoevolutionary synthesis.* New York: Harper & Row.

Plutchik, E. & Kellerman, H. (1986). *Emotion: Theory, research, and experience: Vol. 3. Biological Foundations of Emotion.* New York: Academic Press.

Porrino, L. J. (1987). Cerebral metabolic changes associated with activation of reward systems. In J. Engel & L. Oreland (Eds.), *Brain reward systems and abuse* (pp. 51–60). New York: Raven Press.

Posner, M. I., Petersen, S. E., Fox, P. T., & Raichle, M. E. (1988). Localization of cognitive operations in the human brain. *Science, 240,* 1627–1631.

Post, R. M., & Uhde, T. W. (1982). Biological relationships between mania and melancholia. *L'Encephale, 8,* 213–228.

Rakic, P., Bourgeois, J-P., Eckenhoff, M. F., Zecevic, M., & Goldman-Rakic, P. S. (1986). Concurrent overproduction of synapses in diverse regions of primate cerebral cortex. *Science, 232,* 232–234.

Robbins, T. W. (1975). The potentiation of conditioned reinforcement by psychomotor stimulant drugs: A test of Hill's hypothesis. *Psychopharmacology, 45,* 103–114.

Roberts, D. C. S., & Zito, K. A. (1987). Interpretation of lesion effects on stimulant self-administration. In M. A. Bozarth (Ed.), *Methods of assessing the reinforcing properties of abused drugs* (pp. 119–132). New York: Springer-Verlag.

Robinson, T. E., Jurson, P., Bennett, J., & Bentgen, K. (1988). Persistent sensitization of dopamine neurotransmission in ventral striatum (nucleus accumbens) produced by prior experience with (+)-amphetamine: A microdialysis study in freely moving rats. *Brain Research, 462,* 211–222.

Rolls, E. T. (1986). Neural systems involved in emotion in primates. In E. Plutchik & H. Kellerman (Eds.), *Emotion: Theory, research, and experience: Vol. 3. Biological foundations of emotion* (pp. 125–143). New York: Academic Press.

Sawaguchi, T., & Goldman-Rakic, P. S. (1991). D_1 dopamine receptors in prefrontal cortex: Involvement in working memory. *Science, 251,* 947–950.

Sawaguchi, T., Matsumura, M., & Kubota, K. (1988). Dopamine enhances the neuronal activity related to a spatial short-term memory task in the primate prefrontal cortex. *Neuroscience Research, 5,* 465–473.

Sawaguchi, T., Matsumura, M., & Kubota, K. (1990a). Catecholamine effects on neuronal activity related to a delayed response task in monkey prefrontal cortex. *Journal of Neurophysiology, 63,* 1385–1400.

Sawaguchi, T., Matsumura, M., & Kubota, K. (1990b). Effects of dopamine antagonists on neuronal activity related to a delayed response task in monkey prefrontal cortex. *Journal of Neurophysiology, 63,* 1401–1412.

Schneirla, T. (1959). An evolutionary and developmental theory of biphasic processes underlying approach and withdrawal. In M. Jones (Ed.), *Nebraska symposium on motivation* (pp. 27–58). Lincoln: University of Nebraska Press.

Schultz, W. (1986). Responses of midbrain dopamine neurons to trigger stimuli in the monkey. *Journal of Neurophysiology, 56,* 1439–1461.

Stein, L. (1983). The chemistry of positive reward. In M. Zuckerman (Ed.), *The biological bases of sensation seeking, impulsivity, and anxiety* (pp. 17–42). Hillsdale, NJ: Erlbaum.

Stewart, J., de Wit, H., & Eikelboom, R. (1984). Role of unconditioned and conditioned drug effects in the self-administration of opiates and stimulants. *Psychological Review, 91,* 51–268.

Sved, A. F., Baker, H. A., & Reis, D. J. (1984). Dopamine synthesis in inbred mouse strains which differ in numbers of dopamine neurons. *Brain Research, 303,* 261–266.

Sved, A. F., Baker, H. A., & Reis, D. J. (1985). Number of dopamine neurons predicts prolactin levels in two inbred mouse strains. *Experientia, 41,* 644–646.

Tellegen, A. (1985). Structures of mood and personality and their relevance to assessing anxiety, with an emphasis on self-report. In A. H. Tuma & J. D. Maser (Eds.), *Anxiety and the anxiety disorders* (pp. 681–706). Hillsdale, NJ: Erlbaum.

Tellegen, A., & Waller, N. G. (1992). Exploring personality through test construction: Development of the multidimensional personality questionnaire. In S. R. Briggs & J. M. Cheek (Eds.), *Personality measures: Development and evaluation* (Vol. 1, pp. 52–109). Greenwich, CT: JAI Press.

Thierry, A-M., Tassin, J. P., & Glowinski, J. (1984). Biochemical and electrophysiological studies of the mesocortical dopamine system. In L. Descarries, T. Reader, & H. Jasper (Eds.), *Monoamine innervation of cerebral cortex* (pp. 233–261). New York: Alan R. Liss.

Watson, D., & Tellegen, A. (1985). Toward a consensual structure of mood. *Psychological Bulletin, 92,* 426–457.

Weinberger, D. R. (1987). Implications of normal brain development for the pathogenesis of schizophrenia. *Archives of General Psychiatry 44,* 660–669.

White, N. (1986). Control of sensorimotor function by dopaminergic nigrostriatal neurons: Influence on eating and drinking. *Neuroscience and Biobehavioral Reviews, 10,* 15–36.

Zuckerman, M. (1983). *Biological bases of sensation seeking, impulsivity, and anxiety.* Hillsdale, NJ: Erlbaum.

II

Developmental Models of Complex Psychopathologies

3

Some Characteristics of a Developmental Theory for Early-Onset Delinquency

GERALD R. PATTERSON

The task of a developmental theory for delinquent behavior is to explain both the stability and the changes in a form that characterizes the trajectories of antisocial individuals over time. In what sense can a behavioral event be both stable and yet change over time? The research strategies and findings that relate to this crucial question constitute a section in the discussions that follows. Given that the focus for the theory is crime, there are several additional concerns that must be addressed, such as why crime rates vary across nations and across time. These issues force us to consider developmental mechanisms in broader contexts and form a second major focus of this chapter.

This chapter describes a very conservative approach to building a developmental theory of antisocial behavior relevant for early-onset delinquent behavior. The a priori model was based on a decade of efforts to intervene in families of antisocial children (Patterson, Dishion, & Chamberlain, 1993). Only those variables that could be readily measured were included in the model, based on reports from multiple agents: mother, father, child, observers, teachers, and peers. A concept was retained only if it could be demonstrated in several samples that the a priori relationships specified were significant and could be replicated. As new means for measuring complex variables such as emotion or cognition are developed, they will be added to the model, provided that they contribute significant and unique variance. We have labeled this conservative, measurement-focused strategy a *performance model* (Patterson, 1977, 1979, 1982; Patterson, Reid, & Dishion, 1992). Some additional characteristics of a performance model will be introduced later in the discussion.

Historically, most developmental theorists have followed the tradition of outlining such a theory in terms of its internal consistency and completeness of what is being explained. Much empirical support rests on laboratory analogue studies, with little attention given to development of measurement models for key variables (e.g., Maccoby, 1993). In a sense, the adequacy of the developmental model lies in the beauty of the theory itself.

In the past century, psychoanalysis has been the prime example of a theory that survives because of the model's completeness and internal consistency. It survives in spite of the fact that the theory is almost entirely innocent of methods of measurement or even laboratory analogue tests for the key concepts. Bowlby's (1969) (cited in Waters, Kondo-Ikemura, Posad, & Richters, 1990) update of psychoanalysis defined modern attachment theory in such a fashion, but then went on to make a fundamental contribution. Bowlby defined some major concepts to facilitate empirical testing. The fact that a beginning has been made in building a measurement model means that it can be used to illustrate the second major characteristic of a performance model as applied to developmental phenomena. In this case, the model must specify the relationship among the variables (mechanisms) designed to explain how changes and stabilities occur. Ainsworth's (cited in Waters et al., 1990) studies of the strange situation provided a powerful assessment of qualitatively different forms of attachment in young toddlers. These studies were summarized by Waters et al. (1990). As shown in Figure 3.1, part of the attachment model is very similar to the position taken by the present writer: that measures of childrearing directly determine some of the variance associated with socialization outcomes. For example, they would expect that earlier childrearing would correlate significantly with later measures of aggression (Patterson, 1982; Patterson, Reid, & Dishion, 1992). However, as Waters et al. point out, the attachment model goes on to add two very important variables thought to mediate the direct impact of parent–child interaction on child adjust-

THE ORIGINS OF PROSOCIAL AND ANTISOCIAL BEHAVIOR

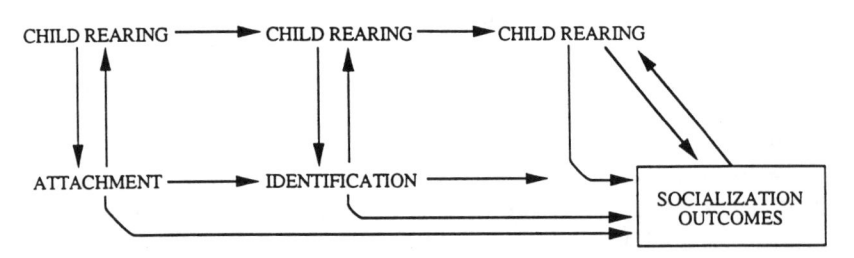

Figure 3.1 Attachment as a candidate for developmental theory. (From Waters, Kondo-Ikemura, Posad, & Richters, 1990.)

ment. They hypothesize that a toddler's level of emotional attachment to the parent directly determines the child's eventual identification with parental values, beliefs, and standards. As shown in the model, childrearing may have some direct effects on child outcomes, but it is also thought to have indirect effects mediated through attachment and identification variables.

There are several straightforward implications of this model. First, a number of investigators have demonstrated very significant relations between childrearing variables and child outcomes. This part of their model is nicely supported. However, in terms of Bowlby's (1969) theory, the most interesting part of their model involves the attachment and identification variables. There are two key hypotheses. Since their current measurement model includes only the attachment concept, my comments will be restricted to that idea. It should be the case that measures of poor attachment as a toddler will correlate significantly with later measures of adjustment (teacher, peer, and observation data).

Second, and even more important, it should be the case that if we enter data describing childrearing, the data will significantly predict later adjustment. But when the attachment score is added, it, too, will make a significant contribution (e.g., attachment tells us something unique that cannot be obtained from measures of childrearing or parent–child interaction).

As pointed out in the review by Fagot and Kavanagh (1990), there have been at least four major efforts to test the second hypothesis. Is the measure of attachment in the strange situation valid? How does it predict later adjustment? The findings, including those from the authors' own study, showed that validity of the measures of attachment tended to be nonsignificant for girls, in general, and for boys from nonrisk normal samples. There do seem to be replicated findings for boys from at-risk samples. Such findings set severe limitations on the generalizability of this particular measure of attachment, but other means for assessing the construct are being developed. These will perhaps fare better (Cox, 1993).

The third requirement for a performance model is that casual status be demonstrated for the mechanisms used to explain developmental changes. Such studies could be carried out at two different levels (Forgatch, 1991). The weakest test would require longitudinal data demonstrating that the changes in the causal variable X covary significantly with changes in the criterion behavior Y. Under certain conditions, cross-lag and other panel designs might be used, but it appears that covariation of change scores makes the strongest case (Stoolmiller & Bank, in press). Most writers would agree that, at best, correlational models can only be used to identify models worthy of being subjected to experimental tests. How this has been done will be sketched out in a later section.

The writer believes that the coercion model is ready to be evaluated as a performance theory. The only other developmental theory for which the measurement model has been even partially worked out is the life course perspective described by Caspi, Elder, and Herbener (1990). The primary focus of this chapter is how the coercion model does and does not meet the requirements for a performance model.

The coercion model is built on a learning theory that Maccoby (1993) and most other psychologists thought of as a defunct explanation for human behavior. The section that follows briefly outlines the nature of several of the deficiencies in early reinforcement theories together with some reasons why they could not, until recently, be applied as an explanation for children's social behavior.

On Being Rescued from the Hall of Debutantes

It is a curious fact that none of psychology's grand theories of human behavior really lend themselves directly to the construction of a performance theory for the development of antisocial behavior. Each of the theories, such as learning theory, drive theory, and social cognitive theory, rests on creditable laboratory findings, but each of them had fatal flaws when efforts were made to translate them into theories that account for behavior in the real world.

For each of the grand theories, the laboratory findings had suggested that potentially the variables in the model could be used to predict events in natural settings. In this sense, each theory was like a debutante decked out in laboratory finery waiting to be asked to dance. As laboratory analogues, each was and is beautiful in its own way. However, the potential is realized only if variables from the model answer questions such as these: Why do such children behave more aggressively in this setting than do other children? Why is this child more aggressive today than yesterday?

As shown in Figure 3.2, the Hall of Psychology's Debutantes is thought to contain four notables who might conceivably have produced a performance theory describing the development of antisocial behavior. Three were derived from the theories of learning and related drive theories extant in the 1960s and 1970s: frustration-aggression theory (Dollard, Doob, Miller, Mowrer, Sears, 1939), imitation (Bandura, 1973), and reinforcement theory (Glaser, 1971). Each of the theories has considerable face validity, (i.e., it seemed that you really could explain aggression this way). Each of them generated volumes of speculations about why and how the variables would explain aggressive behavior in the real world. However, none of these laboratory analogue theories provided a basis for building a measurement model that would test the theory. In the one case where a measurement model was developed, it showed that the frustration-aggression theory was inadequate (Fawl, 1963).

Figure 3.2 Debutante ball.

The most venerable candidate is the frustration-aggression theory (Dollard et al., 1939; Maier, 1961). This theory remains part of everyone's conventional wisdom. Based on a drive theory metaphor about the nature of learning, the model states that drives such as frustration or anger elicit aggressive behaviors. Bandura (1973) provided a devastating review of the laboratory studies demonstrating that even with that set of findings, the model provided an incomplete account of aggressive behavior. For example, some laboratory studies showed that increasing frustration seemed to activate increased cooperation in some children and increased aggression in others (Davitz, 1952). The crucial test was provided by Fawl (1963), who assessed frustrating and aggressive events observed in natural settings and showed that the two variables did not covary significantly. Many events frustrating to children were not followed by aggression, and many aggressive events were not preceded by frustration.

A second and more promising analogue was systematically explored in over a decade of carefully controlled laboratory studies demonstrating that children could learn aggressive responses by merely observing the behavior of models (Bandura, 1973). Most of us remain convinced that much of what children learn about aggression is based on modeling, but the general theory has contributed very little to our understanding about performance (i.e., why one child performs aggressive acts more frequently than another child). The problem lies in the measurement model. A number of investigators have tried, but no one has figured out how to measure imitation as it occurs in natural settings. It remains an analogue theory that cannot be tested as a performance model.

Cognitive science is one of the most exciting developments in modern psychology. It tells us a good deal about thinking and how it works, but the theory doesn't explain how thinking is connected to social behaviors such as aggression. One conclusion reached in reviewing these studies was that there are systematic limitations in thinking itself (Dawes, 1988). Contemporary theories about social cognition tend not to be directly tied to hard cognitive science.

Spivack, Platt, and Shure (1976) developed an intervention model for aggressive children derived from assumptions about disrupted cognitive process that lead to deviant outcomes. Dodge's (1991) primary measure is attributional bias, and Spivack et al. used several measures of impaired cognitive processes. Both groups of investigators used laboratory analogue measures of key cognitive variables. Both groups demonstrated that the analogue measures correlate significantly with measures of antisocial behavior. Although the variance accounted for is small (typically less than 10%), the findings seem quite robust. The next and crucial step will be to carry out modeling studies similar to the one presented in Figure 3.1. Do estimates of cognitive process assessed at $T1$ provide unique information beyond what is contained in measures of aggression at $T1$ in predicting child aggression at $T2$? A more rigorous test would require that changing the child's social cognitions produce changes in the child's aggression. To date, efforts to produce such effects have not been successful, or those that seemed successful could not be replicated. Studies relevant to these general issues are reviewed in Dishion, French, and Patterson, (1995).

Developments in reinforcement theory suggest that reinforcing contingencies provided in natural settings determined the performance rates for aggressive behavior. In the 1960s a number of systematic laboratory studies show that a wide spectrum of positive reinforcers—praise, M&M candies, and pennies—could be used to alter rates of aggressive child behaviors (Bandura, 1973). In natural settings, it was repeatedly demonstrated that manipulation of reinforcing and punishing contingencies significantly altered aggressive behavior in both children and adults (Ribes-Inesta & Bandura, 1976). Also, observations of children in natural settings seemed to identify reinforcing outcomes for aggressive behavior that altered future behaviors (Patterson, Littman, & Bricker, 1967).

Those of us who wished to move on to explain individual differences in rates of aggression encountered an insurmountable problem. In our enthusiasm, we had simply ignored several decades of studies with animal and human subjects that showed conclusively that there was no linear relationship between rate of reinforcement and rates of response. At about the same time, many other investigators were emphasizing other problems with reinforcement theory, such as its presumed failure to explain language development in general and grammatical structure in particular. There were obvious flaws with the extensive work we had done on social reinforcement effects (Eriksen, 1962). But it was not these concerns that led many of us to stop working on a performance theory. It was clear that we could never explain individual differences using such a model. It was also evident that we could not explain why behaviors that were reinforced in one setting generalized to another unless we invoked some very fuzzy assumptions about stimulus generalization. This was very frustrating because our treatment studies showed that changing contingencies led to predictable changes in aggression in natural settings. Our experiments showed that our intervention engineering worked, but it was not possible to develop an empirically based theory about what produced the phenomena in the first place.

In the 1960s, a new idea was developed that could have been used to address concerns about individual difference variance and generalizability. However, the concept of the matching law, as put forth by Herrnstein (1961), was not applied to samples of children until the early 1980s. Its application to problems of aggression will be detailed in a later section.

To cast a performance model as a developmental theory about antisocial behavior requires addressing several specific questions. These are listed in the section that follows. The adequacy of the reactions to these questions also serves as the criterion to be used in evaluating coercion as a developmental theory.

Characteristics of a Developmental Theory

This section briefly outlines the questions to be addressed in the following sections. These questions define the characteristics of a developmental theory of antisocial behavior in children when viewed as a performance theory.

1. The concept of development seems paradoxical. It implies that two processes that appear antithetical occur simultaneously. And it implies a recognizable trajectory over time. There is a sense that the individual is recognizably the same, while in the meantime the form of behavior changes. The antisocial adolescent does not perform exactly the same antisocial acts as she or he did as a child. A developmental theory must be able to describe both change and stability accurately. It must also perform the more difficult task of explaining the dynamic of these processes.
2. The coercion model assumes that the primary direct determinants of antisocial behavior is a breakdown in parenting skills. How are these casual variables to be measured? Can the results be

replicated? Do changes in parenting styles covary with changes in the child's antisocial behavior in longitudinal studies? Finally, do experimental manipulations demonstrate a casual status for these variables? And tangentially, how do you explain the means by which parents and children influence each other?
3. Do the effects of training in the family generalize to the school? How are these effects to be explained?
4. What is the impact of the context in which the family lives (e.g., poverty, stress, single parent, antisocial parent, or depressed parent)?
5. Which variables in the coercion model relate to societal changes in rates of crimes over time?

Contributions of Families and Peers to Early Onset of Antisocial Behavior

The central hypothesis is: Chronic antisocial behavior in children is the direct outcome of a breakdown in parental family management practices (Patterson, 1982; Patterson, Reid, & Dishion, 1992). The five family management skills thought to be primary determinants are discipline, monitoring, family problem solving, parent involvement, and positive reinforcement. These five variables emerged during a decade of effort to develop parent training therapy for parents of antisocial children. Details of how the parents are trained to improve their family management skills are described in Patterson and Forgatch (1987), Patterson (1988), and Forgatch and Patterson (1989). Random assignment comparison studies carried out at the Oregon Social Learning Center and at universities in Georgia and Washington showed that parent training therapy was generally effective for younger antisocial children (ages 3 to 8) (Patterson, Dishion, & Chamberlain, 1993). Although the effects are significant for samples of older antisocial children following treatment, a proportionately smaller number are able to function in the normal range.

It is assumed that interactions with siblings and parents produce a child who is both coercive and socially unskilled (i.e., who has two sets of problems). During the elementary grades, the child will add antisocial skills to his or her repertoire (e.g., lie, cheat, steal, and/or set fires). The details of how this comes about will be covered in a later section. The effect of these failures leads to rejection and school failure. These, in turn, place the child at risk for very early involvement (preadolescence) with the deviant peer group (Dishion, 1990; Dishion, Patterson, Stoolmiller, & Skinner, 1991).

This history of training by family members followed by school failure explains why some children are at risk for early police arrest (Patterson,

DeBarshye, & Ramsey, 1989). Presumably, the antisocial child comes into close contact with deviant peers as a preadolescent because she or he is on the street and unsupervised long before other members of the cohort (Stoolmiller, 1990). The boys with the highest rates of antisocial acts are at greatest risk of being arrested. Event history analyses of the Oregon Youth Study (OYS) showed that this in fact was the case (Patterson, Crosby, & Vuchinich, 1992). The most severely antisocial boys were at greatest risk of arrest prior to age 14. These and related findings will be discussed in greater detail in a later section.

The first problem to be solved involved the means for measuring parenting behavior. In the 1970s, this had seemed an intractable problem in that it had not been possible to replicate correlations between parent practices and child behavior. The National Institute of Mental Health (NIMH) funded several years of development of a multiagent method assessment battery tailored to the five family management practices for a normal sample (Patterson, 1982; Patterson & Stouthamer-Loeber, 1984). Each family management and child adjustment concept was defined by multiagent and multimethod indicators. The assumption was that multiagent-multimethod indicators would lead to more generalizable models (i.e., replicable across studies and sites). The assessment battery was revised and expanded to serve in a longitudinal study of at-risk families in the OYS. Details of the psychometric studies of this assessment battery are presented in Capaldi and Patterson (1989).

The specific hypothesis for the parenting model was: Disrupted parental discipline and monitoring caused antisocial child behavior. Forgatch (1991) summarized the findings from three different at-risk samples that offered strong support for the general parenting model. As shown in Figure 3.3, the a priori model was replicated, and in all cases the parenting variables accounted for a minimum of 30% of the variance in the criterion measure of antisocial behavior. More recently, the model has been extended to include normal preschool boys and girls (Fagot, 1992) and normal adolescents (Metzler & Dishion, 1992).

The writer agrees with the position taken by Forgatch (1991): that the primary role of robust correlational models is to identify worthy candidates for experimental testing. Even the most sophisticated panel analyses cannot establish causal status. Forgatch summarized findings from two experiments demonstrating that altering parent disciplinary practices produced changes in the child's antisocial behavior. Dishion, Patterson, and Kavanagh (1992) described an experiment that used random assignment to parent training that demonstrated that changes in discipline practices were significantly related to changes in the child's antisocial behavior. Three additional experiments are now underway. It is assumed that these clinical trials must be followed by single-subject studies to control more precisely for extraneous variables.

While more tests of the parenting model are needed, serious efforts

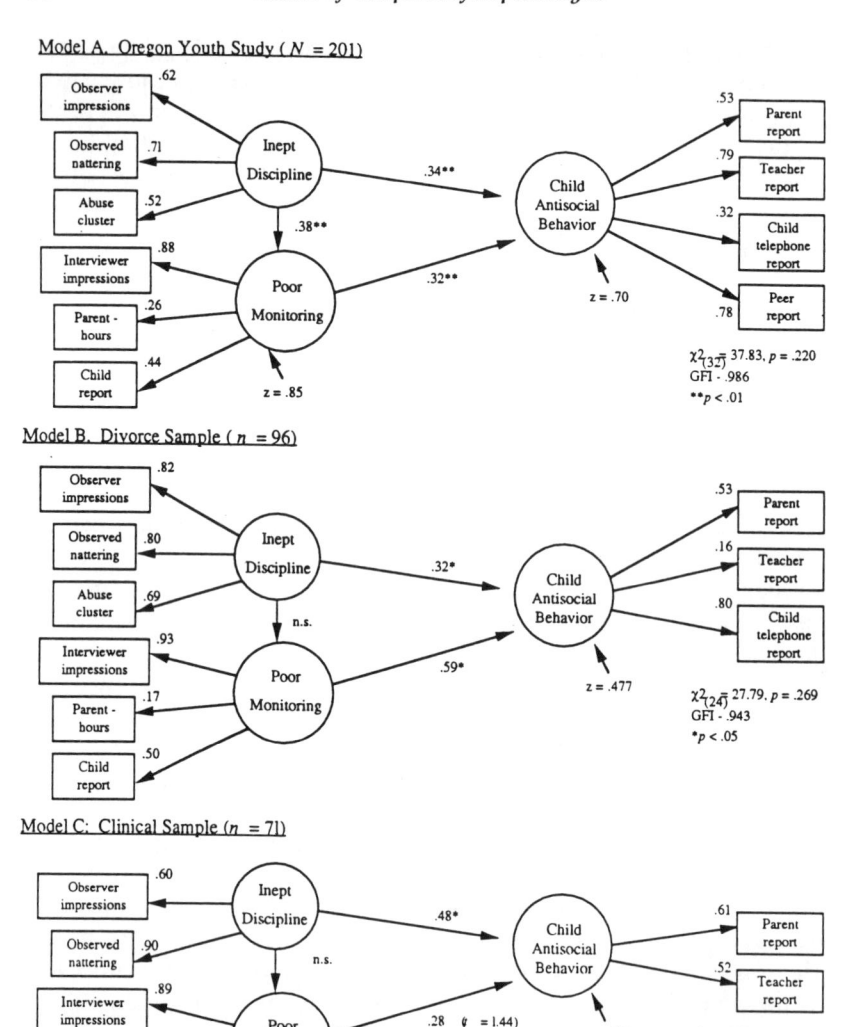

Figure 3.3 Two replications of the parenting training model for high-risk samples. (From Forgatch, 1991.)

have been made to falsify the model, yet it continues to survive. In this sense, it is one of the most thoroughly tested models of children's antisocial behavior now in the literature.

The section that follows examines why one family may be at greater risk than another for disrupted parenting practices.

Context, Social Disorganization, and Family Process
Mediational Models

Within the coercion model, contextual variables (social disadvantage, poverty, divorce, stress, parental depression, and antisocial behavior) are thought to be correlated significantly with child adjustment (Patterson, Reid, & Dishion, 1992). It is hypothesized that these variables increase the risk of antisocial behavior only when they are associated with disrupted parent discipline and monitoring practices. Studies relating to this hypothesis will be reviewed later.

Over the decades, findings from sociological studies of crime have left little doubt that structural variables, such as social disadvantage, neighborhood or community, family size, broken homes and criminality in the parents, are intimately related to delinquency and crime. Generally, the relation between delinquency and these variables is quite modest. However, these early studies did not make clear the mechanisms by which these effects came about. Sampson's (1992) theory of social disorganization asserts that community structures affect the child's adjustment by altering family processes. On this point, the coercion and the Sampson-Laub models (Sampson & Laub, 1994) are in close agreement: The effect of context on child adjustment is mediated through family processes. This perspective integrates structural sociology with current work in developmental psychology (by Sampson and Laub).

Patterson (1983) formulated a general model for examining the impact of stress on the parent—child interaction. The key assumption was that stress was related to increased rates of irritable behavior (e.g., on days when the mother was most stressed, she tended to be most irritable). It was also hypothesized that irritable behaviors were directly related to poor discipline practices, poor problem solving, and disruptions in social interaction in general.

The mediated model for stress effects has received strong support across three different sites (Conger, Patterson, & Gé, 1995; Forgatch, Patterson, & Skinner, 1988; Snyder, 1991). Studies on the effect of social disadvantage have also produced structural equation models consistent with a mediational model (Bank, Forgatch, Patterson, & Fetrow, 1993; Larzelere & Patterson, 1990; Laub & Sampson, 1988; Sampson & Laub, 1994).

Not all contextual variables have the same relation to disrupted parenting practices. The next section considers the possibility that some contextual variables, such as stress or depression, may cause disrupted parenting but that other contextual variables do not, even though they satisfy the requirements of a mediational model. For example, social disadvantage and divorce may be marker variables for subsamples of parents who are characteristically inept in their parenting practices. Unemployment may also belong to this class of contextual variables. The underlying assumption is that certain types of individuals, such as antisocial adults, are particularly vulnerable to economic and psychological pressures that lead to low social status, divorce, and unemployment. The hypothesis is that the antisocial individual is more vulnerable and, therefore, at greater risk of ending up as a member of a contextual class including divorced, unemployed, and disadvantaged people.

Contextual Variables and Societal Rates

This discussion is speculative. Certain elements of the Sampson (1992) model of social disorganization are combined with components of the coercion model in an attempt to account for some of the variation in crime rates. It is generally assumed that certain social processes generate simultaneous increases in the prevalence of unskilled parents and the prevalence of difficult-to-train infants. Sampson's social disorganization theory specifies how changes in contextual variables, such as economic cycles, set in motion what the writer would characterize as a dual process that leads to the production of antisocial children.

The process is described in Figure 3.4. According to the coercion model, it is the interaction between these two variables that determines the highest risk of an antisocial child as an outcome (Patterson, Reid, & Dishion, 1992). A number of writers have shown that difficult infants, as a group, are at significant risk for later adjustment problems; however, it is the difficult infant with an unskilled mother who is most at risk (e.g., the effect is an interactive one) (U. Bronfenbrenner, personal communication, 1993; Werner, 1989). What set of societal variables increases the density of difficult-to-train infants and also increases the supply of unskilled parents?

Society's Contributions to Increased Rates

The focus is on variables that might relate to increasing the density of single parents, but a general model would attempt to account for families with frequent transitions. However, there are certain types of individuals who are at increased risk of achieving single-parent status and then becoming involved in multiple transitions. The transitions model accounts for about three out of four boys in the OYS involved in early arrest. Additional models must be generated to account for early arrest in intact families, which comprises about one-fourth of the early-onset cases. The process described in Figure 3.4 is a preliminary step in attempting to understand variations in crime rates.

Sampson (1987) carried out an elegant series of modeling studies based on data from a sample of metropolitan centers. The young men

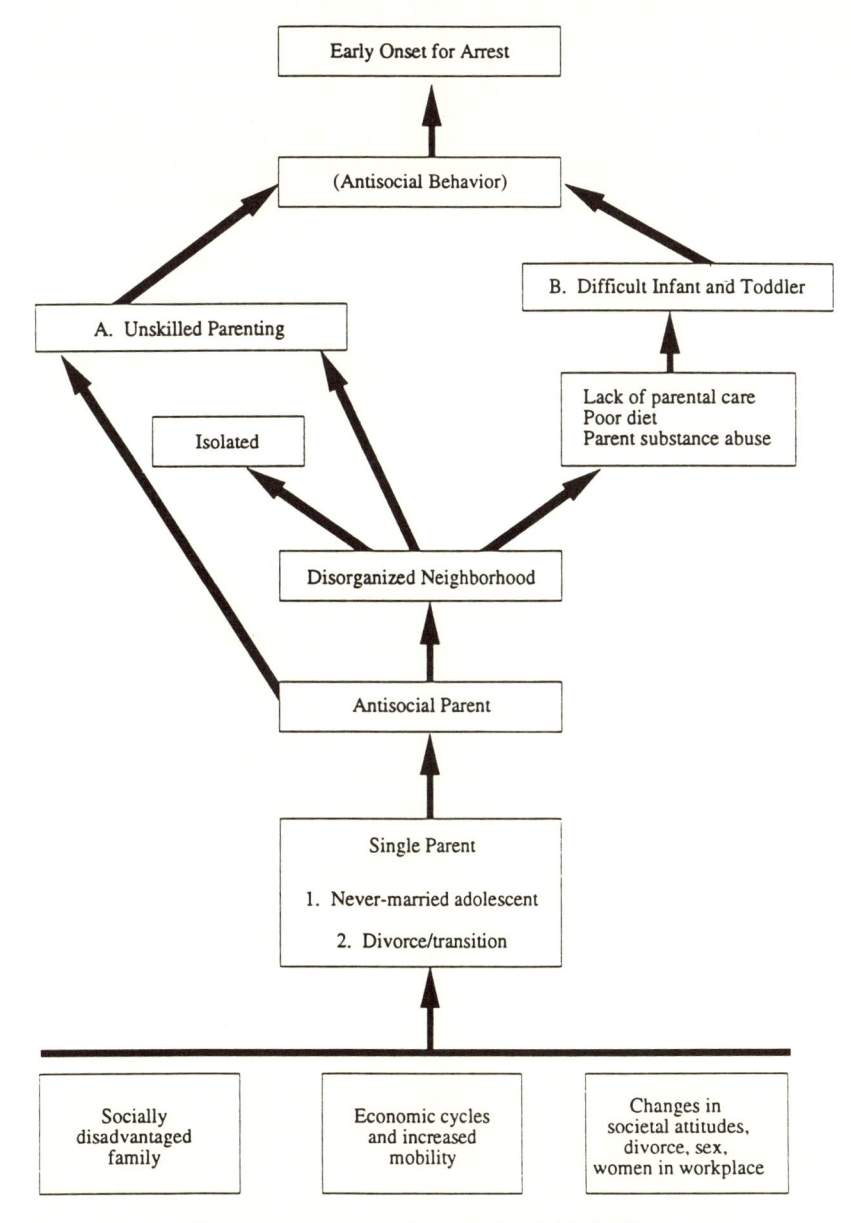

Developmental Theory for Early-Onset Delinquency

Figure 3.4 Two paths to antisocial behavior.

cannot support a family, but they do procreate. The models showed that disrupted family processes were related to antisocial outcomes for the children. The same model applied to both Blacks and Whites living in these disadvantaged settings. The obvious indirect effect—a failed economy—is an increase in the number of young, single mothers, many of whom had never been married. A later section will examine the possibility that some young adults are more vulnerable than others to such societal pressures as economic cycles.

Sampson's (1992) social disorganizational theory underscores a second and related set of outcomes that have profound implications for a model concerned with crime rates: drift to disorganized communities.

Drift to Disorganized Communities

Social disorganization theory would predict that as relatively less skilled parents are affected by disaster, they will tend to drift into areas of large cities where rents and other costs are lowest. Furthermore, in Sampson's (1992) review, this environment isolates the single caretaker not only from family, but from neighbors as well. Supportive, positive reactions from neighbors are replaced by an atmosphere of mistrust and limited communication.

Sampson (1992) pointed out in his review that these ghetto areas were usually characterized by reduced public health services for young pregnant women. Many of these young women subsisted on a substandard diet, and some were also abusing drugs and alcohol. The immediate effect of each of these variables was an increase in the number of low-birth-weight, birth-defective, and premature infants. In other words, the number of difficult-to-raise infants increased.

In a review of primate literature, Sackett (1993) concluded that prenatal factors produced many negative outcomes that had a temperament-like characteristic. He noted that prevalence rates for difficult infants probably reflected primarily constitutional factors (e.g., prenatal circumstances) and secondarily genetic factors. However, in the present context, it is important to note that when the mother and perhaps the father are antisocial, it could well be that genetic contributions play a considerable role, as suggested by Gottesman and Goldsmith (1993). Keep in mind that studies by Werner (1989), Bronfenbrenner (personal communication, 1993), and others strongly suggested that difficult infants raised by skilled parents were not a particular risk for adjustment problems. The key lies in the quality of care.

Sampson (1992) emphasized that rates of crime and the incidence of infant health-related problems are intimately related. Perennial products of industrialized Western societies are cycles of economic failure. Each massive failure increases the supply of young, single mothers, living in isolated circumstances, only marginally skilled as parents. These same conditions also produce an increased supply of difficult-to-raise infants. In summary, cyclic economic conditions can indirectly alter the flow of both difficult infants and unskilled caretakers into disorganized urban areas.

Broken Homes

The preceding discussion rests heavily on the assumption that broken homes in general and single mothers in particular are somehow related to increased rates of crime. The hypothesis is that variables accounting for increases and decreases in the incidence of single mothers define one of several models essential to understanding variations in the rate of crime. The broken-home variable has a venerable history in sociological research on delinquency and crime. However, the careful review by Rutter and Giller (1983) showed inconsistent findings for the relation between crime and broken homes. A decade later, a review of 50 longitudinal studies by Gibbon, Thorpe, and Wilkinson (cited in Utting, Bright, & Henricson, 1993) concluded that the correlation was very weak. At best, that variable was associated with an increase in risk of only 10% to 15%. Most boys from broken homes do not become delinquent, and not all delinquents come from broken homes. Nevertheless, the present writer believes that the number of single mothers in a population may be an important predictor, but its contribution is entirely indirect, as shown in Figure 3.5.

First, it is important to consider that all delinquents are not the same, and that those who are arrested midadolescence or later are quite different from those arrested earlier (Patterson, in press; Patterson & Yoerger, 1993a, 1993b). It is the early-onset delinquents who are society's prime concern. Later in the report, there is a linear relation between age at first arrest and risk of chronic offending. The likelihood of being a chronic offender given an early arrest (prior to age 14.0) was .77. Also, early arrest is related to the risk of violent offending, but late arrest is not. For this reason, the data in Figure 3.5 are limited to early onset as the criterion.

Broken home is such a general term that its usefulness is impaired. For the high-risk subjects in the OYS, Capaldi and Patterson (1991) used the term *frequency of transitions* as an alternative. A shift from an intact family to a single-parent family would be +1, from single parent to stepparent +2, and so on. This new variable showed a linear relation between the number of family transitions and the worsening of child adjustment problems. Families with multiple transitions were at greater risk than were single-parent or intact families. In the present context, this model is extended to a hypothesized linear relationship between early onset (arrest prior to age 14.0) and a history of broken homes.

In keeping with the Capaldi and Patterson (1991) report, it is assumed that the relationship does not reflect the effects of repeated stress incurred as a result of each transition. As an alternative, Capaldi and Patterson demonstrated that families with a large number of transitions were characterized by a significantly higher incidence of disrupted parenting practices. It was hypothesized that the more antisocial the moth-

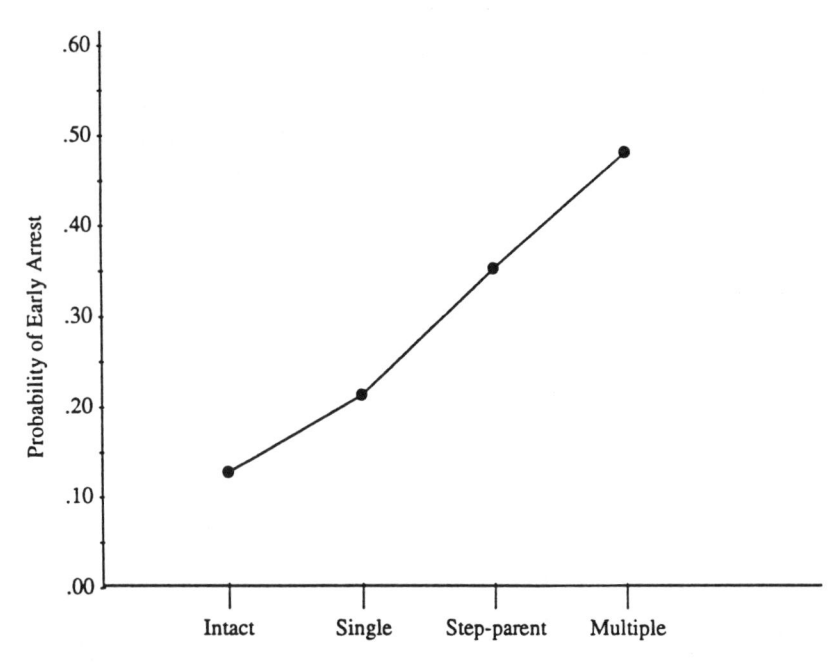

Figure 3.5 Covariation of transition frequency and likelihood of early arrest prior to age 14.

er, the greater the risk of more frequent transitions. Given this hypothesis, it would also follow that more frequent transitions would covary with accompanying disruptions in parenting practices and with an increasing prevalence of antisocial child behavior as an outcome. These analyses strongly supported all of the hypotheses. The general formulation is now extended to the prediction of early arrest.

The OYS began at Grade 4 and, at this point, has continued through age 17. The findings summarized in Figure 3.5 concerned the relation between transition frequency and early onset of arrest. In the sample of 203 at-risk families, 25% of the children had been arrested prior to age 14. The findings showed that intact families contributed less than their share of these serious delinquents. Single mothers contributed twice as many early-onset delinquents as intact families. With each transition, there was a linear increase in the likelihood of early arrest; clearly, families with multiple transitions were most at risk for serious delinquency. The data supported the idea that the pertinent variable is not broken homes per se but frequency of transitions.

Capaldi and Patterson (1991) hypothesized that disruptions in child adjustment associated with transitions were not a function of increasing stressors at each dysfunction, but rather with an increasing risk of having an antisocial parent. Presumably, antisocial men and women are at greater risk of having frequent transitions, as shown by Lahey, Hartdagen, Frick, McBurnett, Connor, and Hynd (1988), Patterson and Capaldi (1991), and Capaldi and Patterson (1991). The next section outlines the key contribution thought to be made by antisocial parents to several aspects of the process.

Antisocial Parents

Even if transitions is used to replace the broken home variable, the vast majority of the children of single-parent, stepparent, or even multiple-transition families still do *not* produce boys with early onset of arrest. As shown in Figure 3.5, the mediating construct is thought to be the antisocial behavior of the parent. As described in Patterson and Dishion (1988), the construct was assessed by four indicators: arrest, motor vehicle violations or license suspension, self-reported substance abuse, and Minnesota Multiphasic Personality Inventory (MMPI) self-reported high scores on hypomania and psychopathic deviation. This key variable makes several different contributions to the overall model.

Context

It is assumed that the relation between context and some family process variables may be bidirectional. Since contextual variables may produce changes in the individual's interactions with family members, the individual may also alter the context. For example, increases in stress or depression may alter patterns of parent–child interaction. On the other hand, the antisocial father may behave in such a manner at work as to get fired from the job. The repeated conflicts engaged in by an antisocial spouse may eventuate in a divorce.

Presumably, some young men, such as Blacks or the poorly educated, are more vulnerable because they have fewer opportunities for employment. We add the hypothesis that young, antisocial men and women are particularly vulnerable to these downturns in the economy. They are assumed to be significantly more vulnerable to disruptions by such natural catastrophes as economic failure and prolonged drought. This is, in part, a function of their lower level of social survival skills in work and human relationships. Caspi and Elder (1988) and Caspi, Elder, and Bem (1987) showed that over their life course, antisocial males tended to be significantly more downwardly mobile than their fathers. A follow-up study (Robins, 1981) of army veterans showed that active combat experience was more disruptive to post-war adjustment for those males who, prior to serving in the army, had been antisocial.

Parenting

It has become our increasing conviction that antisocial parents are very likely to be ineffective in their parenting practices. The deficit is most obvious during discipline confrontations, possibly because of the irritable, explosive style of interacting and problem solving with other family members (Patterson, 1982). This variable had a powerful effect in accounting for variance in parenting skills (Patterson & Capaldi, 1991). It remained significant even after other contextual variables were partialed out (Bank et al., 1993; Capaldi & Patterson, 1991). Some of these structural equation models (SEMs) are shown in Figure 3.6. The SEM showed, for both intact and single-parent families of older boys, that the effect of the antisocial parent on child adjustment was mediated through patterns of disrupted discipline. Some of these findings from both intact and single-parent families are summarized in Figure 3.6. These are complex relationships. For example, social disadvantage relates directly to antisocial behavior, but presumably, its effect is largely a function of identifying a high density of antisocial parents, who tend to be very ineffective in their use of discipline.

Transitions

While Capaldi and Patterson (1991) showed that the mean score of antisocial parents increased as a function of the number of transitions, it would be desirable to have an estimate of how many antisocial parents are at each transition point. Hypothetically, estimates of rates of early-onset arrests would vary as a function of the density of antisocial single parents because this subgroup would be at particular risk for disrupted discipline and monitoring practices. To test these hypotheses, data were examined separately for each of the four indicators of adult antisocial behavior to ensure that the estimate did not simply reflect measurement error. For each indicator, the cutting score for risk was set at 70% or higher.

As shown in Figure 3.7, prevalence rates varied widely as a function of the indicator used. Arrests or license suspensions gave the lowest prevalence estimates, and age of mother at first birth gave the highest prevalence estimate. For intact families, the median risk of having an antisocial mother was around 12%, with about 26% for single mothers, 38% for mothers from stepfamilies, and about 50% for mothers from multiple-transition families. The figures for fathers were comparable but are not included here.

Mobility

If the young adults remained in a normal society, two rather different protective factors might operate to lower the risk of disrupted parenting practices and, in turn, might be related to lower rates of delinquency. First, even though antisocial women are significantly at risk for selecting antisocial men as partners, the effect might be mitigated if the women remained in an extended protective network of family and neighbors to

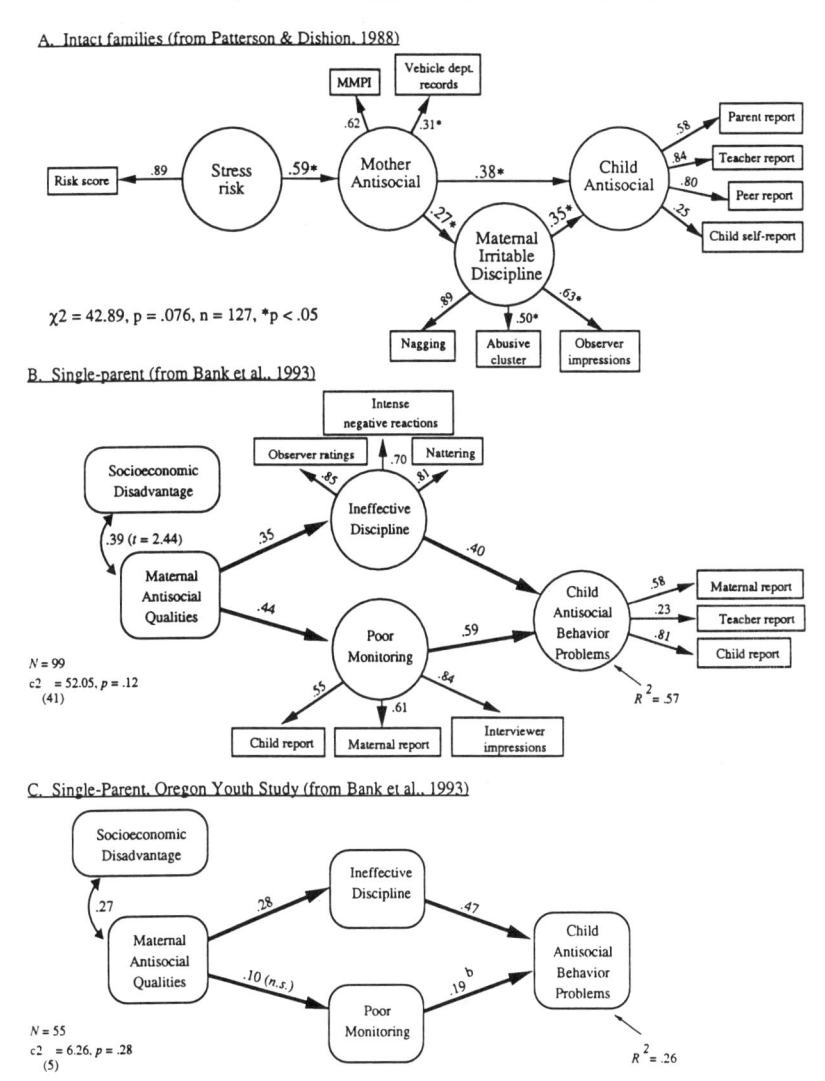

Figure 3.6 Mediated contribution of the antisocial parent to child adjustment. (*a*) Intact families (From Patterson & Dishion, 1988), (*b*) Single-parent family. (From Bank, Forgatch, Patterson, & Fetrow, 1993), (*c*) Single-parent family, Oregon Youth Study. (From Bank, Forgatch, Patterson, & Fetrow, 1993.)

supplement their marginal parenting skills by tracking and reacting to the child outside of the home. Second, the presence of a somewhat more skilled spouse might also vitiate the lack of parenting skills. To the extent that economic cycles contribute to increases in mobility, they would seem to contribute to disrupted parenting skills, perhaps even for intact families (with one or more anitsocial parents).

In summary, the present writer assumes that Sampson's (1992) theo-

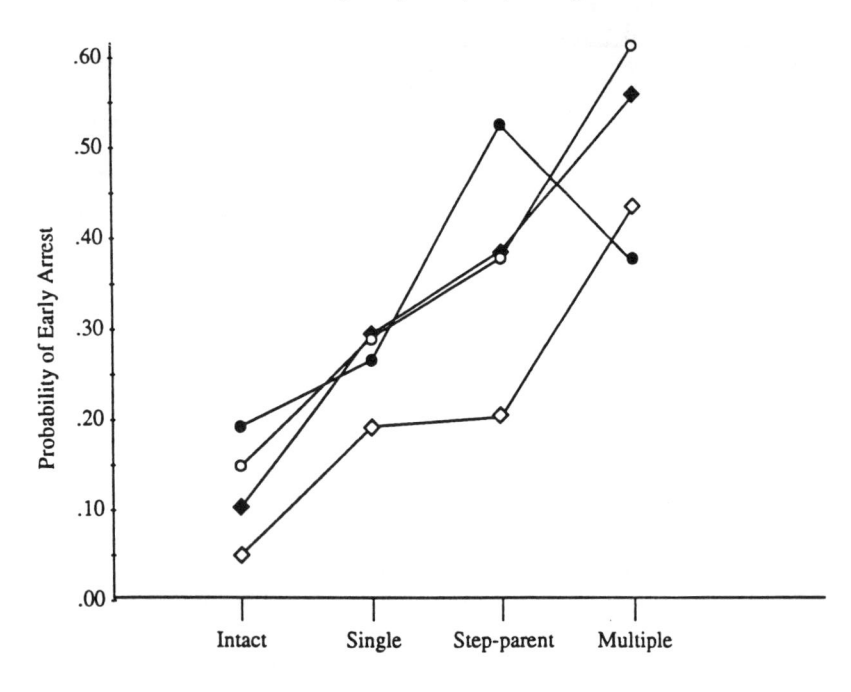

Indicators

◇ Arrest or license suspension (motor vehicle records)
○ First pregnancy prior to age 19.9
● Substance use
◆ High MMPI scores on Mania and Psychopathic Deviate scales

Figure 3.7 Covariation of transition frequency and risk of having an antisocial mother.

ry of social disorganization provides a basis for modeling the process that increases the density of unskilled and isolated parents, with a concomitant increase in the density of difficult-to-train infants. The general model would imply that mothers who are single, as the result of bereavement or due to fathers' absence in recurrent wars, would not necessarily produce larger numbers of antisocial boys (i.e., it is not the father's absence per se that is the issue here).

The central role accorded to parenting practices raises two important questions. First, how do differences in parenting practices produce individual differences in children's antisocial behavior? Second, how do the effects generalize from the socialization training in the home to the school and community, where the parent is no longer directly present? In the following section, modern developments in reinforcement theory are used to address both questions.

Individual Differences in Socialization

As noted earlier, the fact that there is no linear relation between response strength and reinforcement rate meant that the reinforcement theory could not be used to explain why one child was more aggressive than another. To understand individual differences, it is necessary to shift the focus to intraindividual behavior (Patterson, in press; Snyder & Patterson, 1995).

Beginning at the intraindividual level changes the question to "Why is it that, in a given situation, a child does one thing rather than another?" The shift in focus for reinforcement theory was heralded by Herrnstein's (1961) classic paper on the matching law. Updated versions were applied to human behavior almost a decade later and reviewed by McDowell (1988). The shift involves expanding the focus to include not only the reinforcers received for a specific response but also the reinforcers provided for all other responses occurring in that setting. For example, Snyder and Patterson (1995) designed a 10-category code system that contained four child behaviors thought to be coercive, four prosocial, and two neutral. According to the matching law, the relative rate of occurrence for a coercive response should match the relative payoff for that behavior for each child.

The most important reinforcing contingency for coercive behavior in family interaction involves a three-step escape conditioning (or negative reinforcement) sequence: aversive intrusion by a family member, coercive counter by the child, and withdrawal or a positive response by the family member (Patterson, 1982). Most coercive behaviors tend to be relatively innocuous (e.g., noncompliance, whining, temper tantrums, or hitting).

Escape conditioning sequences occur in peer group interaction, as well as in the home. But the peer group adds an important component to the training process. Peers are thought to accelerate the transition from coercive to antisocial acts. It is hypothesized that the coercive child tends to select peers who are likely to provide positive reinforcement for a variety of antisocial behaviors (stealing, lying, substance use, truancy, etc.). The bulk of observation studies carried out thus far indicate that positive reinforcement plays a key role in such behaviors as antisocial (rule-breaking) talk. The details of tests for application of escape conditioning to coercive behaviors are presented in Patterson (1982, in press). The exemplar of this approach is the study by Snyder and Patterson (1995). The tests for peer-dispensed positive reinforcement for antisocial acts are presented in Patterson, Littman, and Bricker (1967), Dishion, Patterson, and Griesler (1994), Dishion, Andrews and Crosby (1995), and Buehler, Patterson, and Furniss (1966).

If the test of the matching law were based on observation data collected in the home, then escape conditioning would be the appropriate reinforcing arrangement. In the Snyder and Patterson (1995) study, an observed conflict episode showed that the mother and preschool child had each exchanged an aversive behavior. The episode ended when the mother behaved in a neutral or prosocial manner. The child's prosocial or coercive response that preceded the mother's submitting was the *reinforced behavior.* As shown in Figure 3.8, the relative success of each prosocial and coercive response was calculated separately for each child. (The two neutral responses are not included.) The relative rate of payoff correlated with the relative rate of occurrence (not shown in the figure) for each of the 10 responses was .59 for the problem child and .76 for the nonproblem child. From an intraindividual standpoint, each child was actively selecting behaviors to match the payoffs in the home envi-

Problem Child

Positive verbal .143
Positive nonverbal .000
Comply .333
Talk .259

Negative verbal .478
Negative nonverbal .500
Noncomply .100
Command .392

Nonproblem Child

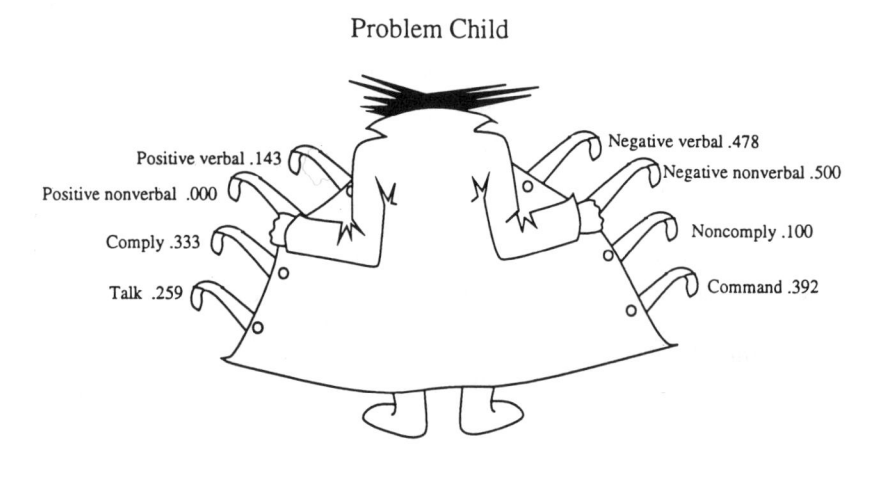

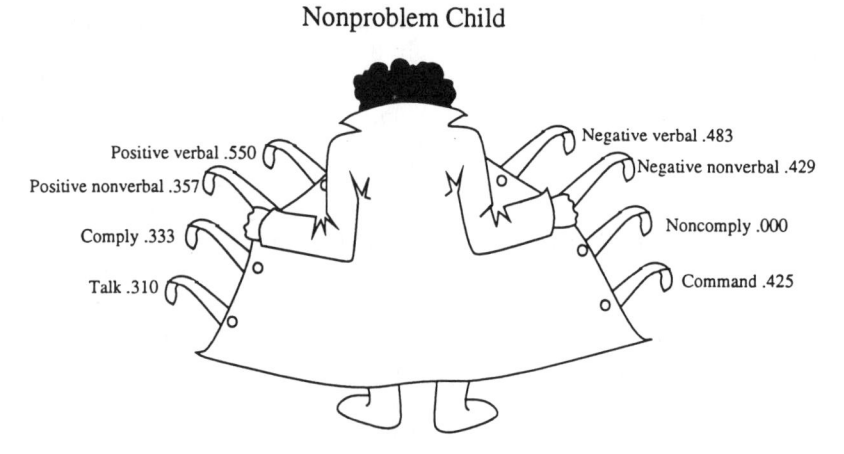

Positive verbal .550
Positive nonverbal .357
Comply .333
Talk .310

Negative verbal .483
Negative nonverbal .429
Noncomply .000
Command .425

Figure 3.8 Relative payoffs for coercive and prosocial reactions for two boys. (From Snyder & Patterson, in press)

ronment. In the Snyder and Patterson study, the median correlation for the 10 problem children was .64 and for the 10 nonproblem children it was .60.

The first observation in homes showed that the density of aversive intrusions was much higher in clinical settings than in normal families (Patterson, 1982). In problem families, parents and male and female siblings were all significantly more aversive when interacting with the problem child than were comparable members of normal families when interacting with the target child. The data showed that in clinical samples, all family members were more likely to counterattack than were their counterparts from normal families. However, the same data revealed the surprising fact that coercive child behaviors worked as well in coping with aversive family members in homes of normal families as they did in clinical samples (Patterson, 1982, Table 7.8). Maccoby (1993) clearly showed the inability of a negative reinforcement model to explain individual differences.

The information in Figure 3.8 points to a solution to the problem. (The raincoats with the hooks will be explained later.) It turns out that in a normal family, there are simply more things the child can do to cope effectively with the aversive intrusion by the mother. In normal families, the payoffs for prosocial reactions are as high as or higher than the payoffs for coercive reactions. For example, 55% of the normal child's positive verbal reactions successfully terminated conflict compared to 48% of negative verbal reactions. In contrast, the problem child was constrained to use only coercive reactions. None of the child's prosocial efforts to cope exceeded base rate payoffs. Thus, the normal child may be able to use both prosocial and coercive techniques, but the problem child discovers that only coercive techniques pay off. Snyder and Patterson's (1995) across-subject analyses showed that the normal child was significantly more likely to use neutral nonverbal gestures and to shut down as a means of coping; by comparison, the problem child relied significantly more often on command or negative verbal or nonverbal responses.

The intraindividual analyses showed that family systems vary in the coping strategies they permit. Using this information, there are several bridges that can be constructed to account for individual differences. If the child's coercive reaction to intrusions (the intraindividual estimate) is explained by the matching payoffs he or she receives, then only one other piece of information is needed. How often do aversive intrusions occur? In the Snyder and Patterson (1995) study, the base rate estimate for aversive mothers was 13.2% for the problem dyads and 8.1% for the nonproblem dyads. An equation that combines information about each child's likelihood of reacting coercively with information about the likelihood of aversive intrusion generates a score that accounts for 78% of the variance in rates of child coerciveness observed several weeks later (Snyder & Patterson).

Note that it is extremely important to base utility estimates, payoffs, and individual difference equations on much larger samples than those used thus far. Much of this discussion rests on fewer than 100 families; the discussion of the Snyder and Patterson (1995) matching law cases rests on about 10 hours of observation required for only 20 families. Therefore, the present discussion of individual differences must be thought of as illustrative rather than confirmatory. The limited data now available indicate, however, that in principle, it is possible to remove reinforcement theory from the hall of debutantes and introduce it into the real world of children's antisocial behavior.

Generalization Across Settings and Time

From the developmental theorists' perspective, Maccoby (1993) noted that the demise of the early reinforcement model was due to its failure to explain language development. But, in larger part, it was due to the models assumed failure to explain "out-of-sight compliance." Since no data were cited, Maccoby assumed that there was little or no correlation between compliance observed in the presence of the parent and compliance observed in settings where the parent was absent.

The explanation of generalization from the home to the community and across time is, of course, the major task for developmental theorists (Maccoby, 1993), who, along with sociologists, provided a common solution to this complex problem. Generalization is explained by the idea that somehow the child internalizes parental (and thus societal) values. It is this internal gyroscope that then guides the individual across time and settings, giving a sense of coherence to the individual life course. Although it is difficult to measure, these internal gyroscopes "feel" right to the man or woman on the street and to the many investigators as well. The question concerns our ability to measure these variables and the extent to which they account for significant amounts of variance in predicting children's aggression. Relevant findings will be briefly reviewed in a later section. In the next section, we will examine the potential contribution of concepts from modern learning theory to this same problem.

Lucretian Seekers: A Mechanism for Generalizability

There was a brief interlude during which personality and social learning theorists seemed in close accord. For example, in Mischel's (1968) somewhat selective review of earlier studies, he concluded that measures of personality traits did not generalize across either time or setting. Many social learning theorists also believed that reinforcement schedules probably shifted over time and were certainly different across settings. In fact, some theorists believed that each child's history of reinforcement was unique; in effect, reinforcement perspectives lead ultimately to a completely idiographic approach.

Given the data available in the 1960s and the nature of both reinforcement and measurement theory, these perspectives seemed plausible. However, recent findings have shown that they are quite wrong. For example, the review of longitudinal studies by Olweus (1979) showed across-time stabilities of children's antisocial behavior that averaged .67 across a wide spectrum of measures and time intervals. When aggregated measures (Epstein, 1979) were employed across the setting, correlations were about the same as those obtained across time (Wright, 1983). In one study, multiple indicators were used in the home to define the antisocial trait; a year later, multiple indicators were used in the classroom setting to define this trait. The across-time, across-setting path coefficient was .72 (Ramsey, Patterson, & Walker, 1990)!

A review of across-time and -setting studies by Patterson, Crosby, and Vuchinich (1992) raised the question of why behaviors, such as aggression, are stable across time and settings. For example, in the generalizability study by Jones, Reid, and Patterson (1975), analyses of variance components for the observation data showed that normal boys varied their performance of deviant behavior across settings, but problem boys did not. Several variables are relevant to this question. First, the patterns of action and reaction form overlearned structures (Patterson, Crosby, et al., 1992). As with driving a car, once the conflict units are overlearned, their employment requires very little cognitive processing. Smith and Lazarus (1990) emphasize the utility in differentiating between conceptual and schematic processes. Well-practiced coercive behaviors are examples of automatic or schematic processes. These overlearned behaviors are brought from home to the school.

The reinforcement-based socialization theories of the 1960s overlooked the possibility that as the child develops, she or he is not just a passive recipient. In the process of acquiring coercive and prosocial skills, the child might become an active agent who alters his or her own social environment (e.g., changes the behavior of parents, siblings, teachers, and peers; Patterson, 1982). In effect, the skilled coercer can elicit an aversive response from an otherwise noncoercive teacher or peer and then successfully counterattack. However, we suspect that the most important mechanism contributing to generalizability across settings has to do with the fact that, once trained, the coercive and antisocial child becomes an active seeker. It is hypothesized that the child actively selects from among settings and persons in order to maximize the immediate payoffs for his or her limited repertoire of prosocial skills and extensive repertoire of coercive skills. The socially unskilled problem child will seek settings on the playground (and in the community) that are relatively unsupervised by adults. Most of the studies of the seeker processes have focused on antisocial boys selecting peers. The boy also selects from among peers who are most likely to reinforce him for the repertoire he brings to the setting (Dishion, French, & Patterson, 1995). Those peers with a repertoire most closely matching that of the problem child would themselves tend to be relatively coercive and unskilled. Presumably, such a match would maximize the mutual receipt of reinforcers (Dishion, French, & Patterson).

Antisocial boys find others who support their behaviors. In this sense, it can be said that the antisocial boy has great self-control (i.e., he is doing what he always does). We suspect that this applies as a general case. For example, an individual will enter business or politics and select a sample of constituents and colleagues who reinforce his or her own pattern of work ethic and values about sexual or fiducial honesty. Selection and matching of repertoires to available payoffs are the two components of self-control built on the foundation laid down during compliance training.

At this point, substantial support for the impact of the child on the parent is shown in the bidirectional effects studies by Lytton (1977), Barkley (1991), and our own studies, as well as that of Vuchinich, Bank, and Patterson (1992). Accordingly, some data showed that individuals tend to prefer like individuals (Kandel, 1978), and they become more similar over time. For example, Dishion, Patterson, and Griesler (1994) showed a significant correlation between the antisocial trait of the target child and that of the "guy he hangs out with." The longitudinal data also showed that these children tended to make these same kinds of selections. However, the seeker hypothesis specifies a match in observed repertoires. The implication is that such a match ensures a mutuality of reinforcement that will keep the dyad going.

Dishion, Andrews, et al. (1995) coded the videotapes from interactions of antisocial and nonantisocial dyads for adolescent boys from the OYS at-risk sample. They tested the hypothesis that antisocial talk would more likely be reinforced (with laughter) in antisocial rather than normal dyads. They also tested the hypothesis that the relative rate of reinforcement for antisocial talk would match the relative rate of occurrence for antisocial talk. Both hypotheses were supported.

In *On the Nature of the Universe,* the Roman philosopher Lucretius introduces a useful metaphor when discussing how atoms combined to form molecules (Lucretius, 1965). He suggested that each atom is equipped with a set of hooks and that colliding hooks combine atoms to form a molecule. In applying this metaphor to the problem of generalization across settings, each child is pictured as wearing a raincoat with an array of hooks on each side. On the right side are hooks representing his or her prosocial sets of skills and on the left side are hooks for coercive behaviors. Presumably, the Lucretian seeker moves through settings and his or her peer group, with the raincoat open on the left or right side. As shown in Figure 3.9, when two members with matching hook arrangements meet, they form a dyad.

A. Seeking

B. Dynamic Homophily

Figure 3.9 The Lucretian seeker: On forming a dyad. (From Lucretius, 1965.)

Although antisocial boys are indeed rejected, Cairns and Cairns (1991) have shown that these boys have many friends. Longitudinal analyses showed that their relationships tended to be of somewhat shorter duration than those of nonantisocial dyads (Dishion, Andrews, et al., 1995). The data showed this was related significantly to the frequent use of coercive exchanges with peers. The selection of deviant peers may serve two related functions. First, it contributes to the generalization of antisocial behavior across time and settings. Second, it contributes to generating new forms of antisocial behavior. We shall return to this topic briefly in a later section.

Is There a Cognitive Connection?

Those with a cognitive persuasion argued that generalizability across settings and time is directly determined by some internalized form of self-control (Maccoby, 1993; Schonfeld, 1990; Shaffer & Brody, 1982). In each setting, the child perceived the risk of deviant behaviors and, after comparing utilities, decided whether or not to be involved. Patterson (1990) took the position that cognitive mechanisms could, in principle, account for individual differences in aggression, but there was little or no convincing empirical support for it (i.e., the findings did not meet the requirements for a performance model). Some evidence for this will be reviewed in the section that follows.

Within the coercion model, successfully training the toddler to about 70% compliance with adult requests was viewed as a necessary but not sufficient condition for adequate socialization (Patterson, Reid, & Dishion, 1992; Patterson & Yoerger, 1993a). It was hypothesized that observation-based measures of child compliance and accompanying coercive behaviors, such as temper tantrums, would provide a significant base for predicting future out-of-control behaviors. A partial test of this hypothesis by Patterson and Duncan (1993) showed that preschool measures of noncompliance and temper tantrums significantly predicted teacher ratings of fighting and confirmed a parent–teacher definition of opposition defiant disorder in second grade.

If parents are not effective in training the child to compliance when they are present in the room, then the child will also be noncompliant when parents are out of sight. In effect, a failure to train for compliance means that the child has not been trained to follow explicit rules. Presumably, if the child does not follow explicit rules, then she or he tends not to follow implicit rules either. Therefore, the noncompliant child will not follow the myriad explicit and implicit rules embedded in the classroom and playground situations. Many studies have shown that laboratory analogue measures of resistance to temptation, delay of gratification, or moral knowledge correlated significantly with observation-based measures of noncompliance in young children. Most recently, for example, Kochanska (1991) showed that observed toddler compliance with mothers' requests correlated .34 with moral orientation assessed when the child was 8 to 10 years of age.

Patterson (1990) and Patterson (in press) outlined the design for a study to demonstrate that measures of inner mechanisms of self-control would make the unique contribution claimed for them. The design required at least a brief longitudinal design with child aggressiveness measured at $T1$ and $T2$. One would assume that measures of inner control at $T1$ explain why the child was aggressive at that time; thus, these measures would serve as the best basis for predicting future aggression. Thus far, three tests using this design have failed to confirm the hypothesized unique contribution of cognitive mechanisms.

Low verbal intelligence is thought by some theorists to be an estimate of impaired executive function (Moffitt & Henry, 1989; Wilson & Herrnstein, 1985). Given this assumption, one would expect measures of IQ at age 8 to correlate negatively with peer ratings of aggression, as shown in the longitudinal study by Huesmann, Eron, and Yarmel (1987). However, Patterson and Duncan (1993) showed that these same findings supported the counterhypothesis: that high levels of child coerciveness imply that socializing agents will be relatively unsuccessful in teaching the child either academic or social skills. The negative correlation in the Huesmann et al. study supports either a cognitive or a coercion point of view. Furthermore, the coercion model predicts that aggression in children anticipates impaired future achievements. In keeping with this view, measures of childhood aggression were significantly related to lower adult IQs (Huesmann et al., 1987). High levels of child aggressiveness also predicted impaired adult achievement in the work force (Caspi, Elder, & Herbener, 1990). Does low IQ (impaired executive function) predict future aggression? Based on the Huesmann et al. study, the answer is "No."

A second longitudinal study showed, as expected, that a measure of verbal intelligence assessed during the preschool years correlated negatively with a measure of coerciveness collected at the same time. If one assumes that low verbal intelligence is an estimate of impaired executive function that explains high rates of coerciveness, then entering it next in a multivariate analysis should demonstrate that the prior contribution of the coercion variable was reduced. The findings offered no support for this hypothesis (Patterson & Duncan, 1993).

An empirical question is, how much variance in predicting future antisocial behavior can one account for by introducing measures of cognitive or social cognitive mechanisms? Those tests have not offered strong empirical support for the utility of cognitive mechanisms as explanations. The connection, if there is one, is yet to be established. For the moment, a cognitive theory of antisocial behavior remains firmly planted in the Hall of Debutantes. Correlations for cognitive variables do not provide causal status. A behavioral alternative seems eminently testable; however, only the study of Dishion, Andrews, et al. (1995) provide empirical support for the seeker hypothesis. An empirical base for understanding generalizability of social behavior has hardly been established.

Developmental Changes

The study of developmental changes in deviant behavior requires a very careful specification of what is changing together with the mechanisms that bring about changes. Presumably, one fundamental question for the developmental theorist involves the explanation for changes in forms of behavior. In a paradoxical sense, change and stability define a life trajectory. As noted earlier, an important consideration when examining the utility of a developmental theory is how well it addresses this question. For the sake of brevity, the relevant studies will only be briefly summarized here.

Some SEM studies for 2-year intervals found stabilities as high as .93 (Patterson, 1992). Then how can there be a high order of change concurrent with a high order of stability? This general question has been considered in a series of publications (Patterson, 1992, 1993, in press). The paradox is readily resolved if one considers that questions about stability are concerned only with the ordinal rankings of individuals along some underlying dimension (trait) assessed at two or more points in time. While the individual is frequently engaging in a trait behavior that is stable over time, there may be qualitative shifts in what she or he is doing. What she or he is doing may change in intensity or form, as well as in some other ways noted in the discussions that follow.

Stability and Changes in Mean Level

Given a stability correlation of .67, Olweus (1979) suggests that about 55% of the variance represented errors of measurement. However, some of the score changes may represent intraindividual growth or changes over time (i.e., not measurement error but systematic changes that can be identified).

Rogosa and Willett (1985), McArdle and Epstein (1987), and others pointed out that stability correlations ignore potential changes that may have taken place at the same time. During the same interval in which individual differences were shown to be highly stable, the OYS data showed a significant increase in mean level of antisocial behavior (Patterson, 1992).

It seems obvious that our developmental model must study the variance associated with individual growth (changes in mean level) over time. We can think of each individual with a growth curve defined by three or more points in time. Some individuals will show increases in mean level, while others will show declines or no change. This generates the variance associated with intraindividual growth. Modeling these growth curves not only makes it possible to describe the shape of the growth for a group but also includes covariates that account for these changes (McArdle & Epstein, 1987; Stoolmiller & Bank, in press; Willett, Ayoub, & Robinson, 1991).

The analyses of changes in antisocial behavior in the OYS from grades 4 through 8 showed that, indeed, such a subgroup existed (Patterson, 1993). The shift in mean level for this age group was in close agreement with findings from a longitudinal study by Cairns and Cairns (1991) and with cross-sectional data by Achenbach and Edelbrock (1983). It was also interesting to note that the covariates relating to antisocial behavior for younger boys were different from the covariates relating to boys who later became aggressive (Patterson, 1993). High stability did not mean that systematic changes in ordinal rankings were not occurring.

Changes in Intensity

Often in conflict situations, if one family member escalates in amplitude, she or he will, in the short run, "win" that particular exchange (Patterson, 1982). In the next round, one or both members are more likely to begin the exchange at a higher level of intensity. Escalation is thought to characterize repeated conflicts between spouses and uncontrolled conflicts among family members. The key hypothesis is: The more frequent the aversive exchanges, the greater the likelihood of high-amplitude, coercive behavior (threats, hitting, attacking with an object) (Reid, 1986).

Escalation in amplitude is thought to proceed in an orderly fashion, moving from high-frequency, relatively trivial incidents to low-frequency, more severe ones. Presumably, this training is well underway during the preschool years, and the progression continues well into adolescence. Details of the studies testing these assumptions are summarized in Patterson (in press). They showed that escalation is more likely to have a successful outcome in clinical families than in normal families; escalation also occurs more frequently in clinical families. The findings also showed that the occurrence of problem behaviors moves from trivial episodes in the preschool years to more severe events in early grade school.

Changes in the Form of Antisocial Acts

The clinical impression is that the form of pathology changes steadily over time, moving from one expression of a symptom to another. For example, delinquent acts represent a major change, not only in the form of antisocial behavior but also in the settings where the acts occur. Is there a systematic progression whereby the child moves from stealing from the mother's purse to shoplifting and burglary? If so, what determines the change in form at each of these points? The problem has always been to find a means for testing such hypotheses.

Inspection of the data from several longitudinal projects suggests that between Grades 4 and 9 there seemed to be regular increases in certain forms of antisocial behavior, such as substance use and truancy, as well as in most forms of delinquent behavior (Patterson, 1993). A latent growth model (LGM) was applied to the OYS to demonstrate, first, that substance use and truancy showed similar intraindividual growth patterns during this interval (i.e., a boy who increased in one also tended to increase in the other). Second, it was assumed that both the starting level (intercept) and the growth or slope were determined by the level of involvement with deviant peers and with the amount of unsupervised time available to the child. Both hypotheses were supported. For example, the increase in involvement with deviant peers and in-street time available accounted for 54% of the variance in the parameter estimating intraindividual variance. The data supported the hypothesis that the deviant peer group was intimately involved in training for new forms of antisocial behavior.

Qualitatively New Problems

If the longitudinal data collected cover a wide spectrum, it will become apparent that antisocial behavior, and probably most forms of pathologic behavior as well, produced predictable reactions from the social environment (e.g., rejection, contempt, verbal attacks, being fired from a job). These reactions, in turn, altered the behavior of the target person. The general effect produced a "cascade" of qualitatively new problem behaviors (Patterson & Yoerger, 1993a). The findings showed that a symptom may elicit reactions from the social environment that produces new problems that are qualitatively different from the original symptom. In effect, antisocial behavior in children may be an indirect cause of behaviors such as depressed mood. If so, then depression and antisocial behavior are not comorbid; rather, they are part of the same process.

A Recognizable Trajectory

Three major changes have been described; all of them occurred under conditions of high stability. But how can it be said that they are part of the original measure of the antisocial trait?

There are several ways of addressing this interesting problem. One alternative is to demonstrate that change variables serve a function similar to that served by the initial measure (Asendorpf, 1992). A simpler approach is to demonstrate that the new and old variables all load significantly on a second-order factor that changes systematically over time. The loadings on this second-order factor must shift over time because at younger ages the new forms and new problems did not occur with sufficient frequency to load on the factor. The findings from the first test of this hypothesis are summarized in Figure 3.10 (Patterson, 1993). In the example, academic failure served as the qualitatively new problem, and substance use and police arrest described changes in form that began in early adolescence. As expected, the changes in factor loadings seemed orderly and systematic. As a sufficient number of boys displayed

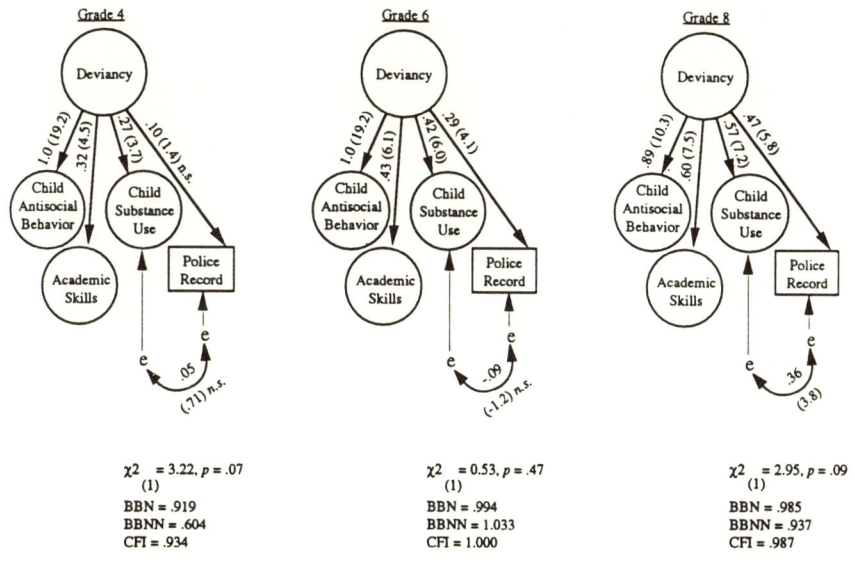

Figure 3.10 What is changing remains the same. (From Patterson, 1993.)

the characteristic, each of the changes loaded significantly on a core factor still clearly defined as antisocial.

Early-Onset Delinquency

Longitudinal studies of delinquent behavior typically found that about half of the boys arrested make no further contribution to crime statistics (i.e., they were transitory; see Wilson & Herrnstein, 1985). On the other hand, a very small group of offenders accounted for 50% to 60% of the arrests for their cohort. Finally, the vast majority of violent crimes were committed by chronic offenders (Capaldi & Patterson, 1993; Farrington & Hawkins, 1991). It is hypothesized that most of the chronic offending delinquency can be explained by an early onset model described in Patterson et al. (1989), Patterson, Capaldi, and Bank (1991), Patterson and Yoerger (1993a), and Patterson, Crosby, et al. (1992). This section briefly outlines the key findings for the early onset model.

It is well known that boys who began their crime careers during preadolescence are at particular risk for chronic offending (Farrington & Hawkins, 1991; Glueck & Glueck, 1950). It is assumed that the extremely antisocial child overwhelms parental efforts to supervise and is out on the street at an earlier age than contemporaries. Presumably, it is the interaction (statistical) between the antisocial trait score and early involvement with deviant peers that produces early delinquent activity.

The higher the rate, the more likely these children will be apprehended at an early age.

As noted earlier, the prime determinants of antisocial child behavior are thought to be disrupted discipline and lack of supervision. One would, therefore, expect that disrupted parenting practices would be significant predictors of early police arrest. A multivariate analyses of OYS data showed that both the discipline and the social disadvantage constructs were significantly related to hazard rates for arrest by age 14.0 (Patterson, Crosby, et al., 1992). However, the early-onset model hypothesized that the effects of faulty parenting on delinquency would be mediated by the interaction term for the antisocial trait and early timing for deviant peer involvement (Patterson & Yoerger, 1993b). In both instances, where the antisocial construct was introduced as a predictor, the contribution of parenting behavior became nonsignificant (Patterson & Capaldi, 1991; Patterson, Crosby, et al.)

Our preliminary analysis of the predicting power of the interaction term (antisocial trait by timing for deviant peer) shows promise as the best predictor of early arrest (Patterson & Yoerger, 1993b). By adding those boys who scored above the median at Grade 4 on both antisocial and deviant peer involvement, 68 were identified at risk. Of these, .471 were arrested prior to age 14. This predictive power identifies the model as potentially useful for prevention field trials.

Several characteristics of offender data suggest that it would be useful to arbitrarily set the cutting score for early arrest at 13.9 years or less (Patterson & Yoerger, 1993a). Two hypotheses follow from this decision. First, early and late starters should be characterized by different determinants; second, the outcomes should be significantly different. Preliminary studies of different determinants for early and late starters are promising (Patterson & Yoerger, 1993b). For the OYS, analyses showed that late starters were intermediate between early starters and nondelinquent samples on several variables describing family process and adjustment skills (i.e., early starters were more deviant than late starters, who in turn were more deviant than nondelinquents.)

Chronicity

A direct test of the differential outcomes hypothesis is relatively straightforward. Chronic offending (three or more arrests) should be significantly higher in the early- rather than the late-start offenders. The data from the OYS are summarized in Figure 3.11. As shown, 100% of the boys (10) arrested prior to age 10 had at least three police arrests prior to age 17. In order to provide more robust estimates, the remainder of the figure data was summarized for two adjacent ages. (For example, for boys aged 10 and 11, the risk of chronic offending was .80.) To make the estimates comparable, they were based only on the 3 years following the

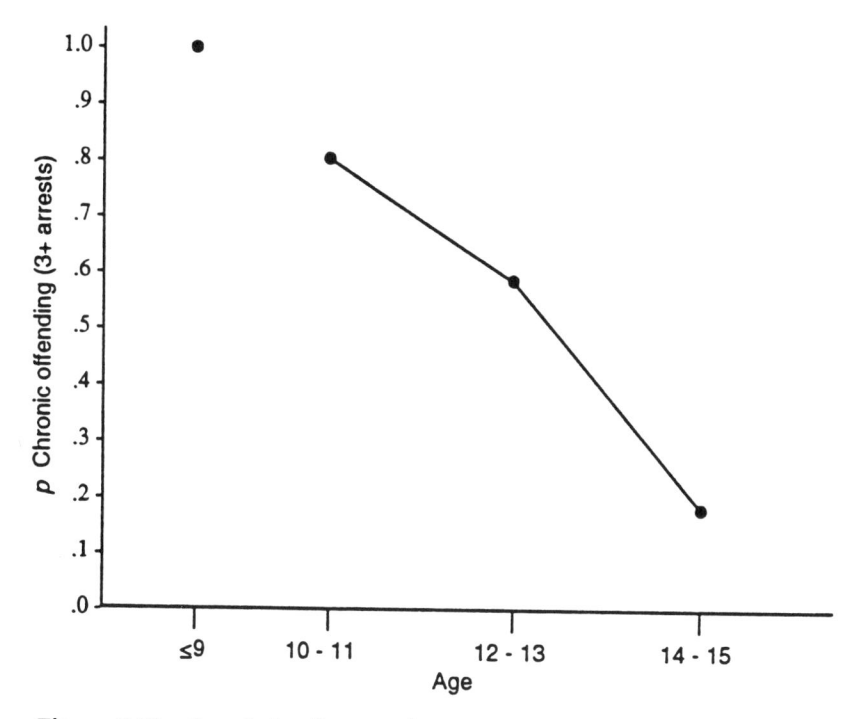

Figure 3.11 Covariation for age of arrest, onset, and chronicity (*N* = 206).

first arrest. There was an almost linear relation between age of first arrest and risk of chronic offending. At age 14.0, there was a sharp drop in the risk of chronic offending.

The data reviewed by Blumstein, Cohen, Roth, and Visher (1986) for three longitudinal studies showed that with three juvenile offenses, the probability of an adult offense ranged from .55 in one study to .90 in another. It seems, then, that adult offending is related to juvenile chronicity.

Violence

According to the coercion model, the more frequent the performance of trivial coercive or antisocial acts, the greater the risk of escalation to more severe acts (Patterson, in press). To test the hypothesized relation between chronicity and violence, Capaldi and Patterson (1993) identified 17 boys in the OYS with one or more arrests for violent crimes (e.g., asault, robbery). The likelihood of an arrest for violence (*A*) given chronic offending (*B*) was .55; the comparable figure for Farrington and Hawkins's (1991) data for adults was .49. Although about half of the high-rate delinquents were violent, almost every violent boy was a frequent offender. The $p\ A/B$ was .940. In other words, a theory that explains early onset identifies most of the chronic offenders. Identifying chronic offenders, in turn, identifies most of the violent offenders. It seems reasonable to hypothesize that a single early-onset model may account for most of society's primary concerns about delinquency.

Implications

This chapter had two general purposes. One was to outline the important characteristics of a performance theory. The emphasis was on the use of multimethod-multiagent indicators to define each of the key independent and dependent variables in the model. Although it is beyond the purview of this chapter, there is now a series of studies concerned with matters such as shared method variance, generalizability of models, and reporter bias that further emphasizes the need for more adequate measurement models for contemporary theories of delinquency.

It was demonstrated that the general measurement strategy seemed to work when applied to testing the parenting model for early antisocial behavior in boys. The model replicated across samples and across sites (i.e., disrupted parental discipline, monitoring, and problem solving) was related to adjustment problems in young boys (and girls). The two or three experiments carried out thus far demonstrated that the parental variables may operate as causal variables. As predicted, the highly antisocial boy was at greatest risk for early police arrest. We are currently preparing a second at-risk sample to determine whether the early-onset model can be replicated.

One of the key features of a developmental model is its ability to account for stability and change. The relevant studies were only briefly reviewed in this chapter. More detailed analyses of the mechanisms that account for stability and change are presented in Patterson and Bank (1989) and Vuchinich et al. (1992). The studies of changes in intensity are reviewed in Patterson (in press), changes in form in Patterson (1993), and qualitative changes in Patterson and Yoerger (1993a). In general, the studies demonstrated that change and stability are not antithetical (i.e., they occur simultaneously during development). It was also shown that the changes are orderly and systematic (i.e., over time they define a second-order deviancy factor). What is lost in the emphasis on changes is the sense that the trajectory is really describing manifestations of the same old thing. The well-known stability correlations showed that in terms of behavior, the child is indeed father of the man. Form, settings, and reinforcers change, but the sense of a second-order deviancy factor still exists, as suggested in the writings of Gottfredson and Hirschi (1990).

The general findings support the idea that the boy who is at grave risk of early police arrest is extremely aggressive in grade school and is already involved with deviant peers. The prediction is accompanied by a low false-positive error rate (53%) and an even lower false-negative error rate (22%). The data showed that more than three out of four members of the early-onset group became chronic offenders by age 17; furthermore, more than half of the chronic offenders were violent.

Taken together, the general pattern of findings suggests that it has been a strategic error to classify all delinquent boys as members of a single class that requires a general theory of delinquency. It seems far more efficient to focus our efforts to explain and predict on this smaller subset of early-start delinquent youth.

In some ways, the most interesting aspect of the early-onset formulation has to do with the role of contextual variables. Sociological theory coordinates economic cycles with an increasing density of single mothers and difficult-to-rear infants. However, by themselves, the prevalence of single mothers and difficult infants accounts for only a small amount of variance in the variations in crime rates. It is assumed that the coercion model identifies that mechanisms that would dramatically increase the amount of variance accounted for; presumably, the single mother who is antisocial is at greatest risk for disruptions in parenting skills. In turn, the difficult-to-raise infant with a mother unskilled in parenting will be at greatest risk for antisocial problems. It seems, then, that the effect of economic cycles on crime rates is mediated by mechanisms from both social disorganizational and developmental theories.

As a final note, it seems that the present effort to update a behavioral-reinforcement perspective and apply it to personality theory is in good company. Staats (1993) has outlined a comprehensive formulation whose general orientation is quite similar to that of the coercion model. His psychological behaviorism uses principles from learning theory to account for individual differences. He takes the position that personality consists of learned basic behavioral repertoires, which serve as determinants for settings and individuals sampled in future interactions. The present writer believes that an understanding of social behaviors requires two components. One consists of reliance on observation data to understand social interaction sequences; and the second is a functional analyses of these interaction sequences. The two components must be an integral part of the effort to understand and predict what people do.

Acknowledgments

The writer gratefully acknowledges the support provided by Research Grant MH 46690 from the NIMH section on Violent Behavior and Traumatic Stress and Research Grant MH 38318 from the NIMH section on Mood, Anxiety, and Personality Disorders. The ideas expressed are a direct outcome of frequent discussions with my colleagues Lew Bank, Tom Dishion, Marion Forgatch, John Reid, Mike Stoolmiller, and Karen

Yoerger. It is these frequent discussions that gradually framed the questions being asked. Fortunately, some of these colleagues were also uncommonly skilled in finding statistical analyses that could increase the fit between the questions and the data.

References

Achenbach, T. M., & Edelbrock, C. S. (1979). *Child behavior checklist.* Bethesda, MD: National Institute of Mental Health.

Achenbach, T. M., & Edlebrock, C. S. (1983). *Manual for the Child Behavior checklist and the revised Child Behavior profile.* Burlington, VT: Thomas M. Achenbach.

Asendorpf, J. B. (1992). Beyond stability: Predicting inter-individual differences in intra-individual change. *Europena Journal of Personality, 6,* 103–117.

Bandura, A. (1973). *Aggression: A social learning analysis* (p. 388). Engelwood Cliffs, NJ: Prentice-Hall.

Bank, L., Forgatch, M. S., Patterson, G. R., & Fetrow, R. A. (1993). Parenting practices: Mediators of negative contextual factors. *Journal of Marriage and the Family, 55,* 371–384.

Barkley, R. A. (1991). The use of psychopharmacology to study reciprocal influences in parent–child interaction. *Journal of Abnormal Child Psychology, 9*(3), 303–310.

Blumstein, A., Cohen, J., Roth, J. A., & Visher, C. A. (Eds.). (1986), *Criminal careers and career criminals* (Vols. I and II). Washington, DC: National Academy Press.

Bowlby, J. (1969). *Attachment and loss. Vol. 1: Attachment.* New York: Basic Books.

Buehler, R. E., Patterson, G. R., & Furniss, J. M. (1966). The reinforcement of behavior in institutional settings. *Behaviour Research and Therapy, 4,* 157–167.

Cairns, R. B. & Cairns, B. D. (1991). Social cognition and social networks: A developmental perspective. In D. J. Pepler & K. H. Rubin (Eds.), *The development and treatment of childhood aggression* (pp. 249–278). Hillsdale, NJ: Erlbaum.

Capaldi, D. M., & Patterson, G. R. (1989). *Psychometric properties of fourteen latent constructs from the Oregon Youth Study.* New York: Springer-Verlag.

Capaldi, D. M., & Patterson, G. R. (1991). Relation of parental transitions to boys' adjustment problems: I. A linear hypothesis. II. Mothers at risk for transitions and unskilled parenting. *Developmental Psychology, 27,* 489–504.

Capaldi, D. M., & Patterson, G. R. (1993, March). *The violent adolescent male: Specialist or generalist?* Paper presented at the Society for Research in Child Development conference, New Orleans.

Caspi, A., & Elder, G. H. (1988). Childhood precursors of the life course: Early personality and life disorganization. In M. Hetherington, R. M. Lerner, & M. Perlmutter (Eds.), *Child development in life span perspective* (pp. 115–142). Hillsdale, NJ: Erlbaum.

Caspi, A., Elder, G. H., & Bem, D. J. (1987). Moving against the world: Life course patterns of explosive children. *Developmental Psychology, 23,* 308–313.

Caspi, A., Elder, G. H., Jr., & Herbener, E. (1990). Childhood personality and the prediction of life-course patterns. In L. Robins & M. Rutter (Eds.), *Straight and devious pathways from childhood to adulthood* (pp. 13–35). Cambridge: Cambridge University Press.

Conger, R., Patterson, G. R., & Gé, X. (1995). It takes two to replicate: A mediational model for the impact of parents' stress on adolescent adjustment. *Child Development, 66,* 80–97.

Cox, M. (1993, July). *Transition to parenthood and families with young children.* Paper presented at the workshop on Conceptual and methodological models for understanding family processes related to child mental health, National Institute of Mental Health, Bethesda, MD.

Davitz, J. R. (1952). The effects of previous training on post-frustration behavior. *Journal of Abnormal and Social Psychology, 47,* 309–315.

Dawes, R. M. (1988). *Rational choice in an uncertain world* (p. 348). San Diego, CA: Harcourt Brace Jovanovich.

Dishion, T. J. (1990). The peer context of troublesome child and adolescent behavior. In P. Leone (Ed.), *Understanding troubled and troubling youth: Multidisciplinary perspective* (pp. 128–153). Newbury Park, CA: Sage.

Dishion, T. J., Andrews, D. W., & Crosby, L. (1995). Adolescent boys and their friends in adolescence: Relationship characteristics, quality, and interactional process. *Child Development, 66,* 139–151.

Dishion, T. J., French, D., & Patterson, G. R. (1995). The development and ecology of antisocial behavior. In D. Cichetti & D. Cohen (Eds.), *Manual of developmental psychopathology* (pp. 421–471). New York: Wiley.

Dishion, T. J., Patterson, G. R., & Griesler, P. C. (1994). Peer adaptation in the development of antisocial behavior: A confluence model. In L. R. Huesmann (Ed.), *Current Perspectives* (pp. 61–95). New York: Plenum Press.

Dishion, T. J., Patterson, G. R., & Kavanagh, K. A. (1992). An experimental test of the coercion model: Linking theory, measurement, and intervention. In J. McCord & R. Tremblay (Eds.), *The interaction of theory and practice: Experimental studies of intervention* (pp. 253–282). New York: Guilford Press.

Dishion, T. J., Patterson, G. R., Stoolmiller, M., & Skinner, M. L. (1991). Family, school, and behavioral antecedents to early adolescent involvement with antisocial peers. *Developmental Psychology, 2,* 172–180.

Dodge, K. A. (1991). The structure and function of proactive and reactive aggression. In D. J. Pepler & K. H. Rubin (Eds.), *The development and treatment of childhood aggression* (pp. 201–216). Hillsdale, NJ: Erlbaum.

Dollard, J., Doob, L. W., Miller, N. E., Mowrer, O. H., & Sears, R. R. (1990). *Frustration and aggression.* Newbury Park, CA: Sage. (Original work published 1939)

Epstein, S. (1979). The stability of behavior: I. On predicting most of the people much of the time. *Journal of Personality and Social Psychology, 37,* 1097–1126.

Eriksen, C. W. (Ed.), (1962). *Behavior and awareness: A symposium of research and interpretation.* Durham, NC: Duke University Press.

Fagot, B. L. (1992). Assessment of coercive parent discipline. *Behavioral Assessment, 14,* 387–406.

Fagot, B. L., & Kavanagh, K. (1990). The prediction of antisocial behavior from avoidant attachment classifications. *Child Development, 61,* 864–873.

Farrington, D. P., & Hawkins, J. D. (1991). Predicting participation, early onset, and later persistence in officially recorded offending. *Criminal Behaviour and Mental Health, 1,* 1–33.

Fawl, C. I. (1963). Disturbances experienced by children in their natural habitats. In R. G. Barker (Ed.), *The stream of behavior* (pp. 99–126). New York: Appleton-Century-Crofts.

Forgatch, M. S. (1991). The clinical science vortex: A developing theory of antisocial behavior. In D. J. Pepler & K. H. Rubin (Eds.), *The development and treatment of childhood aggression* (pp. 291–315). Hillsdale, NJ: Erlbaum.

Forgatch, M. S., & Patterson, G. R. (1989). *Parents and adolescents living together: II. Family problem solving.* Eugene, OR: Castalia.

Forgatch, M. S., Patterson, G. R., & Ray, J. A. (in press). Divorce and boys' adjustment problems: Two paths with a single model. In E. M. Hetherington (Ed.), *Stress, coping, and resiliency in children and the family.* Hillsdale, NJ: Erlbaum.

Forgatch, M. S., Patterson, G. R., & Skinner, M. L. (1988). A mediational model for the effect of divorce on antisocial behavior in boys. In E. M. Hetherington & J. D. Aresteh (Eds.), *Impact of divorce, single parenting, and step-parenting on children* (pp. 135–154). Hillsdale, NJ: Erlbaum.

Glaser, R. (Ed.), (1971) *The nature of reinforcement* (p. 380). New York: Academic Press.

Glueck, S., & Glueck, E. (1950). *Unraveling juvenile delinquency.* Cambridge, MA: Harvard University Press.

Gottesman, I. I., & Goldsmith, H. H. (1993). *Developmental psychopathology of anitsocial behavior: Inserting genes into its ontogensis and epigensis.* Paper presented at the 27th Minnesota Symposium on Child Psychology, C. Nelson (Ed.), University of Minnesota.

Gottfredson, M. R., & Hirschi, T. (1990). *A general theory of crime.* Stanford, CA: Stanford University Press.

Herrnstein, R. J. (1961). Relative and absolute strength of response as a function of frequency or reinforcement. *Journal of Experimental Analysis of Behavior, 4,* 267–272.

Huesmann, L. R., Eron, L. D., & Yarmel, P. W. (1987). Intellectual function and aggression. *Journal of Personality and Social Psychology, 52,* 232–240.

Jones, R. R., Reid, J. B., & Patterson, G. R. (1975). Naturalistic observation in clinical assessment. In P. McReynolds (Ed.), *Advances in psychological assessment* (Vol. 3, pp. 42–95). San Francisco: Jossey-Bass.

Kandel, D. B. (1978). Homophily, selection, and socialization in adolescent friendships. *American Journal of Sociology, 84*(2), 427–436.

Kochanska, G. (1991, April). *Child compliance and noncompliance in the origins of conscience.* Paper presented at the meeting of the Society for Research in Child Development, Seattle.

Lahey, B. B., Hartdagen, S. E., Frick, P. J., McBurnett, K., Connor, R., & Hynd, G. W. (1988). Conduct disorder: Parsing the confounded relation to parental divorce and antisocial personality. *Journal of Abnormal Psychology, 97,* 334–337.

Larzelere, R. E., & Patterson, G. R. (1990). Parental management: Mediator of the effect of socioeconomic status on early delinquency. *Criminology, 28,* 301–324.

Laub, J. H., & Sampson, R. J. (1988). Unraveling families and delinquency: A reanalysis of the Gluecks' data. *Criminology, 26,* 355–380.

Lucretius. (1965). *On the nature of the universe.* A new verse translation, with an introduction by James H. Mantinband. New York: Fredrick Ungar.

Lytton, H. (1977). Do parents create, or respond to, differences in twins? *Developmental Psychology, 13,* 456-459.

Maccoby, E. E. (1993). The role of parents in the socialization of children: An historical overview. *Developmental Psychology, 28*(6), 1006–1017.

Maier, N. R. F. (1961). *Frustration: The study of behavior without a goal.* Ann Arbor: University of Michigan Press.

McArdle, J. J., & Epstein, D. (1987). Latent growth curves within developmental structural equation models. *Child Development, 58,* 110–133.

McDowell, J. J. (1988). Matching theory in natural human environments. *The Behavior Analyst, 11,* 93–109.

Metzler, C. E., & Dishion, T. J. (1992, May). *A model of the development of youthful problem behaviors.* Paper presented at the 18th Annual Convention of the Association for Behavior Analysis, San Francisco.

Mischel, W. (1968). *Personality and assessment.* New York: Wiley.

Moffitt, T. E., & Henry, B. (1989). Neuropsychological assessment of executive functions in self-reported delinquents. *Development and Psychopathology, 1,* 105–119.

Olweus, D. (1979). Stability of aggressive reaction patterns in males: A review. *Psychological Bulletin, 86*(4), 852–875.

Patterson, G. R. (1977). A three-stage functional analysis for children's coercive behaviors: A tactic for developing a performance theory. In D. Baer, B. C. Etzel, & J. M. LeBlanc (Eds.), *New developments in behavioral research: Theories, methods, and applications. In honor of Sidney W. Bijou* (pp. 59–79). Hillsdale, NJ: Erlbaum.

Patterson, G. R. (1979). A performance theory for coercive family interaction. In R. B. Cairns (Ed.), *The analysis of social interactions: Methods, issues, and illustrations* (pp. 119–162). Hillsdale, NJ: Erlbaum.

Patterson, G. R. (1982). *A social learning approach: III. Coercive family process.* Eugene, OR: Castalia.

Patterson, G. R. (1983). Stress: A change agent for family process. In N. Garmezy & M. Rutter (Eds.), *Stress, coping, and development in children* (pp. 235–264). New York: McGraw-Hill.

Patterson, G. R. (1988). Family process: Loops, levels, and linkages. In N. Bolger, A. Caspi, G. Downey, & M. Moorehouse (Eds.), *Persons in context: Developmental processes* (pp. 114–151). New York: Cambridge University Press.

Patterson, G. R. (1990). Some comments about cognitions as causal variables. *American Psychologist, 45,* 984–985.

Patterson, G. R. (1992). Developmental changes in antisocial behavior. In R. D. Peters, R. J. McMahon, & V. L. Quinsey (Eds.), *Aggression and violence throughout the life span* (pp. 52–82). Newbury Park, CA: Sage.

Patterson, G. R. (1993). Orderly change in a stable world: The antisocial trait as a chimera. *Journal of Consulting and Clinical Psychology, 61,* 911–919.

Patterson, G. R. (in press). Coercion as a basis for early age of onset for arrest. In J. McCord (Ed.), *Coercion and punishment in long-term perspective.* New York: Cambridge University Press.

Patterson, G. R., & Bank, C. L. (1989). Some amplifying mechanisms for pathologic processes in families. In M. R. Runnar & E. Thelen (Eds.), *Systems and development: The Minnesota symposium on child psychology, 22,* (pp. 159–167). Hillsdale, NJ: Erlbaum.

Patterson, G. R., & Capaldi, D. M. (1991). Antisocial parents: Unskilled and vulnerable. In P. A. Cowan & E. M. Hetherington (Eds.), *Family transitions* (pp. 195–218). Hillsdale, NJ: Erlbaum.

Patterson, G. R., Capaldi, D., & Bank, L. (1991). An early starter model for predicting delinquency. In D. J. Pepler & K. H. Rubin (Eds.), *The development and treatment of childhood aggression* (pp. 139–168). Hillsdale, NJ: Erlbaum.

Patterson, G. R., Crosby, L., & Vuchinich, S. (1992). Predicting risk for early police arrest. *Journal of Quantitative Criminology, 8,* 335–355.

Patterson, G. R., DeBaryshe, B. D., & Ramsey, E. (1989). A developmental perspective on antisocial behavior. *American Psychologist, 44,* 329–335.

Patterson, G. R., & Dishion, T. J. (1988). Multilevel family process models: Traits, interactions, and relationships. In R. A. Hinde & J. Stevenson-Hinde (Eds.), *Relationships within families: Mutual influences* (pp. 283–310). Oxford: Clarendon.

Patterson, G. R., Dishion, T. J., & Chamberlain, P. (1993). Outcomes and methodological issues relating to treatment of antisocial children. In T. R. Giles (Ed.), *Handbook of effective psychotherapy* (pp. 43–88). New York: Plenum Press.

Patterson, G. R., & Duncan, T. (1993). *Tests for continuity for preschool coercion progression.* Unpublished manuscript.

Patterson, G. R., & Forgatch, M. S. (1987). *Parents and adolescents living together: I: The basics.* Eugene, OR: Castalia.

Patterson, G. R., & Forgatch, M. S. (1990). Initiation and maintenance of processes disrupting single-mother families. In G. R. Patterson (Ed.), *Depression and aggression in family interaction* (pp. 209–245). Hillsdale, NJ: Erlbaum.

Patterson, G. R., Littman, R. A., & Bricker, W. (1967). Assertive behavior in children: A step towards a theory of aggression. *Monographs of the Society for Research in Child Development, 32*(5), 1–43.

Patterson, G. R., Reid, J. B., & Dishion, T. J. (1992). *A social learning approach: IV. Antisocial boys.* Eugene, OR: Castalia.

Patterson, G. R., & Stouthamer-Loeber, M. (1984). The correlation of family management practices and delinquency. *Child Development, 55,* 1299–1307.

Patterson, G. R., & Yoerger, K. (1993a). Developmental models for delinquent behavior. In S. Hodgins (Ed.), *Mental disorders and crime* (pp. 140–172). Newbury Park, CA: Sage.

Patterson, G. R., & Yoerger, K. (1993b, March). *A model for late onset delinquency.* Paper presented at the meeting of the Society for Research in Child Development, New Orleans.

Ramsey, E., Patterson, G. R., & Walker, H. M. (1990). Generalization of the antisocial trait from home to school settings. *Journal of Applied Developmental Psychology, 11,* 209–223.

Reid, J. B. (1986). Social-interactional patterns in families of abused and non-abused children. In C. Zahn-Waxler, E. M. Cummings, & R. Iannotti (Eds.), *Altruism and aggression: Biological and social origins* (pp. 238–255). New York: Cambridge University Press.

Ribes-Inesta, E., & Bandura, A. (Eds.). (1976). *Analyses of delinquency and aggression.* Hillsdale, NJ: Erlbaum.

Robins, L. N. (1981). *What effect did Viet Nam have on veterans' mental health?* Unpublished manuscript.

Rogosa, D. R., & Willett, J. B. (1985). Understanding correlates of change by modeling individual differences in growth. *Psychometrika, 50,* 203–228.

Rutter, M., & Giller, H. (1983). *Juvenile delinquency: Trends and perspectives.* Middlesex, U.K.: Penguin.

Sacket, G. (1993, July). *Why children in the same family are so different: Revisited.* Paper presented at the Second Social Interactional Chautauqua, Eugene, OR.

Sampson, R. J. (1987). Urban Black violence: The effect of male joblessness and family disruption. *American Journal of Sociology, 93,* 348–382.

Sampson, R. J. (1992). Family management and child development: Insights from social disorganization theory. In J. McCord (Ed.), *Facts, frameworks, and forecasts, Vol. 3 of Advances in criminological theory* (pp. 63–91). New Brunswick, NJ: Transaction.

Sampson, R. J., & Laub, J. H. (1992). Crime and deviance in the life course. *Annual Review of Sociology, 18,* 63–84.

Sampson, R. J., & Laub, J. H. (1994). Urban poverty and the family context of delinquency: A new look at structure and process in a classic study. *Child Development, 65,* 523–540.

Schonfeld, I. S. (1990). A developmental perspective and antisocial behavior: Cognitive functioning. *American Psychologist, 45*(8), 983–984.

Shaffer, D. R., & Brody, G. H. (1982). Parental and peer influences on moral development. In R. W. Henderson (Ed.), *Parent–child interaction: Theory, research, and prospects* (pp. 83–124). New York: Academic Press.

Smith, C. A., & Lazarus, R. S. (1990). Emotion and adaptations. In L. A. Pervin (Ed.), *Handbook of personality: Theory and research* (pp. 609–637). New York: Guilford Press.

Snyder, J. J. (1991). Discipline as a mediator of the impact of maternal stress and mood on child conduct problems. *Development and Psychopathology, 3,* 263–276.

Snyder, J. J., & Patterson, G. R. (1995). Individual differences in social aggression: A test of a reinforcement model of socialization in the natural environment. *Behavior Therapy, 26,* 371–391.

Spivack, G., Platt, J., & Shure, M. B. (1976). *The problem solving approach to adjustment.* San Francisco: Jossey-Bass.

Staats, A. W. (1993). Personality theory, abnormal psychology, and psychological measurement. *Behavior Modification, 17*(1), 8–42.

Stoolmiller, M. (1990, December). *Parent supervision, child unsupervised wandering, and child antisocial behavior: A latent growth curve analysis.* Unpublished doctoral dissertation, University of Oregon, Eugene.

Stoolmiller, M., & Bank, L. (in press). Autoregressive effects in structural equation models: We see some problems. In J. Gottman & G. Sackett (Eds.), *The analysis of change.* Hillsdale, NJ: Erlbaum.

Utting, D., Bright, J., & Henricson, C. (1993). Crime in the family: Improving child rearing and preventing delinquency. *Occasional Paper, 16.* London: Family Policy Studies Centre.

Vuchinich, S., Bank, L., & Patterson, G. R. (1992). Parenting, peers, and the stability of antisocial behavior in preadolescent boys. *Developmental Psychology, 28,* 510–521.

Waters, E., Kondo-Ikemura, K., Posad, G., & Richters, J. E. (1990). Learning to love: Mechanisms and milestones. In M. Gunnar & L. A. Sroufe (Eds.), *Minnesota symposia on child psychology* (Vol. 23, pp. 217–255). Hillsdale, NJ: Erlbaum.

Werner, E. E. (1989). Children of the garden island. *Scientific American, 260,* 107–111.

Willett, J. B., Ayoub, C. C., & Robinson, D. (1991). Using growth modeling to examine systematic differences in growth: An example of change in the function of families at risk of maladaptive parenting, child abuse, or neglect. *Journal of Consulting and Clinical Psychology, 59,* 38–47.

Wilson, J. Q., & Herrnstein, R. J. (1985). *Crime and human nature.* New York: Simon & Schuster.

Wright, J. C. (1983). *The structure and perception of behavioral consistency.* Unpublished doctoral dissertation, Stanford University, Stanford, CA.

4

Markers, Developmental Processes, and Schizophrenia

BARBARA A. CORNBLATT, ROBERT H. DWORKIN,
LORRAINE E. WOLF, AND L. ERLENMEYER-KIMLING

Clinical, self-report, and experimental studies have converged to implicate attention in the biology of schizophrenia. Clinically, impaired attention has consistently been described as a prominent characteristic of schizophrenia in the literature, beginning with the early descriptions of Kraepelin (1919). Phenomenologically, schizophrenic patients have described a distressing inability to focus on information in the environment (e.g., Freedman & Chapman, 1973). Experimentally, laboratory studies spanning at least 40 years have demonstrated that objectively measured attentional dysfunctions are displayed by schizophrenic patients and by their first-degree relatives—especially, their at-risk offspring (Cornblatt & Keilp, 1994; Erlenmeyer-Kimling & Cornblatt, 1992).

More recently, researchers interested in genetics have begun to investigate the value of impaired attention as a biobehavioral indicator or marker—that is, as a deficit measured at the behavioral level that indicates the presence of the schizophrenic disease gene(s) (Cornblatt & Keilp, 1994; Erlenmeyer-Kimling, 1987). In this chapter, we will review the evidence suggesting that abnormal attention is a strong candidate marker of a biological susceptibility to schizophrenia. In addition, we will be interested in the extent to which attentional markers also predict illness in at-risk children and play a role in its pathogenesis—that is, contribute to symptom development. Our discussion will center on three major topics:

1. The nature of the attentional deficit in schizophrenia.
2. The data supporting impaired attention as a valid marker of the schizophrenia genotype.

3. Developmental findings that suggest a model for the role of attention dysfunction in the formation of schizophrenic symptoms, especially those related to inadequate social skills.

We will rely heavily on the data collected over the course of the New York High Risk Project (NYHRP), a longitudinal prospective study of children who are either at high or low risk for schizophrenia (see Cornblatt & Erlenmeyer-Kimling, 1985; and Erlenmeyer-Kimling & Cornblatt, 1992, for reviews). Prospective studies of the young at-risk offspring of schizophrenic parents provide a direct way to assess the role of attention in both the etiology and development of schizophrenia, as antecedent deficits can be studied unconfounded by clinical symptomatology. Of the many high-risk studies initiated in the late 1960s and early 1970s, the NYHRP is the only one that has continually followed and tested at-risk subjects from early childhood through midadulthood. In addition, abnormalities of attention have been a primary focus of the NYHRP since its inception; thus, the developmental data collected over the course of the NYHRP offer a unique opportunity to understand the relationship between attention and schizophrenia.

Nature of the Attentional Deficit

In a phenomenological study of schizophrenic patients, Freedman and Chapman (1973) reported that a common complaint of patients was an inability to maintain their focus on critical information from the environment and a tendency to be distracted by irrelevant stimuli. Such findings led to a large number of studies of attention that found schizophrenics to be abnormally distractible. It gradually became apparent, however, that there were significant methodological difficulties with much of this research (as pointed out by the Chapmans; e.g., Chapman & Chapman, 1975; Chapman, Chapman, & Raulin, 1976). Recent findings suggest that distractibility is not specific to schizophrenia and that it is likely to be a state, rather than a stable trait, indicator (Cornblatt, Lenzenweger, Dworkin & Erlenmeyer-Kimling, 1985). It has also become increasingly clear that the general construct of attention is comprised of a number of subcomponents, of which distractibility is only one (e.g., Mirsky, Anthony, Duncan, Ahearn, & Kellam, 1991; Wolf & Halperin, 1987). As a result, research concerned with attentional abnormalities has rapidly grown and extended into a number of new directions since the early distractibility studies (see reviews by Erlenmeyer-Kimling & Cornblatt, 1987; Nuechterlein & Dawson, 1984).

To date, the single component of attention that has been most solidly associated with the biology of schizophrenia is sustained attention, as measured by some form of the Continuous Performance Test or CPT

(Cornblatt & Keilp, 1994). The CPT is actually not a single test, but rather a family of measures that share a number of common features. These are (1) the rapid presentation of a long series of stimuli; (2) the requirement that a subject respond whenever a designated target or target sequence occurs amid the series; and (3) a relatively low probability that a target will appear (generally around 20% of the time). In addition, a constant, externally paced presentation rate that is not under the subject's control appears to be a critical feature of the CPT tasks used most successfully in schizophrenia research. Although there are a few auditory versions of the CPT, the majority have been presented visually, either on a rear projection screen (earlier versions used a slide projector) or on a video monitor (later, computerized measures).

Because of its similarity to measures typically used in vigilance research (Parasuraman & Davies, 1977), the CPT was originally thought to tap an inability to sustain attention over time in schizophrenic patients. However, differences between control subjects and schizophrenic patients are generally apparent from the outset of any given CPT task and are maintained at a fairly stable level throughout task performance. Thus, attentional deficits in schizophrenia appear to involve a reduced information processing capacity rather than a decline in attention over time. In the majority of studies administering the CPT to schizophrenic patients, the most common types of attention difficulties are either a failure to detect target stimuli (increased omission errors or "misses") or, in more sophisticated signal detection analyses, a reduction in d' (d-prime), a measure of sensitivity to differences between stimuli. These findings are consistent with patients' self-reported inability to focus on critical information in the environment.

Interestingly, although attentional capacity appears compromised at all age levels, schizophrenic patients nevertheless display normal developmental changes in the *pattern* of attentional processing. For example, on the identical pairs version of the CPT (i.e., the CPT-IP; Cornblatt, Risch, Faris, Friedman, & Erlenmeyer-Kimling, 1988; Cornblatt, Winters, & Erlenmeyer-Kimling, 1989b), normal adolescents are able to attend to spatial stimuli more accurately than to verbal stimuli, while normal adults perform equivalently with both types of stimuli. Psychotic adolescents, like normal adolescents, also perform better on spatial than on verbal tasks, although their performance on both is poorer than that of normal adolescents (Cornblatt, 1993). Adult schizophrenic patients, like adult normal controls, perform equivalently on both spatial and verbal tasks, though their level of performance is profoundly impaired on both compared to adult normals. These findings again suggest that the impairment in attention involved in schizophrenia is not a reflection of a deficient processing strategy or a deficit in a particular component of attention (such as susceptibility to distraction), but rather a general lowering of processing capacity.

Marker Status of Impaired Attention

Definition of Biobehavioral Markers.

Data accumulated over more than three decades of CPT research suggest that impaired capacity to attend to information in the environment is a biologically based dysfunction that can serve as a behavioral marker of the schizophrenia genotype. As discussed here, biobehavioral markers are abnormalities that are expressed phenotypically (i.e., behaviorally) and indicate the likely presence of a disease gene or genes, regardless of the extent to which the illness is expressed clinically.

The role of such markers is schematically represented in Figure 4.1. In this model, the schizophrenic genotype is viewed as leading to structural, functional, and/or biochemical abnormalities in the brain. Recent examples of such possibilities are the temporal lobe reductions reported by Shenton et al. (1992), depressed frontal lobe functioning or hypofrontality investigated in depth by Weinberger and colleagues (e.g., Weinberger, 1988; Weinberger, Berman, & Zec, 1986) and the long suspected involvement of a dopamine imbalance in schizophrenia (Creese, Burt, & Snyder, 1976; see Robbins, 1990, for review).

It is further assumed that such brain anomalies lead directly to dysfunctions in neurobiologically driven behaviors, such as in a variety of information-processing abilities, including the capacity to attend to information in the environment. For example, while the brain–marker link is not yet understood, it is possible that impaired attention is related to a specific structural abnormality, such as in the basal ganglia (Cornblatt & Keilp, 1994) or, alternatively, to an excess of dopamine in specific brain areas.

In the model presented here, while a biobehavioral marker such as impaired attention is thought to signal the presence of the underlying disease gene, it does not necessarily indicate that the clinical illness will be fully expressed. In fact, it is assumed that the gene and marker can be associated with a variety of clinical phenotypes, ranging from schizophrenia, as represented in the topmost box on the outcome side of the model, through a number of milder forms of illness in the middle (including schizotypal personality disorders and schizophrenia-related personality disorder features), to clinically normal phenotypes on the bottom (see Erlenmeyer-Kimling, in press; Siever & Davis, 1991, for further discussion of this approach).

So conceptualized, biobehavioral markers of the genotype differ substantially from molecular markers (such as restriction fragment length polymorphisms or simple sequence repeat polymorphisms). For example, as discussed above, a biobehavioral marker is of interest primarily as a signal of the likely presence of a disease gene. It provides no information about the possible location of the gene on the chromosomes, nor does it necessarily imply mode of transmission. By contrast, a molecular

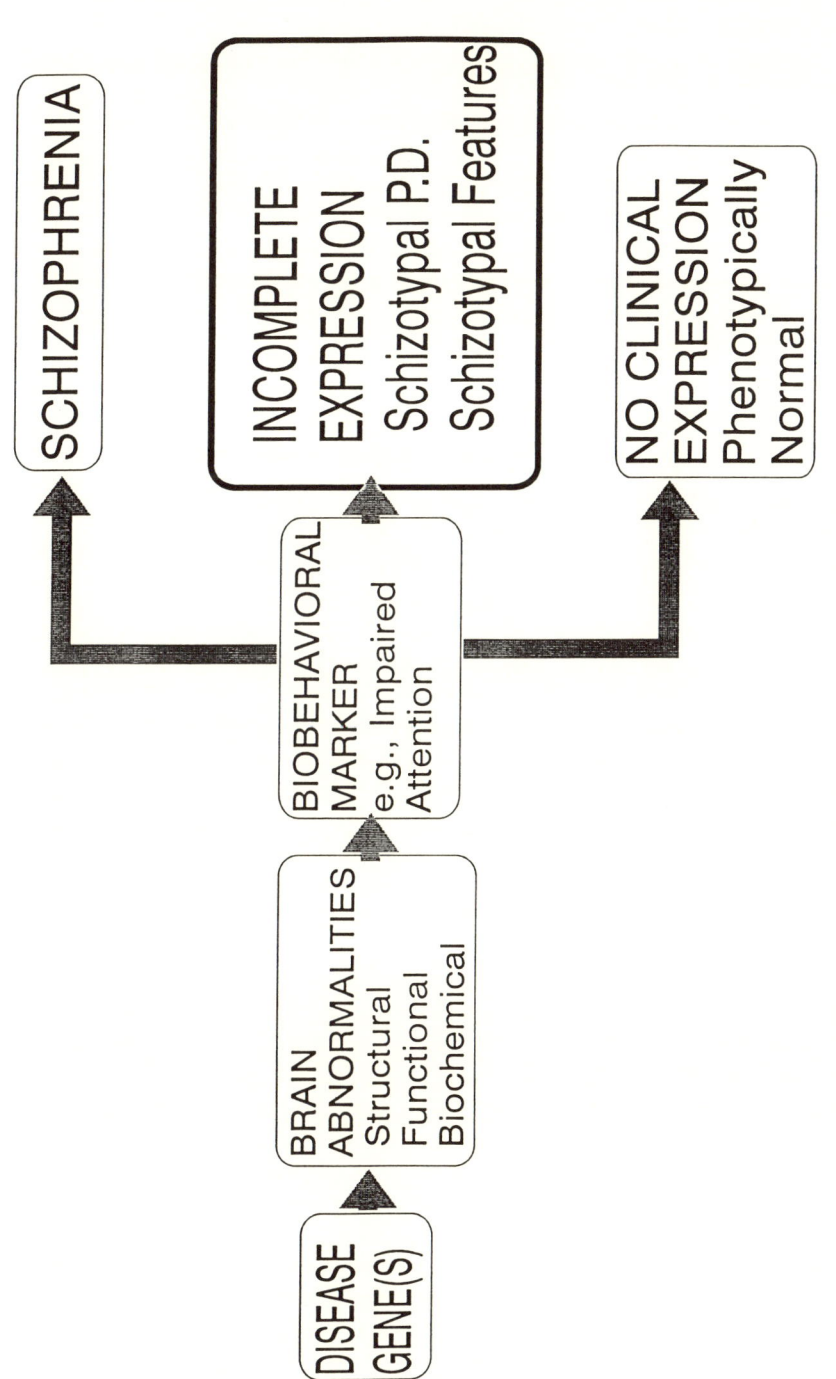

Figure 4.1 Model of the speculated role of biobehavioral markers.

marker functions primarily to indicate the physical location of a gene (Gershon & Goldin, 1986; Weeks et al., 1990).

Furthermore, although a molecular marker and a disease gene are very close to each other on a chromosome, they do not necessarily, or even usually, have a functional relationship. Therefore, the role of a linkage marker is to point to the location of the disease gene, but the marker typically has nothing to do with the illness process. By contrast, biobehavioral markers are considered likely to play a substantial role in the pathophysiology of the illness (Gershon & Goldin, 1986). For example, as will be discussed in detail later, a chronic inability to process information efficiently may have a direct influence on the development of specific personality traits or features.

Role of Biobehavioral Markers in Schizophrenia Research

The goals expected from identifying behavioral markers of schizophrenia have changed in recent years. In the early high-risk studies, such indicators were of interest to the extent that childhood deficits were able to predict later schizophrenia. A primary goal of such research was to identify children at true risk (as opposed to statistical risk), who could then be specifically targeted to receive preventive intervention.

With the advent of modern genetics, however, this view of the role of biobehavioral markers has been substantially expanded—partly as a result of the emerging difficulties in applying molecular techniques to psychiatric illnesses (Cornblatt & Keefe, 1991a; Erlenmeyer-Kimling, in press). For example, compared with successes in illnesses such as Huntington's disease, cystic fibrosis, and Duchenne's muscular dystrophy, the search for molecular markers of complex disorders such as schizophrenia—and psychiatric illnesses in general—has proven less fruitful (Cornblatt & Keefe, 1991a, 1991b).

A major complication in genetic studies of mental illness results from difficulties in defining the phenotype. Identification of "affected" cases (i.e., those assumed to carry the schizophrenia gene or genes) is primarily based on standard diagnoses that are difficult to make and rely largely on clinical judgment (even when using structured assessments). Family studies (e.g., Kendler, Ochs, Gorman, Hewitt, Ross, & Mirsky, 1991; Kety, 1985; Kety, Rosenthal, Wender, Schulsinger, & Jacobsen, 1975; Squires-Wheeler, Bassett, & Erlenmeyer-Kimling, 1989) suggest that expression of the disease gene(s) includes mild schizophrenia-related personality characteristics that would not typically lead to a formal diagnosis of schizophrenia. Therefore, subjects at the mild end of the schizophrenia spectrum—many of the cases falling into the middle box of our model in Figure 4.1—tend to be misclassified as nonaffected in pedigrees, elevating the rate of false negatives. Even more problematic for linkage analysis, the lack of clarity at the diagnostic boundaries of the major psychiatric disorders (e.g., between schizophrenia and affective disorders) can frequently lead to false-positive identifications.

Consequently, pedigree classifications of affected cases based on clinical characteristics alone can result in substantial false-positive and false-negative identifications. These difficulties in defining the ill phenotype have, in turn, led to increasing recognition of a need for biobehavioral markers of the genotype that are independent of clinical symptoms (Cloninger, 1987; Cornblatt & Keefe, 1991a; Erlenmeyer-Kimling, in press; Gershon & Goldin, 1986; Goldin, Nurnberger, & Gershon, 1986).

As a result, considerable interest has been directed to studying biobehavioral markers in populations likely to carry the schizophrenia gene but not necessarily to express the full illness. These populations include (1) at-risk offspring of schizophrenic parents studied prior to disease onset; (2) the clinically unaffected or mildly symptomatic adult first-degree relatives of schizophrenic patients; and (3) nonpsychotic at-risk subjects who have no family history of schizophrenia but who are nevertheless characterized by schizophrenia-related personality disorders and features, such as those identified psychometrically (e.g., Chapman, Chapman, & Raulin, 1976; Lenzenweger, 1993) or in clinic settings (Siever & Davis, 1991). In this chapter, we will consider these to be at-risk populations, with the implication that these subjects are at risk for carrying the schizophrenia gene, although not necessarily for expressing the full clinical illness. Such subjects are optimal for studying the biological mechanisms involved in schizophrenia, as they are free of many of the confounding conditions characterizing research with schizophrenic patients, such as chronic psychosis, generalized performance deficits, long-term medication use, and frequent hospitalizations.

Attention: A Biobehavioral Marker of Schizophrenia?

In their review, Cornblatt and Keilp (1994) provide considerable evidence that impaired attention, as measured by the major versions of the CPT, is likely to be a biobehavioral marker of the schizophrenia genotype. This conclusion is based primarily on the extent to which research using the CPT has fulfilled the criteria listed below, which have been suggested by several investigators (Cloninger, 1987; Erlenmeyer-Kimling, 1987; Gershon & Goldin, 1986; Holzman, Kringlen, Mattysse, Flanagan, Lipton, Cramer, Levin, Lange, & Levy, 1988; Moldin & Erlenmeyer-Kimling, 1994).

1. Association between the marker and schizophrenia in the population (i.e., patients differ from normal controls). This is the most robust finding about impaired attention in the schizophrenia literature. It is clear from the review of over 40 studies (Cornblatt & Keilp, 1994) that affected schizophrenic patients display profound performance deficits relative to a variety of normal and psychiatric controls across all standard versions of the CPT. Moreover, when appropriate CPT tasks are used—most notably, the more difficult Identical Pairs (CPT-IP) and Degraded Stimulus (DS CPT) versions—various at-risk populations show performance deficits consistent with those characterizing the affected patients.

2. *Specificity to schizophrenia.* Although not as solidly established as differences between schizophrenics and normals, attentional abnormalities—or, at least, particular patterns of attentional abnormalities—appear to be specific to psychosis and possibly to schizophrenia. For example, Cornblatt, Lenzenweger, and Erlenmeyer-Kimling (1989a) found that affectively disturbed patients displayed attentional abnormalities on the CPT-IP that were clearly different from those characterizing schizophrenic patients. Schizophrenics showed a global deficit across verbal and spatial tasks, and were primarily characterized by low hit rates and high numbers of random commission errors. By contrast, affective patients were impaired only on spatial tasks and made an excessive number of false alarm errors.

3. *State independence.* A great deal of evidence suggests that deficits in sustained attention are independent of clinical state in schizophrenia. Deficits relative to control groups are apparent in both acutely ill and clinically remitted patients, thus indicating that impaired attention is not a product of the psychotic state. Similarly, deficits in sustained attention in schizotypes are independent of anxiety and depression (Lenzenweger, Cornblatt, & Putnick, 1991). Furthermore, the few studies conducted on affected patients tested both on and off medication indicate that while attention is somewhat improved with treatment, it is not fully normalized (Cornblatt & Keilp, 1994).

4. *Heritability of the trait.* Although research in this area is very limited, the findings that have been reported indicate that attention is heritable in normal families (Cornblatt et al., 1988) and that abnormalities in attention tend to be transmitted in the families of schizophrenic patients (Grove, Lebow, Clementz, Cerri, Medus, & Iacono, 1991; Kendler et al., 1991).

5. *Predating the illness.* The high-risk investigations conducted by Erlenmeyer-Kimling and colleagues (e.g., Cornblatt & Erlenmeyer-Kimling, 1985; Erlenmeyer-Kimling & Cornblatt, 1978; 1992) and by Nuechterlein (1983), involving the more difficult CPT versions, have produced solid evidence for a dysfunctional attentional trait in children at risk for schizophrenia. In these studies, the children are tested several years before symptoms typically appear. Moreover, in the NYHRP, attentional dysfunctions detected in then behaviorally normal children were found to predict behavioral disturbances subsequently emerging in the adolescents at risk for schizophrenia but not in those at risk for affective disorders or in normal controls (Cornblatt & Erlenmeyer-Kimling, 1985; Erlenmeyer-Kimling & Cornblatt, 1992; Erlenmeyer-Kimling, Cornblatt, & Golden, 1983).

6. *Cosegregating with illness.* Gershon and Goldin (1986) define cosegregation as follows: "among relatives who manifest the marker, the prevalence of illness is higher than among relatives who do not" (p. 115). They add that such cosegregation (a) should be assessed only in families in which the proband has both the marker and the illness, (b) is more robust than a population association (i.e., criterion 1), and (c) can offset genetic heterogeneity, since a given family would be expected to have only one form of the disorder.

As yet, little attention had been directed to this issue in marker research. However, some preliminary evidence supporting cosegregation of the attentional marker with schizophrenia-related illness has been provided in a recent study by Steinhauer, Zubin, Condray, Shaw, Peters, and van Kammen (1991). Early results, comparing d' derived from the Degraded Stimulus (DS) version of the CPT among schizophrenic patients, their siblings, and normal controls, indicate that (1) schizophrenic patients had significantly lower (poorer) d' than the normal controls; (2) siblings with spectrum disorders had d' similar to those of the patient probands; and (3) siblings with no schizophrenia-like features had d' similar to those of the normal controls. Similarly, as part of a family study now underway in Germany, Maier, Franke, Hardt, Hain, & Cornblatt (submitted) have administered the CPT-IP to schizophrenic patients, their siblings, and matched normal controls; preliminary findings indicate that siblings are intermediate between patients and controls on both the spatial and verbal conditions. Despite the preliminary findings reported in both studies, however, no direct evidence of cosegregation of attention and the clinical illness has yet been reported in the literature.

Based on integration of the above findings, we believe that it is very likely that a reduced capacity to attend to information in the environment is a marker of the genotype underlying at least one major form of schizophrenia (Cornblatt & Keilp, 1994) and that research should now focus on the role of this deficit in the development of the disorder.

Attention and Schizophrenic Symptoms: A Possible Interaction

Longitudinal data collected over a 20-year developmental period on subjects from the initial sample of the NYHRP, many of whom are now characterized by schizophrenia-related personality disorder (SRPD) features, have led us to propose a model of the role of impaired attention in the development of various clinical features of illness. We subsequently tested the predictions generated by this model on the younger, independent replication sample also being followed in the NYHRP. In the following sections, we will discuss this model and the data that support it.

NYHRP: Overview

The NYHRP is a prospective longitudinal study, started by Erlenmeyer-Kimling in 1971 (e.g., Erlenmeyer-Kimling & Cornblatt, 1987), of subjects at either low or high risk for adult mental illness. Children were considered to be at high risk for schizophrenia if one or both of their parents were schizophrenic and to be at high risk for affective disorder, but not for schizophrenia, if one or both parents had a major affective disorder. They were considered to be at low risk for both illnesses if their parents had no history of mental illness.

The study began with a single sample, referred to as Sample A. As indicated in Table 4.1, when first recruited, Sample A consisted of just over 200 children between the ages of 7 and 12 years (mean age, 9.5 years). Sixty-three of these children were at risk for schizophrenia (HRSz group), 43 were at risk for major affective disorder (HRAff), and 100 were normal controls (NCs) at low risk for both disorders.

Approximately 6 years after the first testing of Sample A, a second sample (Sample B) was added, consisting of 150 risk children between 7 and 12 years old. This somewhat smaller sample included 46 HRSz, 39 HRAff, and 65 NC children during the initial test round.

To fully understand the design of the HR study, it is important to note that risk for illness is statistical. When the study began, based on empirical findings, it was expected that about 10% to 15% of the subjects in the schizophrenic risk group would eventually develop schizophrenia. We had, however, no a priori means of predicting which subjects would comprise the "true risk" group.

The major goal of the NYHRP was to find deficits in early childhood that would predict which of the subjects at statistical risk were at true risk and would actually develop schizophrenia and related illnesses. These deficits are considered likely to be biobehavioral markers of a biological susceptibility, as discussed above.

Based on the data collected over the study period of the NYHRP, we have concluded that of all of the domains studied, impaired attention has the most potential to be such a marker of schizophrenia. The early findings supporting this conclusion can be summarized as follows:

Table 4.1. NYHRP: Number of Subjects in Samples A and B

	Schizophrenia Risk Group	Affective Risk group	Normal Controls
Sample A	63	43	100
Mean age (years)	9.68	9.30	9.43
Sample B	46	39	65
Mean age (years)	8.76	9.34	9.00

Note: Sample A was initially tested between 1971 and 1972, and Sample B was initially tested between 1977 and 1979.

1. During every test round of the NYHRP, more HRSz children displayed attentional deficits than did either NCs or HRAff children. This is consistent with earlier patient findings suggesting that attention might be specifically related to the schizophrenia diatheses. (Cornblatt & Erlenmeyer-Kimling, 1985; Erlenmeyer-Kimling & Cornblatt, 1987, 1992)

2. Moreover, for children in the HRSz group, attentional deficits that were detected at about 9 years of age remained stable throughout development. That is, in nearly every case, those children in the HRSz group who displayed early attentional impairments continued to do so during every subsequent test round. Conversely, virtually no HRSz subjects showing attentional abnormalities at older ages had not done so during the first round of testing at age 9. By contrast, the few HRAff and NC subjects displaying attentional deficits did so sporadically, with no subject in either comparison group being attentionally deviant across all test rounds (Cornblatt et al., 1989b; Winters, Cornblatt, & Erlenmeyer-Kimling, 1991). These findings suggest that in subjects with a liability for schizophrenia, disturbed attention is a long-standing trait that can be detected as soon as it can be reliably measured.

3. Finally, relatively early data from the NYHRP indicated that of the HRSz children who were found to have attentional deviance at around age 9 (when they were behaviorally normal), 93% (13 of 14) in Sample A and 86% (6 of 7) in Sample B were considered moderately to severely disturbed by the time they were in midadolescence (Cornblatt, 1990, 1991). Disturbances were defined nonspecifically as problems in school, with peers, or at home (Cornblatt & Erlenmeyer-Kimling, 1985; Erlenmeyer-Kimling et al., 1983). Conversely, of the subjects with both a genetic risk for schizophrenia and impaired attention, only one subject in each sample appeared to develop normally. This pattern was not displayed by individuals without a biological susceptibility to schizophrenia: No relationship was found between childhood attention and adolescent adjustment either in HRAff subjects or NCs (Cornblatt, 1990, 1991).

Attention and Adult Personality

It can be concluded from the early NYHRP findings discussed above that in individuals at genetic risk for schizophrenia, impaired childhood attention predicts general psychopathology and possibly schizophrenia, although the magnitude of the latter relationship is still being explored. However, as pointed out in Figure 4.1 and in the accompanying discussion, interest in subjects at risk has recently expanded to include individuals who carry the gene and the marker but who do not necessarily express the full clinical illness (Cornblatt, Lenzenweger, & Dworkin, 1992; Erlenmeyer-Kimling, in press).

In Figure 4.1, it is assumed that an as yet undetermined proportion of first-degree relatives of schizophrenic individuals carry the schizophrenic gene or genes (Gottesman & Shields, 1976) and that many of these individuals will display the attentional marker under study. Subjects thought to have both the gene and the marker, but no signs of the clinical illness (i.e., those in the bottom box in Figure 4.1), represent clinical false negatives and considerably complicate the study of both etiology and biobehavioral markers. The first group, the diagnosed schizophrenic patients, also pose formidable problems for research concerned with etiology and process because of the presence of such confounding conditions as a generalized performance deficit and long-term medication use and illness. Thus, the middle group, which may be the largest of the three, appears to be optimal for studying the way in which markers are involved in the emergence of illness.

Applying this strategy specifically to the study of attention, we (Cornblatt et al., 1992) examined the relationship between attentional dysfunctions detected in early childhood and the emergence of personality disturbances in adulthood in all nonpsychotic subjects in Sample A of the NYHRP. It was expected that few, it any, of these subjects would undergo a psychotic episode after the completion of these analyses, as they were already well past the age of greatest risk for schizophrenia. However, many of the subjects in the two risk groups displayed a range of SRPD features.

The two main goals of the analysis were to determine:

1. The extent to which the nonpsychotic schizophrenia risk subjects were characterized by early childhood attentional dysfunctions, thereby establishing the potential of this sample to function as a risk population.
2. The influence of chronic attentional abnormalities on adult behavioral adjustment.

The study was limited to subjects in Sample A of the NYHRP because outcome could not be established with confidence for the younger subjects in Sample B, who are still in the age range of greatest risk for illness. Sample A subjects were included if:

1. They had not received a Research Diagnostic Criteria (RDC) diagnosis of schizophrenia or other psychosis by age 27, as determined during follow-up clinical contacts.
2. They had been assessed on the full attentional battery administered during the study's first round of testing (at which time their mean age was 9.9).
3. They had been interviewed on the Personality Disorder Examination (PDE, 1985 version; Loranger, Susman, Oldham, & Russakoff, 1987) during the project's fifth round of assessments, at

which time they were approximately 24 years old (see Squires-Wheeler et al., 1989, for details). The PDE is a semistructured interview assessing DSM-III-R Axis II personality disorders.

The resulting sample included 39 HRSz, 39 HRAff and 86 NC subjects. Childhood attention was measured by an attentional deviance index (ADI) developed by Cornblatt & Erlenmeyer-Kimling, which consisted largely of response indices generated by the early version of the CPT administered during the first round of testing (see Cornblatt & Erlenmeyer-Kimling, 1985; Cornblatt et al., 1989b, for more details). The higher the ADI score, the more deviant the subject's attention. Personality features were assessed according to two factors derived from the schizoid, schizotypal, histrionic, narcissistic, avoidant, and dependent personality disorder PDE scales.

Major Results: Attention

Even after removal of all HRSz subjects who would later become psychotic, group differences in childhood attention remained. That is, HRSz subjects free of psychosis as adults nevertheless displayed significantly poorer childhood attention than either HRAff or normal control subjects. HRAff subjects, on the other hand, did not differ from NCs in childhood attentional abilities. Therefore, the nonpsychotic group of HRSz subjects can be considered an appropriate risk population in that a substantial proportion of these subjects are characterized by the attentional trait marker but not by the fully expressed illness.

Major Results: Personality Disorders

The two factors resulting from the PDE analyses reported by Cornblatt et al. (1992), both of which were related to attention, are summarized in Tables 4.2 and 4.3. The first factor, labeled "social sensitivity," consisted of nine items, which are listed in Table 4.2. (Items were included if they had loadings of .45 or above.) The second factor, consisting of seven high loading items and labeled "social indifference," is presented in Table 4.3.

In addition to these two factors, a composite scale was derived by changing the direction of the scores on factor 1 and then combining it with factor 2. This was based on our assumption that subjects who are both socially insensitive (low scores on factor 1) and socially indifferent (high scores on factor 2) would tend to be socially withdrawn and isolated. We thus consider this composite scale to measure social isolation.

Table 4.2. Items Loading on Factor 1: Social Sensitivity

Variable	Loading Factor
1. Feelings easily hurt by criticism or disapproval	.69
2. Constantly seeking reassurance, approval, or praise	.57
3. Reacts to criticism with feelings of rage, shame, or humiliation	.56
4. Afraid of appearing foolish or being embarrassed	.56
5. Excessive social anxiety	.52
6. Has difficulty initiating projects or doing things on his/her own	.46
7. Preoccupied with feelings of envy	.46
8. Unwilling to get involved with people unless certain of being liked	.46
9. Entitlement: expectation of special favors without assuming reciprocal responsibilities	.45

Source: Cornblatt et al. (1992). Reprinted with permission of the *British Journal of Psychiatry*.

Major Results: Association Between Childhood Attention and Adult Personality

For subjects in both the HRAff and NC groups, no relationship was found between the childhood ADI and the three personality dimensions (i.e., social sensitivity, social indifference, and social isolation). However, all three were significantly related to attention in the HRSz group, with the ADI correlating $-.37$ with social sensitivity, .34 with social indifference, and .40 with social isolation (for all three correlations, $p < .05$).

Table 4.3. Items Loading on Factor 2: Social Indifference

Variable	Loading Factor
1. Is aware of but indifferent to the feelings of others	.79
2. Is uninterested in the feelings of other people	.72
3. Avoids social or occupational activities that involve significant interpersonal contact	.59
4. Almost always chooses solitary activity	.56
5. Suspiciousness or paranoid ideation	.58
6. Appears or claims to be indifferent to the praise and criticism of others	.53
7. Avoids everday activities for fear that they will be too fatiguing or physically uncomfortable	.51

Source: Cornblatt et al. (1992). Reprinted with permission of the *British Journal of Psychiatry*.

Major Conclusions

Based on these findings, we reached the following conclusions:

1. The greater prevalence of childhood attentional dysfunctions in the nonpsychotic offspring of schizophrenic parents compared to subjects in the two comparison groups supports abnormal attention as being a marker of the schizophrenia genotype.
2. Chronic attentional dysfunctions do appear to have a specific role in personality formation in individuals with a biological susceptibility to schizophrenia, even when the full illness is avoided. This seems to be related to the development of social skills and interactions.

Model of the Role of Attention in Personality Development

Based on these conclusions, we have proposed a heuristic model (Cornblatt et al., 1992), represented in Figure 4.2 and summarized as follows:

1. In subjects with a biological liability for schizophrenia, impaired attention is likely to be a chronic disturbance evident throughout development.
2. A chronic attentional impairment interferes with the efficient processing of information in the environment, especially subtle and highly complex interpersonal cues and communications.
3. Impaired attention is particularly disruptive of the processing of social information. This is because successful understanding of social cues requires sustained attention and continual processing of shifting interpersonal information. Difficult versions of the CPT are assumed to reflect specifically the ability to process rapidly shifting information that cannot be slowed or adjusted and that must be continually attended to over time.
4. Developmentally, these processing deficiencies take their toll by making interactions with others increasingly difficult and stressful.

We then proposed two possible outcomes for the predisposed person with this type of social information processing deficit, as indicated by the two arms of the model. On the right, as the individual matures, continued attempts to initiate or maintain relationships with other people create escalating stress, which, in turn, exacerbates symptoms and, in some cases, acts as an environmental trigger for the full clinical expression of the disease.

Alternatively, as indicated on the left, some individuals with the schizophrenia diathesis expressed as a chronic attentional disorder are able to reduce interpersonal stress by actively avoiding intense interper-

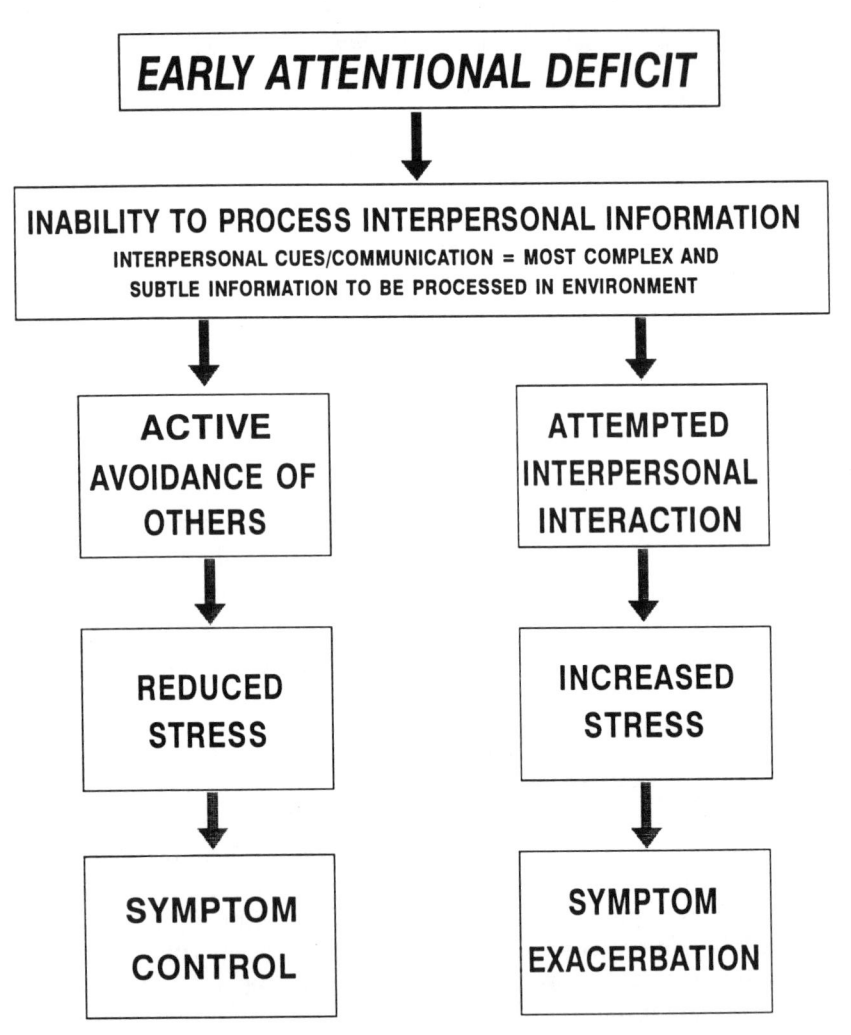

```
┌─────────────────────────────────────┐
│     EARLY ATTENTIONAL DEFICIT       │
└─────────────────────────────────────┘
                  ↓
┌─────────────────────────────────────┐
│ INABILITY TO PROCESS INTERPERSONAL INFORMATION │
│  INTERPERSONAL CUES/COMMUNICATION = MOST COMPLEX AND │
│  SUBTLE INFORMATION TO BE PROCESSED IN ENVIRONMENT   │
└─────────────────────────────────────┘
         ↓                       ↓
┌──────────────┐         ┌──────────────┐
│   ACTIVE     │         │  ATTEMPTED   │
│ AVOIDANCE OF │         │ INTERPERSONAL│
│   OTHERS     │         │ INTERACTION  │
└──────────────┘         └──────────────┘
       ↓                        ↓
┌──────────────┐         ┌──────────────┐
│   REDUCED    │         │  INCREASED   │
│    STRESS    │         │    STRESS    │
└──────────────┘         └──────────────┘
       ↓                        ↓
┌──────────────┐         ┌──────────────┐
│   SYMPTOM    │         │   SYMPTOM    │
│   CONTROL    │         │ EXACERBATION │
└──────────────┘         └──────────────┘
```

Figure 4.2 Hypothesized role of attention deficits in the development of social dysfunctions in individuals with a biological susceptibility to schizophrenia. (From Cornblatt et al., 1992. Reprinted with permission from the *British Journal of Psychiatry*.

sonal contacts and situations where they are required to relate actively to other people. We speculate that for these people, the avoidance of others may function as a compensatory mechanism. We also speculate that a reduced capacity to attend to information leads to an inability to understand and communicate with others, resulting in interpersonal insensitivity and indifference and, eventually, in social isolation. However, in these individuals, it is the ability to tolerate this isolation that helps to protect them against the intrusive, stressful interactions that can exacerbate symptoms.

More Recent Evidence in Support of the Model from Sample B

We acknowledge that we have presented an unusual view of social isolation that is more typically considered to be an undesirable early prodromal symptom or vulnerability marker of schizophrenia and related illnesses. However, additional support for our model has been provided by preliminary data obtained from Sample B of the NYHRP. In these data, which have not been previously reported, the association between childhood attentional deviance and social competence measured in middle to late adolescence was examined.

Attention was measured in behaviorally normal Sample B subjects at a mean age of approximately 9 years, using an ADI scale comparable to the index previously developed for Sample A (Cornblatt et al., 1989b). Ratings of social competence, described in detail elsewhere (Dworkin et al., 1991, 1993, 1994), were based on items selected from the Premorbid Adjustment Scale (PAS; Cannon-Spoor, Potkin, & Wyatt, 1982) assessing peer relationships, adaptation to school, degree of interest in life (i.e., hobbies and interests), and social-sexual adjustment (in offspring 12 years of age and older).

Social competence ratings were derived from two sources of information. The first consisted of a 30-minute, semistructured, videotaped interview with each participating child conducted by a child psychiatrist. The second source of information consisted of items selected from interviews with each subject's parents, which were comparable to those in the children's interviews and tapped three major areas of interest: peer relationships, school adjustment, and degree of interest in life.

As reported by Dworkin et al. (1994), no differences were found between the three subjects groups (i.e., HRSz, HRAff, and NCs) in childhood social competence. However, by early adolescence (mean age = 12.3 years) and continuing into midadolescence (mean age = 15.4 years), HRSz subjects had significantly poorer social competence than did either HRAff subjects or NCs.

In Table 4.4, the relationships between childhood attention and social competence based on the child interviews (Dworkin et al., 1994) are presented for Sample B subjects in each of the three age periods (i.e., 9.0, 12.3, and 15.4 years).[1] As was found earlier for Sample A, in normal control subjects, no significant relationship between childhood attention and later social skills was found at any age. For HRSz subjects, however, although childhood attention deficits did not relate to childhood social competence, a highly significant association did emerge by midadolescence. The more deviant childhood attentional skills were, the more HRSz subjects began to have social problems as they progressed through adolescence.

In contrast with previous Sample A findings, Sample B HRAff subjects also showed a relationship between childhood attention and social competence. However, the pattern of this association differed considerably

Table 4.4. Correlations Between Attention and Social Adjustment at Different Ages in HRSz Subjects, HRAff Subjects, and NC Subjects

	Mid-Childhood	Early Adolescent	Mid-Adolescent
Mean age (in years)	(9.0)	(12.3)	(15.4)
HRSz subjects	.13	.28	.70***
	(35)	(28)	(24)
HRAff subjects	.70***	.55***	.44*
	(26)	(25)	(21)
NC subjects	.07	.25	.30
	(48)	(42)	(36)

*$p < .05$
**$p < .01$.
***$p < .001$.

from that characterizing the group at risk for schizophrenia. HRAff subjects showed an association that was strongest in childhood and gradually declined throughout adolescence. In contrast, HRSz subjects showed a relationship that gradually increased across development. In the latter case, attentional abnormalities did not appear to affect childhood social adjustment. However, by midadolescence, the period at which HRSz individuals showed a significant impairment in social competence relative to other subjects, a markedly strong association with attention emerged.

Thus, the current findings for Sample B complement our earlier Sample A results. In Sample A, impaired attention in HRSz subjects is associated with a tendency to be socially isolated when these subjects were young adults. In Sample B, data collected at earlier ages support a developmental perspective and suggest a gradually increasing association between chronically impaired attention and social competence. In keeping with the model discussed earlier, we can further speculate that during childhood, social interactions may not be highly demanding of information processing skills. However, with the onset of adolescence, interpersonal interactions may make increasing demands on the ability to rapidly process complex information. In the Sample B HRSz subjects, attention shows an increasing association with social competence as social functioning begins to decline relative to other subjects in the sample. Thus, it may be that for subjects with a biological risk for schizophrenia, a chronic attentional deficit begins to be socially debilitating when interpersonal interactions start becoming most demanding of information processing skills. This interaction may, at least in part, account for the decline in social competence observed in adolescence for Sample B HRSz subjects compared to HRAff and NC subjects.

Future Directions

As mentioned above, we are proposing a relatively unorthodox interpretation of the role of social isolation in the clinical expression of schizophrenia. In essence, we suggest that for some genetically susceptible individuals, avoidance of other people may be therapeutic. To fully support this view, several additional research steps need to be followed.

First, while the Sample B findings newly reported here indicate that the relationship between attention and poor peer relationships can be observed as soon as social competence declines in HRSz subjects, there is no direct evidence supporting this as a causal relationship. It is tempting to assume that impaired attention leads to dysfunctional social skills, as attentional deficits are detectable in HRSz children at considerable earlier ages (i.e., by 9 years of age), while social skills do not appear to decline until early adolescence (i.e., around 12 years of age). However, it is also possible that both deficits are due to a third underlying abnormality (e.g., both may be related to a dysfunction in the frontal lobes) that affects these functions at different developmental stages. Clearly, a causal relationship between impaired attention and the development of social skills would have important implications for both treatment and intervention programs. Thus, there is a major need for further research that disentangles the developmental course of attention from that of social skills.

An additional way of assessing the validity of our model would be to compare premorbid functioning of schizophrenic patients with that of schizotypal individuals. Our model predicts that chronic social deficits and social isolation should characterize schizotypals. By contrast, schizophrenics with attentional deficits should not be characterized by the same degree of premorbid asociality. Research focusing on such comparisons can potentially contribute to our understanding of the role of social isolation as a buffer helping to avoid fully expressed psychosis.

We have two additional recommendations for future research. First, although we have concluded that the evidence supporting impaired attention as a marker is quite compelling, additional work is necessary. More research is needed to establish the extent to which attention, in general, and attentional abnormalities, in particular, are genetically transmitted. Furthermore, the degree to which attentional deficits co-segregate with the clinical illness in families needs to be more fully explored.

Second, with regard to understanding the pathogenesis of schizophrenia, developmental studies of attention in normal subjects, and an understanding of the underlying biology of attention in both normal subjects and in those at risk for psychiatric disorders, are essential.

In conclusion, it should be emphasized that schizophrenia is increasingly viewed as a neurodevelopmental disorder (Weinberger, 1986). Research in developmental psychopathology, such as the work on high-risk populations discussed in this chapter, is thus optimal for tracing the unfolding of the disorder and for isolating those abnormalities that critically contribute to the pathogenesis of the illness. Once such pathodevelopmental processes are identified, major steps in understanding the etiology and prevention of schizophrenia can be taken.

Note

1. We have not presented parental reports of social competence because these did not relate to childhood attention for any of the groups at any age. This lack of consistency with the analyses based on the child interviews was unexpected, and we have no explanation for it.

References

Cannon-Spoor, H. E., Potkin, S. G., & Wyatt, R. J. (1982). Measurement of premorbid adjustment in chronic schizophrenia. *Schizophrenia Bulletin, 8,* 470–484.

Chapman, L. J., Chapman, J. P., & Raulin, M. L. (1976). Scales for physical and social anhedonia. *Journal of Abnormal Psychology, 85,* 374–382.

Chapman, L. J., & Chapman, J. P. (1975). How to test hypotheses about schizophrenic thought disorder. *Schizophrenia Bulletin, 12,* 42–59.

Cloninger, C. R. (1987). Genetic principles and methods in high-risk studies of schizophrenia. *Schizophrenia Research, 13,* 515–523.

Cornblatt, B. A. (1990). *Do attentional problems in children of schizophrenics predict adult psychopathology?* Presented at the 29th annual meeting of the American College of Neuropsychopharmacology, San Juan, Puerto Rico, December 10–14.

Cornblatt, B. A. (1991). *Childhood attentional problems and adult psychopathology.* Presented at the annual meeting of the Society for Biological Psychiatry, New Orleans, May 18–12.

Cornblatt, B. (1993). *The Elmhurst First Episode Project: Overview and preliminary findings.* Presented at the annual meeting of the Society for Biological Psychiatry, San Francisco, May 21.

Cornblatt, B. A., & Erlenmeyer-Kimling, L. (1984). Early attentional predictors of adolescent behavioral disturbances in children at risk for schizophrenia. In N. F. Watt, E. J., Anthony, L. C. Wynne, & J. E. Rolf (Eds.), *Children at risk for schizophrenia: A longitudinal perspective* (pp 198–212). New York: Cambridge University Press.

Cornblatt, B., & Erlenmeyer-Kimling, L. (1985). Global attentional deviance as a marker of risk for schizophrenia: Specificity and predictive validity. *Journal of Abnormal Psychology, 94,* 470–486.

Cornblatt, B. A., & Keefe, R. S. E. (Eds.). (1991a). The genetics of mental illness, *Social Biology* (Special Section), *38,* 163–218.

Cornblatt, B. A., & Keefe, R. S. E. (1991b). Genetics and mental illness: An overview. *Social Biology* (Special Section), *38,* i–v.

Cornblatt, B. A., & Keilp, J. G. (1994). Impaired attention: A trait indicator of the schizophrenia genotype and contributor to the clinical phenotype. *Schizophrenia Bulletin, 20,* 31–46.

Cornblatt, B. A., Lenzenweger, M., Dworkin, R. & Erlenmeyer-Kimling, L. (1985). Positive and negative schizophrenics symptoms, attention and information processing. *Schizophrenia Bulletin, 11,* 397–408.

Cornblatt, B. A., Lenzenweger, M., Dworkin, R. H., & Erlenmeyer-Kimling, L. (1992). Childhood attentional dysfunctions predict social deficits in unaffected adults at risk for schizophrenia. *British Journal of Psychiatry, 161,* (Suppl. 18):59–64.

Cornblatt, B. A., Lenzenweger, M., & Erlenmeyer-Kimling, L. (1989a). The Continuous Performance Test, Identical Pairs Version: II. Contrasting attentional profiles in schizophrenic and depressed patients. *Psychiatry Research, 29,* 65–85.

Cornblatt, B. A., Risch, N. J., Faris, G., Friedman, D., & Erlenmeyer-Kimling, L. (1988). The Continuous Performance Test, Identical Pairs Version (CPT-IP): I. New findings about sustained attention in normal families. *Psychiatry Research, 26,* 223–238.

Cornblatt, B. A., Winters, L., & Erlenmeyer-Kimling, L. (1989b). Attentional markers of schizophrenia: Evidence from the New York High Risk Study. In S. C. Schulz & C. A. Taminga (Eds.), *Schizophrenia: Scientific progress* (pp. 83–92). New York: Oxford University Press.

Creese, I., Burt, D. R., & Snyder, S. H. (1976). Dopamine receptor binding predicts clinical and pharmacological potencies of antischizophrenic drugs. *Science, 192,* 481–483.

Dworkin, R. H., Bernstein, G., Kaplansky, L. M., & Lipsitz, J. D., Rinaldi, A., Slater, S. L., Cornblatt, B. A., Erlenmeyer-Kimling, L. (1991). Social competence and positive and negative symptoms: A longitudinal study of children and adolescents at risk for schizophrenia and affective disorder. *American Journal of Psychiatry, 148,* 1182–1188.

Dworkin, R. H., Cornblatt, B. A., Friedman, & R., Kaplansky, L. M., Lewis, J. A., Rinaldi, A., Shilliday, C., & Erlenmeyer-Kimling, L. (1993). Childhood precursors of affective versus social deficits in adolescents at risk for schizophrenia. *Schizophrenia Bulletin, 19,* 563–577.

Dworkin, R. H., Lewis, J. A., Cornblatt, B. A., & Erlenmeyer-Kimling, L. (1994). Social competence deficits in adolescents at risk for schizophrenia. *Journal of Nervous and Mental Disease, 182,* 103–108.

Erlenmeyer-Kimling, L. (1987). Biological markers for the liability to schizophrenia. In H. Helmchen, & F. Henn (Eds.), *Biological perspectives of schizophrenia* (pp. 451–463). Chichester, U.K.: Wiley.

Erlenmeyer-Kimling, L. (in press). A look at the evolution of developmental models of schizophrenia. In S. Mattysse, D. Levy, & J. Kagan, (Eds.), *Psychopathology: The evolving science of mental disorder.* Cambridge: Cambridge University Press.

Erlenmeyer-Kimling, L., & Cornblatt, B. (1978). Attentional measures in a study of children at high-risk for schizophrenia. In L. Wynne & R. Cromwell (Eds.), *The nature of schizophrenia* (pp. 359–365). New York: Wiley.

Erlenmeyer-Kimling, L., & Cornblatt, B. (1987). High-risk research in schizophrenia: A summary of what has been learned. *Journal of Psychiatric Research, 21,* 401–411.

Erlenmeyer-Kimling, L., & Cornblatt, B. (1992). A summary of attentional findings in the New York High-Risk Project. *Journal of Psychiatric Research, 26,* 405–426.

Erlenmeyer-Kimling, L., Cornblatt, B., & Golden, R. (1983). Early indicators of vulnerability to schizophrenia. In S. Guze, F. Earls, & J. Barrett (Eds.), *Childhood psychopathology and development* (pp. 33–56). Chichester, U.K.: Wiley.

Freedman, B., & Chapman, L. (1973). Early subjective experience in schizophrenic episodes. *Journal of Abnormal Psychology, 82,* 46–54.

Gershon, E. S., & Goldin, L. R. (1986). Clinical methods in psychiatric genetics I. Robustness of genetic marker investigative strategies. *Acta Psychiatrica Scandinavica, 74,* 113–118.

Goldin, L. R., Nurnberger, J. I., Jr., & Gershon, E. S. (1986). Clinical methods in psychiatric genetics II. The high risk approach. *Acta Psychiatrica Scandinavica, 74,* 119–128.

Gottesman, I. I., & Shields, J. A. (1976). A critical review of recent adoption, twin and family studies of schizophrenia: Behavioral genetics perspectives. *Schizophrenia Bulletin, 2,* 360–407.

Grove, W. M., Lebow, B. S., Clementz, B. A. Cerri, A., Medus, C., & Iacono, W. G. (1991). Familial prevalence and co-aggregation of schizotypy indicators: A multi-trait family study. *Journal of Abnormal Psychology, 100,* 115–121.

Holzman, P. S., Kringlen, E., Mattysse, S., Flanagan, S. D., Lipton, R. B., Cramer, G., Levin, A., Lange, K., & Levy, D., A single dominant gene can account for eye-tracking dysfunction and schizophrenia in offspring of discordant twins. *Archives of General Psychiatry, 45,* 641–647.

Kendler, K. S., Ochs, A. L., Gorman, A. M., Hewitt, J. K., Ross, D. E., & Mirsky, A. F. (1991). The structure of schizotypy: A pilot multitrait twin study. *Psychiatry Research, 36,* 19–36.

Kety, S. S. (1985). Schizotypal personality disorders: An operational definition of Bleuler's latent schizophrenia? *Schizophrenia Bulletin, 11,* 590–594.

Kety, S. S., Rosenthal, D., Wender, P. H., Schulsinger, F., & Jacobsen, B. (1975). Mental illness in the biological and adoptive families of adoptive individuals who have become schizophrenic: A preliminary report based on psychiatric interviews. In R. R. Fieve, D. Rosenthal, & H. Brill (Eds.), *Genetic research in psychiatry* (pp. 147–165). Baltimore: Johns Hopkins University Press.

Kraeplin, E., Barclay, R. M., & Robertson, G. M. (1919). (trans). *Dementia praecox and paraphrenia.* Edinburgh: E & S Livingstone.

Lenzenweger, M. F. (1993). Explorations in schizotypy and the psychometric high-risk paradigm. In L. Chapman, J. Chapman, & D. Fowles (Eds.), *Progress in experimental personality and psychopathology research* (pp. 66–116). New York: Springer.

Lenzenweger, M., Cornblatt, B., & Putnick, M. (1991). Schizotypy and sustained attention. *Journal of Abnormal Psychology, 100,* 84–89.

Loranger, A. W., Susman, V. L., Oldham, J. M., & Russakoff, L. M. (1987). The personality disorder examination: A preliminary report. *Journal of Personality Disorders, 1,* 1–13.

Maier, W., Franke, P., Hardt, J., Hain, C., & Cornblatt, B. (submitted). Attentional abilities and measures of schizotypy: Variation and covariation in a high risk sample compared to controls. *Pschiatry Research.*

Mirsky, A. F., Anthony, B. J., Duncan, C. C., Ahearn, M. B., & Kellam, S. G. (1991). Analysis of the elements of attention: A neuropsychological approach. *Neuropsychology Review, 2,* 109–145.

Moldin, S. O., & Erlenmeyer-Kimling, L. (1994). Measuring liability to schizophrenia: Progress report 1994: Editor's introduction. *Schizophrenia Bulletin, 20,* 25–30.

Nuechterlein, K. H. (1983). Signal detection in vigilance tasks and behavioral attributes among offspring of schizophrenic mothers and among hyperactive children. *Journal of Abnormal Psychology, 92,* 4–28.

Nuechterlein, K. H., & Dawson, M. (1984). Information processing and attentional functioning in the developmental course of schizophrenic disorders. *Schizophrenia Bulletin, 10,* 160–203.

Parasuraman, R., & Davies, D. R. (1977). A taxonomic analysis of vigilance performance. In R. R. Mackie (Ed.), *Vigilance: Theory, operational performance and physiological correlates* (pp. 559–574). New York: Plenum.

Robbins, T. W. (1990). The case for frontostriatal dysfunction in schizophrenia. *Schizophrenia Bulletin, 16,* 391–402.

Shenton, M. E., Kikinis, R., Jolesz, F. A., Pollack, S. D., LeMay, M., Wible, C. G., Hokama, H., Martin, J., Metcalf, D., Coleman, M., & McCarley, R. W. (1992). Abnormalities of the left temporal lobe and thought disorder in schizophrenia. *New England Journal of Medicine, 327,* 614–612.

Siever, L. J., & Davis, K. L. (1991). A psychobiological perspective on the personality disorders. *American Journal of Psychiatry, 148,* 1647–1657.

Squires-Wheeler, E., Basset, A., & Erlenmeyer-Kimling, L. (1989). DSM-III-R schizotypal personality traits in offspring of schizophrenic disorder, affective disorder, and normal control parents. *Journal of Psychiatric Research, 23,* 229–239.

Steinhauer, S. R., Zubin, J., Condray, R., Shaw, D. B., Peters, J. L., & van Kammen, D. P. (1991). Electrophysiological and behavioral signs of attentional disturbance in schizophrenics and their siblings. In C. A. Taminga, & S. C. Schulz (Eds.), *Schizophrenia research: Advances in neuropsychiatry and psychopharmacology.* (Vol. 1, pp. 169–178). New York: Raven Press.

Weeks, D. E., Brzustowicz, L., Squires-Wheeler, E., Cornblatt, B., Lehner, T., Stefanovich, M., Bassett, A., Gilliam, T. C., Ott, J., & Erlenmeyer-Kimling, L. (1990). Report of a workshop in genetic linkage studies in schizophrenia. *Schizophrenia Bulletin, 16,* 673–686.

Weinberger, D. R. (1986). The pathogenesis of schizophrenia: A neurodevelopmental theory. In H. A. Nasrallah & D. R. Weinberger (Eds.), *Handbook of schizophrenia: (Volume 1. The neurology of schizophrenia* (pp. 397–406). Amsterdam: Elsevier.

Weinberger, D. R. (1988). Schizophrenia and the frontal lobes. *Trends in Neuroscience, 11,* 367–370.

Weinberger, D. R., Berman, K. F., & Zec, R. F. (1986). Physiologic significance of dorsolateral prefrontal cortex in schizophrenia I: Regional cerebral blood flow evidence. *Archives of General Psychiatry, 43,* 114–124.

Winters, L., Cornblatt, B., & Erlenmeyer-Kimling, L. (1991). The prediction of psychiatric disorders in late adolescence. In E. Walker (Ed.), *Schizophrenia: A life-course developmental perspective* (pp. 123–137). New York: Academic Press.

Wolf, L. E., & Halperin, J. M. (1987). Attention in psychiatrically disturbed children: what are we really measuring? *Journal of Clinical & Experimental Neuropsychology, 9,* 61.

5

Developmental Psychopathology in the Context of Adolescence

JEANNE BROOKS-GUNN AND ILANA ATTIE

Intergrating Development and Psychopathology

Developmental psychopathology offers a compelling paradigm from the perspective of those who study the normative processes of development, those who focus on the processes underlying the emergence and maintenance of psychopathology, and those who integrate the two (Cicchetti & Cohen, in press; Cicchetti & Schneider-Rosen, 1984; Rutter, 1986; Sroufe & Rutter, 1984). Most research focuses either on individuals who already have a disorder or on normative development in individuals who do not have a disorder. Developmental psychopathological frameworks have been valuable for work in both research traditions. Less often studied is the integration of development and psychopathology in a framework that gives equal weight to each. An example is the study of the development processes preceding the onset of a disorder or the developmental course of a group of individuals, some of whom will go on to have a disorder and some of whom will not. Very few prospective, developmentally oriented studies exist.

Multidimensional models are common in the study of various disorders and normative processes. However, current research does not always integrate findings from social, cultural, biogenetic, personality, family, school, and peer domains. How problems arise within these domains, the associations among them, and their links with disorders are not always addressed. In part, this lack of integration is due to the methodological and sampling difficulties inherent in designing, mounting, and funding multidomain studies. Problems are even more daunting when the disorder and normative process approaches are melded. Large samples are necessary to chart individuals' developmental trajectories if the goal is to identify various groups vis-à-vis the emergence of problem behavior and frank disorders. Adding the necessity of including various groups of individuals who vary with respect to the likelihood of exhibiting a disorder is another complexity and a methodological constraint.

A developmental perspective on the study of psychopathology is thought to take into account the continuities and discontinuities between normal growth and psychopathology, age-related changes in modes of adaptation and symptom expression, behavioral reorganizations that occur around salient developmental transitions, internal and external sources of competence and vulnerability, and the effects of development on pathology and of pathology on development (Achenbach, in press; Attie & Brooks-Gunn, 1992, p. 35; Carlson & Garber, 1986; Cicchetti, 1984; Rutter, 1986). Integral to this approach is delineating patterns of continuity and change as these are manifest across the life span via cross-sectional and longitudinal research on populations at high and low risk for specific forms of psychopathology.

Why Focus on Adolescence?

In this chapter, we explore the development of psychopathology in the context of one particular age group, albeit one that spans a decade and includes two major transitions. The adolescent period is one in which multiple normative changes occur, both during the transition to adolescence and during the transition out of adolescence (Brooks-Gunn & Petersen, 1984; Feldman & Elliott, 1990; Gunnar & Collins, 1988; Lerner & Foch, 1987). These challenges must be negotiated by all youth, even though they are potential sources of risk to physical and emotional health.

Generally, although adolescents in Western countries are quite healthy, 11% increases in morbidity have been reported for this age group over the past 20 years (Office of Technology and Assessment, 1991; World Health Organization, 1990). Significant morbidity has been seen in terms of suicide, substance abuse, sexually transmitted diseases, accidents, depression, and eating disorders (Millstein, Petersen, & Nightingale, 1991; Petersen et al, 1993).

Our focus in this chapter is on two clusters of mental health problems—depression and eating. We are particularly concerned with the spectrum of eating and depressive problems, rather than with just frank disorders. Throughout the chapter, the term *disorder cluster* is used to connote a range from symptoms to problems to disorders.

While the majority of teenagers handle adolescent transitions without severe disruptions in their relationships, affective states, or behavioral manifestations of problems, some experience clinical signs of distress that are more than the transitory experiences of individuals managing multiple and novel events across a number of domains. Some of these symptoms become chronic, and some of them become severe enough to meet diagnostic criteria for psychopathology. The focus of this chapter is on the intersection between the normative changes associated with adolescence and the emergence of transient problems, as well as the intersection between the exhibition of transient problems and chronic problems.[1]

Eating and Depressive Disorders in the Context of Adolescence

These intersections between development and psychopathology in the context of adolescence are illustrated in this chapter by focusing on two symptom and disorder clusters—eating and depressive problems and disorders. These two clusters are intertwined with adolescence in that both exhibit large increases in adolescence compared to childhood rates. After the adolescent transition, girls are more likely to exhibit these disorders, or signs of these disorders, than are boys. These gender linkages remind us that boys and girls have quite different adolescent experiences that need to be taken into account when studying the emergence of psychopathology. Taken together, these facts suggest that the developmental challenges of adolescence (including biological, social, cognitive, and intrapsychic changes) and the gender divergences in the meaning of these challenges, as well as the challenges themselves, might be contributing to the onset of eating and depressive problems and disorders. An additional feature of relevance is that eating and depressive problems and disorders occur quite frequently in adolescent girls. Certain groups of girls are particularly vulnerable to these two disorder clusters, making it possible to conduct prospective research on high-risk groups in order to study emergence and maintenance in a developmental framework.

A Comparative Approach

We have chosen to look at these two disorder clusters in order to compare and contrast the approaches taken to studying each. We hasten to add that very little truly comparative research exists. Consequently, the research literatures on eating and depression are somewhat separate (with the exception of work on comorbidity). Considering the two disorder clusters simultaneously provides a heuristic approach that highlights the need for more comparative work. Links are made between the research on eating and depression whenever possible, without being impossibly speculative.

Similarities Across Eating and Depressive Disorder Clusters

Similarities across the eating and depressive disorder clusters are striking, over and above the links to age and gender. Many (but not all) of the risk factors identified in the literature are similar; both disorders involve affective and biological dysregulation; and both disorders are linked, either as antecedents or as concomitants, with stressful life events.

Risk Factors

We believe that it is useful to see how risk and continuity play out in these two disorder clusters that are studied separately even though several features are shared. Not only do these two disorders converge in terms of gender and developmental period of onset, but they may be seen as disorders of dysregulation. They are also disorders that are believed to have a biological component (although the research on eating disorders is weaker than that on depression), as well as to involve family system dysfunction (although the research on depression is not as well developed as that on eating disorders). The experience of major and stressful life events is thought to play a role in some cases of both disorders (with the research on eating disorders suggesting a more developmental or age-bounded effect than the work on depression). The onset of puberty is thought to be implicated, although it is not clear whether the more social or biological aspects of puberty are more important (with the research on eating disorders presenting stronger evidence for such links than the research on depression). The meaning of becoming a woman, and the implications for individuation and relationships, also have been considered relevant for both disorder clusters.

Similarities in Dysregulation of Physiology and Affect

The interpretation and experience of affective states and their regulation are central to both disorder clusters. We have characterized eating disorders as a "dysregulation of eating behavior involving the complex interaction of biological, affective, social, and cognitive processes that override the normal physiological regulatory pressures of hunger and satiety" (Attie & Brooks-Gunn, 1995, p. 333; Polivy & Herman, 1987). However, eating disorders cannot be considered to be solely dysregulations of appetite. There is little evidence, for example, that individuals with anorexia nervosa and individuals who severely restrict their food intake do not experience hunger. Indeed, they may feel hungry almost constantly but tolerate food deprivation in response to psychological imperatives (Polivy & Herman, 1987). Chronic dietary restraint renders them vulnerable to disinhibition of self-control, that is, to binge eating, in response to a variety of triggering factors. At the same time, individuals with bulimia nervosa typically report difficulty in knowing when they are full at the end of a meal, suggesting an impairment of satiety.

Depression also involves dysregulation, in this case in affective mood states and related behaviors rather than in eating behavior and the affect associated with it. Additionally, dysregulation is thought to occur in a variety of neuroendocrine processes, suggesting a central role of biology. Regardless of the way in which the onset of a depressive episode is triggered, biological dysregulation is the result. Thus, even environmental frameworks have to consider dysregulation. This has been called the *final common pathway* model (Akiskal & McKinney, 1973). While this term has not been applied to eating disorders, it is quite appropriate in that, regardless of the mechanisms underlying the onset of an eating disorder, biological dsyregulation may be the consequence.

Another similarity between the dysregulation seen in depression and anorexia nervosa is that once an episode is underway (regardless of the original etiology or etiologies), the disorders seem to "take on a life of [their] own" (Shelton, Hollon, Purdon, & Loosen, 1991, p. 212). In both cases, the biological features may impact mood, thought processes, and behavior. In the case of anorexia nervosa, weight loss and starvation have specific physiological effects, which seem to alter body images as well as food imagery; it may be difficult to treat a women with anorexia until some weight had been regained, although disagreement exists on this point. Bulimia nervosa may not have such biological concomitants (although some work suggests that it is responsive to some antidepressants; if this turns out to be true, then some of the biological substrates underlying bulimia may also contribute to some forms of depression).

Depression impacts various hypothalamic-pituitary (HP) axes as well, although HP axis dysregulation is believed to be more likely at the beginning of a depressive episode or preceding an episode than it is for anorexia or bulimia nervosa (although work on the neuroendocrine processes preceding an episode of eating disorder is preceding at a rapid pace; Brooks-Gunn, Petersen, & Compas, 1995; Petersen, Compas, Brooks-Gunn, Stemmler, Ely, & Grant, 1993; Puig-Antich, 1986).

Stressful Life Events and Distress

Another line of research relevant to the possible features underlying both problem behavior and clinical disorders focuses on stressful events. In the eating literature, this has been generally referred to as *distress*, which may predispose a girl to diet (Streigel-Moore, Silberstein, Frensch, & Rodin, 1989). Dieting in and of itself may provoke distress, which could result in exaggerated dieting behavior or at least more distress (Rosen, Tacy, & Howell, 1990). One of the major stressors associated with dieting is that it is not always successful; dieting may result in weight fluctuations and metabolic changes that lead to less efficient weight loss and increased weight gain rather than weight loss (Attie & Brooks-Gunn, 1995; Heatherton & Baumeister, 1991; although see Brownell & Rodin, 1994, for an alternative view). Repeated attempts to diet may result in lowered self-esteem, as well as disinhibition in eating and other realms of life. Once an individual enters a spiral of dysregulation, the cycle of dieting, overeating, dietary failure, and affective distress may deepen and be difficult to break (Baumeister, 1990). Whether such spirals are associated with the progression from dieting to eating disorders is not known. Also, these models are not specific to adolescents, but have been developed on females more generally, with most work focusing on adult women (Lowe, 1993; Polivy & Herman, 1987).

The literature on depression has taken a slightly different tack. Given the clear links between stressful life events and depression episodes in adults, exploration of such associations during the adolescent years has been undertaken, paralleling the work with adults (Brooks-Gunn, 1991; Compas, 1987a, 1987b). The work of our research group is a case in point. We have explored the role of life events in girls' depressive affect over a 4-year period. Change in life events yearly is modeled simultaneously with change in depressive symptom scores yearly. This model provides a strong test of the link between life events and depression, since change is being predicted and since the occurrence of life events is being examined each year; therefore change in life events may be entered into regression equations. As expected, an increase in possibly stressful life events predicts rises in depressive symptomatology. Girls who are 12 to 14 years of age report more stressful life events than younger or older girls in our work. This pile-up of events predicts the rise in depressive symptomatology in this age period (Brooks-Gunn, 1991).

While consistent with literature on the predictors of the onset of clinical depressive episodes, this study, as well as other research in the area, does not deal directly with the issue of why some girls who experience a large number of stressful life events simultaneously go on to exhibit signs of clinical depression, while others do not.

Issues Underlying the Study of Disorder Clusters

This chapter addresses the emergence and maintenance of eating disorders and depression in the context of the adolescent experience. The features of the two disorder clusters are considered first. We focus on the feature similarities of symptoms, problems, and clinically diagnosed pathology for each. Our intent is to highlight possible continuities and discontinuities between symptoms and disorders. The issue of whether or not a continuum exists between more and less severe manifestations of a disorder is perennial, and one that has not been adequately addressed for adolescents. Then the rates of problems and disorders are considered, based on age and gender. Of interest here are not only differences in prevalence, but also variations in the possible symptoms associated with disorders in childhood and adolescence for both sexes. The next section focuses on the adolescent experience and the ways in which it renders some youth vulnerable to the onset of a problem or disorder. Biological, cognitive, and affect changes are considered, as well as the two major contexts in which the adolescent operates—the family and the peer system. A separate section outlines the biological concomitants and possible predictors of clinical syndromes. This literature is reviewed separately from that on the adolescent experience because it does not focus on the biological changes associated with puberty, but rather on those changes that are indicative of biological dysregulation. A brief discussion of familial contributions to eating and depressive disorders follows. It is separate from the work on adolescent experience, as it does not consider adolescents specifically, but rather family contributions more generally across the life span (even when adolescents constitute the sample, their particular needs and experiences are not the focus).

Continuities in Symptoms by Severity of Disorder

One of the greatest challenges in the integration of development into psychopathology (and vice versa) is to chart the nature and degree of continuity between problems and clinical syndromes (see Wilson, 1993, for an example in the eating disorders literature). The issue of a continuum of eating and depressive pathology is complex, given that most individuals who exhibit dieting or binge-restrict cycles do not go on to develop an eating disorder. The same is true of individuals exhibiting depressive affect.

A developmental perspective requires an examination of continuities and discontinuities between problems and disorders, as well as an exploration of why some individuals develop a problem and others do not; why some individuals with a problem go on to develop a disorder; why some individuals continue to have a problem but do not develop a disorder; and why some individuals with a problem return to low levels of symptoms. Distinctions among symptoms as a function of severity are made in order to explore such issues. They are also necessary for classification, particularly with respect to diagnostic criteria. Different terms are often used in making such distinctions, further blurring the boundaries. Here we use the terms *symptoms, problems,* and *disorders* (Petersen et al., 1993).

Disorders are based on DSM diagnostic criteria. Problems are usually defined in terms of cutoff scores on a number of self-report instruments. The cutoff scores are often derived by comparing clinically referred individuals to individuals seen in (more or less) representative samples of children and youth. Number of symptoms and intensity of symptoms are often included and weighted to obtain cutoff scores. Individuals with high scores are considered at risk for developing the particular disorder in question. The existence of symptoms is also based on self-report instruments. Number, intensity, or a combination of the two are used to indicate the existence of depressive affect or dieting. Occurrence of depressive affect or dieting is based on the characteristics of the sample being studied (i.e., individuals above the 30th percentile, or one-quarter of the sample). Each study defines the existence of symptoms somewhat differently, making cross-sample comparisons quite difficult. This is in contrast to the criteria for problems, since so many studies use the same instruments and the reported cutoff scores (i.e., the Eating Attitudes Test [Garner & Garfinkel, 1979] or the Eating Disorders Inventory [Garner, Olmsted, & Polivy 1983] for eating problems and the Center for Epidemiological Studies—Depression [Radloff, 1977; 1991] or the Youth Behavior Checklist [Achenbach & Edelbrock, 1987] for depressive problems). These checklists have childhood and adolescent forms, so that across age comparisons may be made (Child EAT [Maloney, McGuire, & Daniels, 1988]; KEDS [Kids' Eating Disorders Survey; Childress, Brewerton, Hodges, & Jarrell, 1993]; and the Child Behavior Check List [Achenbach, 1991]). Even when these same instruments are used to define the existence of symptoms, investigators use different cutoff points.

Eating Disorders: Problems and Symptoms

Similarities across disorders, problems, and symptoms exist with respect to the following features: attempts to restrict food intake (or to reduce caloric intake after a binge), negative body image, and concerns about weight gain and appearance (Garner, Olmsted, Polivy & Garfinkel, 1984; Polivy & Herman, 1987). However, actual weight differs across groups, as do the means of restricting weight and the severity of concerns about fatness.

A diagnosis of anorexia nervosa requires the behavior of self-induced starvation, a psychopathological fear of becoming fat even though underweight, and a biological abnormality in reproductive functioning, which in females is manifested in primary or secondary amenorrhea (Morgan & Russell, 1975). The actual weight loss requirement has changed over time: It is 15% in DSM-III-R and was 25% in DSM-III. This probably has increased the number of individuals classified as having anorexia nervosa.

Bulimia nervosa generally requires several features: a history of recurrent binges, a fear of becoming fat, and attempts to compensate for the unwanted calories ingested in a binge by self-induced vomiting, strenuous exercising, subsequent fasting, or abuse of laxative and diuretics. In contrast to anorexia nervosa, weight may vary. Distinctions are often made between bulimia nervosa in which weight is low (and self-induced starvation is maintained by low intake, purging, or a combination of the two) and bulimia in which weight is in the normal range or even high.

The features just listed may have differential predictive power for psychopathology. Purging may be the most critical dimension of bulimia nervosa vis-à-vis determining the course and recovery. Laxative abuse may be the most deleterious form of purging (Tobin, Johnson, Steinber, Staats, & Dennis, 1991). In one study of bulimic patients, the vast majority used at least two purging strategies. The number of purging techniques was the best predictor of depression and body disturbance in this sample of identified bulimic women (Tobin, Johnson, & Dennis, 1992).

The criteria for bulimia nervosa have changed from DSM-III to DSM-III-R, being more stringent in the latter than in the former (the converse of what has happened to the criteria for anorexia nervosa). The number of women who are diagnosed as having bulimia nervosa has been reduced as a result (Lancelot, Brooks-Gunn, & Warren, 1991; Stunkard et al., 1986). Interestingly, the women who would be classified as having bulimia nervosa in DSM-III but not in DSM-III-R are less likely to exhibit depressive symptoms and other disturbances than those classified as having bulimia nervosa in DSM-III-R, lending face validity to the change (Lancelot et al., 1991). At the same time, these women have higher depression scores than women who are not classified as bulimic under either diagnostic system. Such results provide some support for notions of continuum underlying eating disorders.

Along the same lines is the work on women who are classified as having so-called subthreshold eating disorders. These individuals meet some but not all of the diagnostic criteria for either anorexia nervosa or bulimia nervosa. This category may contain a relatively large number of individuals. In two of our studies, which are based on adolescent girls and young women from upper-middle-class backgrounds and highly competitive high schools and colleges, one-quarter to one-third of the samples meet criteria for Eating Disorder Not Otherwise Specified (Graber, Brooks-Gunn, Paikoff & Warren, 1994; Warren et al., 1991). Generally, females in this category have higher eating problem scores, lower body images, and more depressive symptoms than individuals with no eating disorder diagnosis; their scores are not as extreme as those with a diagnosis of bulimia or anorexia nervosa. As mentioned before, such results suggest a continuum of disordered eating but provide validity for the diagnostic distinctions made.

Eating problems include restricting food intake (dieting) and binge-restrict cycles. The most widely used scales have subscales for these two types of behavior (Garner & Garfinkel, 1979). Of interest is the fact that high scores on dieting and binging are associated with higher, not lower, weights in our samples of adolescent and young adult women (including females from high academic and athletic achievement environments). Unlike girls with anorexia nervosa, who have been successful in restricting food intake, girls with high eating problem scores have been less successful (alternatively, they may be heavier than girls who do not diet prior to the onset of our studies; Attie & Brooks-Gunn, 1992).

These results also may be valuable when designing studies on the developmental trajectories of individuals. That is, a useful comparison might be made between women who have high eating problem scores, those who meet some but not all of the diagnostic criteria for disorders, and those who are diagnosed with a disorder. Additionally, it might be possible to see if women who end up with a disorder go through intermediate stages on their way to the disorder. Are they likely to be diagnosed as Eating Disorder Not Otherwise Specified first? Comparisons could also be made regarding the timing of different phases or way points. Are certain women likely to have eating problems for a long period of time before developing a disorder, and do they differ in terms of life experiences, personality characteristics, and biological characteristics from those who move from problems to disorders quite rapidly?[2]

A final point needs to be made about symptoms rather then problems. We are hesitant to say much about symptoms because studies are so parochial in their definitions. The major "symptom" in the eating disorder cluster is dieting or reports of restricting food intake. What is important is that dieting has become normative for girls in our society. Normative is certainly not the same as normal.

Depressive Disorders: Problems and Symptoms

Distinctions also are made for various forms of depression, and changes in DSM criteria have been introduced. Of particular interest are the distinctions between Major Depressive Disorder and Dysthymia, which is perhaps akin to the distinction between Anorexia and Bulimia Nervosa, on the one hand, and Unspecified Eating Disorders, on the other. In both cases, little is known about the likelihood that an individual with the less specified, and perhaps less severe, form of either disorder will go on to develop the more specific or more severe forms of depression or eating disorders. It is critical to document such progressions, if they occur, for they might illuminate the processes by which some individuals escape particular problems and other do not.

Depressive problems include depressive symptoms and affect. *Depressive affect* refers to periods of sadness, unhappiness, or dysphoric moods that most individuals experience (Kazdin, 1989). Depressed affect probably represents one of the two broad affective dimensions, specifically negative affect, identified by Watson and Tellegen (1985). Depressive symptoms are often distinguished from depressive mood in terms of the duration, severity, and number of symptoms, as discussed briefly earlier in this chapter.

Feature analyses are less frequent for the depressed disorder cluster than for the eating disorder cluster. Common features in depressive problems and disorders in adolescence may include decreased interest in school, decrease in school performance, lowered self-esteem, social isolation, and negative affective states (Compas, Petersen, & Brooks-Gunn, in press).

Age and Gender as Features of Eating and Depressive Disorders

Rates of eating disorders and depression vary between childhood and adolescence but not between adolescence and adulthood, for the most part. Findings differ somewhat across studies, in part due to sample selection, changes in the definitions of disorders, and techniques used to elicit reports of disorders.

Eating Disorders: Problems and Symptoms

Age Trends

Eating disorders and eating problems are experienced by many adolescents. Anorexia nervosa occurs in about 0.2% of all girls (based on the adult Epidemiological Catchment Area Study; Robins, Carlson, Bucholz, Sussman, & Earls, 1989). In a large two-stage epidemiological study of DSM-III psychiatric disorders in a secondary school population in New Jersey, of 5,596 adolescents surveyed, 12 lifetime cases of anorexia nervosa were identified (lifetime prevalence estimate of 0.2%; Whitaker et al., 1990). For girls, the rate of anorexia nervosa in this study was 0.5%.

The rate is higher in samples at risk for the disorder (i.e., European and American white girls from professional families and girls attending high-achievement, private schools). Perhaps the most widely cited studies are those of Crisp and Szmukler of adolescent girls in Great Britain, where the former found one case per 200 girls and the latter one case per 120 girls. However, recent studies indicate that rates may be creeping up in other ethnic groups and in lower social class groups (Hsu, 1987); the perceived importance of adapting middle-class or upper-middle-class standards may be one reason for the increases (Pumariega, 1986).

The range of estimates for bulimia nervosa in females is 1% to 2.8% for adolescents and young adults (Fairburn & Beglink 1990; Kendler, MacLean, Neale, Kessler, Heath, & Eaves, 1991). In the New Jersey study previously mentioned, the estimate was 1% for bulimia with past or current anorexia and 2.5% for bulimia at normal weight (Whitaker et al., 1990). These rates results those reported in the adult ECA study (Robins et al., 1984).

Childhood rates of eating disorders are low, although prevalence figures are not forthcoming (Lask & Bryant-Waugh, 1992). However, the symptoms seen in children with eating disorders may be somewhat different from those seen in adolescent and adult women. Lask and Bryant-Waugh (1992) have observed that many prepubertal children do not meet the full diagnostic criteria for anorexia nervosa: Children as opposed to adolescents with an eating disorder seem to have lower body fat and are more likely to restrict their fluid intake as well their food intake (Irwin, 1981). Since starvation often results in delayed puberty (Warren, & Brooks-Gunn, 1989a), it is sometimes difficult to know whether a prepubertal 10- or 11-year-old girl with an eating disorder would have already entered puberty if she was not restricting her caloric intake. This fact further complicates comparisons among prepubertal and pubertal children and young adolescents (given that puberty as well as chronological age is used to define the onset of adolescence; Brooks-Gunn & Petersen, 1983, 1984).

One other study warrants mention, both for its methodology and for its results. Two groups of anorectics—one that developed the disorder prepubertally and one that became ill postpubertally—were compared in a retrospective study. The two groups were similar on a variety of familial and personality characteristics—suicide attempts, family problems, and sexual anxiety. They differed in several important aspects, however. One had to do with earlier eating problems and family focus on feeding, which were more common in the prepubertal group. The other difference was that the younger group was more likely to have experienced major stressful life events that might have been a factor in the onset of the disorder (Jacobs & Isaacs, 1986). The focus on possible difference in the etiology, or at least the concomitants, of disorders, as a function of age or gender, is a welcome addition to the field of developmental psychopathology.

Turning to subclinical disorders, we find that perhaps as many as 20% of adolescent girls will or have exhibited bulimic behaviors (Schwartz, Thompson, & Johnson, 1985). This figure does not include girls who engage in unhealthy eating behavior (perhaps less extreme than binge and purge behaviors but still indicative of eating problems); estimates suggest that about 15% may engage in chronic dieting behavior (Attie & Brooks-Gunn, 1995; Killen, Taylor, Telch, Saylor, Maron, & Robinson, 1986; Sallis., 1993; Story, Rosenwinkel, Himes, Resnick, Harris, & Blum, 1991; Whitaker et al., 1990). The overlap between those girls who diet chronically and those who engage in binging and/or purging is large (Story et al., 1991). Estimates for younger girls vis-à-vis chronic dieting and bulumic behaviors are not particularly reliable; however, girls from fourth to sixth grade do engage in unhealthy eating behaviors.

In one study, 3.8% of fifth and sixth graders reported purging (Stein & Reichert, 1990; see also Childress et al., 1993); in another study, 7% of third to sixth graders scored at about the cutoff for the Child EAT (Maloney et al., 1988; see also Alessi, Krahn, Brehm, & Wittekindt, 1989).

Almost no studies have looked at change over time in the manifestation of severe eating problems. Our group has followed a sample of over 100 girls for 8 years—during middle school, high school, and college. At each time point, one-quarter scored about the cutoff point for severe problems using the EAT (Graber, Brooks-Gunn, Paikoff & Warren, 1994). Interestingly, no increase in the number of girls scoring in the high range was found; while continuity was found, a number of girls who were high at one point were not high at others. Little is known about the characteristics of girls who have extreme scores during one phase of adolescence but not during another.

Having been on a diet is now normative for adolescent girls. Normative does not mean that such behavior is normal, or does not have negative health consequences, or does not place girls at risk for such consequences (another example of a behavior that has become normative in adolescence that places teenagers at risk for morbidity is drinking). A large study (over 35,000 middle and high school students in Minnesota) indicates that about two-thirds of adolescent girls reported having dieted in the past 12 months (Story et al., 1991). The incidence increased with the grade in school, although similar rates were reported across social class and geographic residence (suburban, rural, urban).

Another approach to the issue of developmental changes is to consider the nature of eating problems. We have conducted a study using maximum likelihood factor analysis, which allows us to look at the salience of various constructs across age groups (Brooks-Gunn, Rock, & Warren, 1989). Using a form of the EAT-26, we found that the size of the absolute factor loadings increased across three groups of girls—those in 7th to 8th, 9th to 10th, and 11th to 12th grades. Eating problems became more important as girls moved through their adolescent years. This procedure is particularly important in that many studies do not report increases in mean levels of eating problems over this age period.

Gender

Gender divergence in rates of eating disorders and problems occur at the time of adolescence. Prior to adolescence, cases of anorexia nervosa and bulimia appear to occur in boys versus girls in a 1 to 5 ratio (Lask & Bryant-Waugh, 1992). The ratio of females to males for anorexia nervosa is estimated to be 10 to 1 both during the adolescent period and thereafter (Lucas, Beard, O'Fallon, & Kurland, 1991). Likewise, prior to adolescence, boys and girls have quite similar rates. During adolescence, the rates climb more rapidly for girls, so that by the middle to the end of adolescence, girls have a rate twice as high as that of boys (Angold & Rutter, 1992; Bird et al., 1988).

As in the case of age, we may ask whether symptoms, or the meaning of symptoms, are gender linked. While the DSM diagnostic criteria are not bounded by gender, descriptions of eating-disordered symptoms may differ for boys and girls. Generally, males are less concerned with the number of pounds gained or lost and more concerned with achieving a muscular body. Males with eating disorders are more likely than females to belong to subgroups in which weight control is demanded for professional athletic reasons (although female athletes, especially those in ballet, figure skating, and gymnastics, have higher rates of anorexia nervosa than those in other athletic fields or nonathletes; Brooks-Gunn, Attie, Burrow, Rosso, & Warren, 1989; Malina, 1983; Striegel-Moore, 1992). Slender physiques are also preferred in some homosexual male communities and rates of eating disorders may be higher in such contexts (Striegel-Moore, 1992), but not as high as in women generally (Brand, Rothblum, & Solomon, 1992).

Gendered aspects of eating concerns are mirrored in the media. One study reports that 10 times as many diet articles and advertisements are found in magazines aimed at women compared to those directed to same-age men (Andersen & DiDomenico, 1992). The ratio of diet articles (10 to 1) is the same as the ratio of females to males with eating disorders. The authors speculate about the presence of a "dose-response" curve to explain the gendered nature of eating disorders given the cultural incentives for dieting and slim figures in women. Such musings, of course, go way beyond what is known, since it is still unclear whether media and other sociocultural features are associated with eating disorders.

Depressive Disorders: Problems and Symptoms

Age Trends

Clincial depression is more common than eating disorders. The point prevalence for adolescents is about 1% to 3%, and for adults it is about 4% to 5% (Fendrich, Warner, & Weissman, 1990; Rutter, Graham, Chadwich, & Yule, 1976; Weissman, Gammon, John, Merikangas, Prusoff, & Scholomskas, 1987). A recent review suggest that this rate may be higher (Petersen, Compas, Brooks-Gunn, Stemmler, Ely, & Grant, 1993).

In the depression literature, controversy has focused on whether children have the cognitive capacity to experience feelings of hopelessness and to generalize these feelings to the future. Suicidal ideation was once though to be impossible for children, although clinicians have documented cases of suicidal ideation in young children. However, possible differences in the features of clinical disorders in childhood and adolescence need a closer look, as they provide clues to etiological, developmentally bounded similarities and differences. Research has compared children and adolescents vis-à-vis similarities and differences in prepubertal and postpubertal onset of major depressive disorders (Puig-Antich, 1986; Rutter, Izard, & Read, 1986). Generally, this literature suggests a higher likelihood of familial affective disorder in those early-onset cases. It is possible that early onset is due in part to a larger genetic loading for affective disorder. At the same time, residing in a home with a parent who has a disorder is itself a major risk factor for depression (as well as for other mental disorders; Hammen, 1991). Untangling the effects of hereditability and family environment is exceedingly difficult, making it difficult to interpret the findings of familial transmission and early-onset depression.

The rates of depressive symptomatology and depressive affect are estimated to be quite high. About one-sixth of all youth report depressive symptomatology at any point in time (Angold, 1988; Petersen et al., 1993). Additionally, depressive affect of mood states may be reported by as much as one-third of all youth at any point in time (Petersen et al., 1993). Rates are lower for children, although, like the research on eating problems in childhood, the literature of depressive problems in childhood is scanty.

To see whether the nature of depressive problems changes as a function of age, we have looked at the factor structure of constructs across three groups of adolescent girls (Brooks-Gunn et al., 1989). The salience of the construct, including emotional tone (a measure of depressive affect; Petersen et al., 1991), was similar across the three age points (in contrast to what was found for eating problems).

Gender

Depression also may have gendered features. Perhaps the best example is the fact that males and females may have different styles of coping with stressful life events. Females seem to ruminate on problems more than males, a style that may result in more depressive affect being experienced or the meaning of such negative mood states being constructed differently (Nolen-Hoeksema, Girgus, & Seligman, 1991; Seligman, Petersen, Kaslow, Tannenbaum, Alley, & Abramson, 1984). More direct studies of the meaning of depressive symptoms to boys and girls, along the lines of the eating literature, would be welcome.

Behaviors associated with depressive affect also may adhere to gender lines. For example, adolescent boys who are depressed may be more likely to use drugs or to exhibit acting-out behavior than girls (Kandel, Ravies, & Davies, 1991). Such behaviors may mask the depressive symptoms, so that depression may be less likely to be diagnosed in boys than in girls. Studies of comorbidity do suggest different patterns by gender (Lewinsohn, Clarke, Hops, & Andrews, 1990; Lewinsohn, Rohde, Seeley, & Hops, 1991).

The onset of adolescence is believed to be a time of gender intensification (Hill & Lynch, 1983), as boys and girls struggle with what it means to be a male or a female, and as both sexes pay closer attention to how maleness and femaleness are defined culturally and how males and females are treated and portrayed. These differences may result in more stress for girls than for boys, which, in turn, may be associated with the higher rates of depressive disorders and problems for girls (Hill & Lynch, 1983; Petersen, Sarigiani, & Kennedy, 1991). The higher stress of adolescence for girls may take several forms, including the experience of more stressful events, the simultaneous experience of multiple events, the lack of varied opportunities to demonstrate competence, the perceived narrowing of career options, the lack of coping strategies with which to meet the challenges of this time period, and difficulties in forging an independent persona. All have been hypothesized to account for differ-9ences in depression rates (Brooks-Gunn, 1992; Compas, 1987a; Colton & Gore , 1991; Petersen et al., 1991). However, detailed studies of multiple explanations for the gender differences, and longitudinal studies of the various processes underlying depression in boys and girls, are few and far between.

The Adolescent Experience and Emerging Psychopathology

Adolescence is a time of multiple developmental challenges. Change probably occurs in every facet of life (Brooks-Gunn & Petersen, 1991; Feldman & Elliott, 1990; Petersen et al., 1993; Takanishi, 1993). Consequently, conceptual frameworks employed to chart the emergence of specific forms of developmental psychopathology focus on the changes that occur during adolescence.

The possible continuities in symptoms from childhood to adolescence or in childhood predictors of adolescent behavior are not studied as frequently as we would like (notable published exceptions include the work of Block and his colleagues and that of Caspi, Moffit, and their colleagues, who have followed cohorts through childhood and adolescence, with an eye toward problem behaviors associated with depression and eating disorders; other longitudinal studies, while informative, often have not included the type of measures most relevant to a study of these two forms of psychopathology; Brooks-Gunn, Phelps, & Elder, 1991; Robins & Rutter, 1990; Rutter, 1986). The reliance on the developmental challenges of adolescence probably obscures continuity in form or function across the first 18 years of life. For example, in the Block study (Block, 1991; Gjerde & Block, 1991), girls who had high depressive symptomatology scores at age 18 were likely to exhibit inhibited and overcontrolled behavior in the preschool years, while adolescent boys who had high scores were likely to show behavioral organization in the early years characterized as aggressive and low in impulse control. Continuity here is seen in the rank ordering of individuals, not in the form that a behavior takes at each age.

At the same time, a careful look at the contribution of the challenges of adolescence to depression and eating disorders is itself a fairly recent phenomenon. In part, this shortcoming is due to the widely held belief that adolescence itself is a period of almost universal storm and stress for boys and girls alike. This view has had the perverse effect of discounting developmental problems, on the one hand (as adolescents should grow out of their problems), and ignoring developmental variations on the other (Brooks-Bunn & Petersen, 1991; Colten & Gore, 1991; Lerner, 1985; Petersen et al., 1993). Research has demonstrated that many, if not the majority of, adolescents do not experience significant storm and stress but that of those who do, many have subsequent and severe difficulties (Offer, Howard, Schonert, & Ostrov, 1991; Rutter et al., 1976). These alterations represent a sea change in how adolescence is perceived, with increased attention being given to the factors that contribute to the emergence of problem behavior in some young people, as well as those that protect other individuals from problem behavior. Multidimensional, system-level, longitudinal models are in favor, underlying the belief that problem behavior is not the result of single causes or single systems. Much more research focuses on depression than on eating disorders, in part because of the large numbers of young people experiencing depressive affect at any point in time.

We first look at the literature on biological dysregulation and the onset of the two disorder clusters. This work does not always take a developmental perspective. However, it is relevant since dysregulatory processes associated with disorders may differ as a function of age. We then briefly review what is known about the internal changes known to be associated with adolescence—puberty, cognition, and affective states—as they might intersect with the emergence of eating problems and depressive symptomatology. Then two contexts in which the adolescent girls finds herself are considered (albeit briefly). Virtually all of this literature considers problem behavior, not psychopathology (with the exception of the literature on biological dysregulation), given the paucity of studies beginning prior to the onset of a clinical disorder.

Biological Dysregulation and Adolescent Onset of Disorders

Given the rise in the rates of depression and eating disorders during adolescence, biological explanations are almost always suggested when looking at etiology. Developmental approaches have not been used extensively.

In the eating disorder literature, as mentioned in the introduction, a biological concomitants or precursors of eating problems have been studied primarily in terms of whether biological conditions are due only to the effects of starvation or semistarvation. Changes associated with starvation include impaired concentration, loss of general interests, depressive symptomatology, social withdrawal, and a focus on food-related concerns (Garner, 1986), as well as sleep distrubance, amenorrhea, hypotension, bradycardia, reduced core temperature, insensitivity to pain, and lanugo hair (Warren, 1986). Most important for our purpose is the fact that starvation effects are not specific to eating disorders; they are seen in all starving individuals (Keys, Brozek, Henschel, Mickelsen, & Taylor, 1950). Interestingly, obese persons may suffer from the effects of semistarvation when losing weight even though their weight is in the normal rather than the low range.

Research to date does not allow for a separation of the factors contributing to the etiology and those maintaining the disorder. Additionally, how biological factors interact with psychosocial factors in eating disorders is poorly understood. Currently, most biological changes are considered secondary to weight loss. The neuroendocrine changes are thought to be reversible following weight gain (Kaplan & Woodside, 1987; Warren, 1986). With respect to adolescent girls, the onset of anorexia nervosa can cause a reversion to prepubertal hormonal output (nocturnal spiking of luteinizing hormone; Boyar, Finklestein, Roffwarg, Kapan, Wertman, & Hellman, 1972); weight gain signals a return to normal hormonal patterns. Possible exceptions to the reversibility of effects for both adolescent girls and young women include bone demineralization and hypercortisol activity (Salisbury & Mitchell, 1991; Warren, Brooks-Gunn, Fox, Lancelot, Newman, & Hamilton, 1991).

The links between depression and biological dysregulation are quite different from those between eating disorders and biological changes. What is common, however, is that both forms of psychopathology may be triggered by environmental events, and that both major depressive disorder and anorexia nervosa are characterized by biological dysregulation—starvation in the case of eating disorders and stressful life events in the case of depression. A major depressive disorder may follow several different paths (and probably each trajectory exists, with some being more common for particular forms of depression than others). "Depression may be due to: (a) a response to environment events, with biological dysregulation a result of psychosocial factors; (b) a biological difference prior to the occurrence of any environment event for those individuals who go on to have a depressive episode; and (c) a reflection of a genetic susceptibility to experiencing the biological dysregulation associated with depression" (Brooks-Gunn, Petersen, & Compas, 1995). To further complicate matters, the nature of the biological dysregulation seems to differ across individuals (as demonstrated in studies of clinically depressed patients, not all of whom ever exhibit the particular dysregulation under study, and as demonstrated in studies of the differential effectiveness of biological treatments for specific individuals).

While it is beyond the scope of this chapter to review all of the literature on biological concomitants of depression in adolescence (see Brooks-Gunn et al., 1995; Dahl et al., 1991; Puig-Antich, 1986), a few points are relevant to a focus on adolescence. First, while biological work has the potential to provide information on the etiology of depression, almost none of the work has taken a comparative or longitudinal perspective, limiting what may be said about biological underpinnings or about age-related differences. Second, while there is great interest in discovering possible biological markers of depression, little evidence exists (Gold, Goodwin & Chrousos, 1988). This is due in part to what we would accept as evidence (i.e., the necessity to have studies prior to the onset of the first episode to see if biological substrates differed then; see Puig-Antich, 1986). Studies of children and adolescents who are at high risk for developing a depressive disorder (i.e., offspring of affectively disordered parents) constitute a possible approach.

What do we know about biological dysregulation, and what does it tell us about adolescents and psychopathology? It is clear that the limbic system, specifically the HP axes, are affected during a depressive episode. Those axes involving the adrenal (HPA), the thyroid (HPT), the gonadal (HPG), and the somatotropic (HPS) have all been the object of investigation. Additionally, sleep architecture changes and melatonin secretion seem to be affected during depressive episodes (Giles, Jarrett, Roffwarg, & Rush, 1987; Reynolds, Gillen, & Kupfer, 1987). Finally, neurotransmitter systems are altered, with links between these systems and the HP axes being studied at an ever-increasing rate.

What is interesting, vis-à-vis the focus on adolescents, is how little work actually considers the dramatic changes in the HP axes occurring as part of the pubertal process (Brooks-Gunn & Reiter, 1990; Reiter, 1987). Adrenarche occurs in middle childhood as the HPA axis is reactivated after a relatively quiescent time. A few years later, the HPG axis increases in steroid hormones due to releases in inhibition of the HPG axis due to central nervous system system changes.

Comparisons between depressed children and adolescents have been made for HP axes and sleep architecture dysfunction. However, the intersection between these forms of dysregulation and the normal perturbations of puberty have not been the focus of study. Indeed, not all studies even document the pubertal stage of their depressed adolescents, instead categorizing them as prepubertal or postpubertal. This is surprising since puberty is often heralded as one of the factors contributing to the rise in these two disorders (Rutter et al., 1976; Angold & Rutter, 1992).

Almost nothing is known about the HPG axis and depression in adolescence, in part because this system is not believed to be a major contributor to depression in adults. In contrast, studies of depressive affect rather than of clinical depression have looked at the HPG axis (Buchanan et al., 1992).

Puberty, Cognition, and Affective Changes

Puberty and the Body

Pubertal changes are biological, social, and intrapsychic. They are both public and private. They evoke strong feelings in most adolescents, and even in adults, long after puberty is completed (Brooks-Gunn, 1991; Petersen, 1987). We review research on the physiological changes of puberty, the meaning of puberty, and the body image construct here as they are linked to eating and depression disorder clusters.

Physiological Changes

Perhaps the most striking change during the transition to adolescence is the development of a mature body. Puberty is comprised of a series of physiological changes, which themselves often follow different timetables. Both hormonal events and the secondary sexual characteristics that follow may influence girls' behavior (Brooks-Gunn & Reiter, 1990). Hormones may have direct effects upon behavior, or more indirect effects via their effects on internal feeling states or on secondary sexual characteristics. The bodily changes may influence behavior via girls' responses to the changes, others' responses to the changes, or some combination (see Brooks-Gunn, Graber, & Paikoff, 1994; and Graber, Brooks-Gunn, & Warren, 1995, for a discussion of different models underlying possible pubertal influences on affective states).

Two different research traditions have focused on pubertal changes and mental health. The first focuses on disorders and the second on problems. Little has been done on pubertal processes and mental health disorders (see the later review of physiological contributions to depression and eating disorder). The work to date has considered whether the age-related increases in disorders can be linked to puberty specifically rather than to the age range in which puberty typically occurs. Perhaps the best example of this work involves the case record reviews by Angold and Rutter (1992), who report no association between puberty and depressive disorders. No comparable research exists for eating disorders. Hormonal studies have focused on biological dysregulation more generally, rather than on the dysregulations that occur with pubertal change.

The second line of research targets problems as outcomes. The hormonal research on adolescence has focused on affective outcomes, in part because of strong beliefs about early adolescence being a time of storm and stress (Brooks-Gunn, 1991; Holmbeck & Hill, 1991; Petersen, 1988). This research has been reviewed elsewhere (Buchanan, Eccles, & Becker, 1992; Brooks-Gunn et al, 1994; Paikoff & Brooks-Gunn, 1990). Of interest here is the fact that some links have been found between the rapid increases in steroid hormones (and pituitary hormones) and depressive symptoms in girls (Brooks-Gunn & Warren, 1989; Warren & Brooks-Gunn, 1989). This effect seems to be non-linear (see Susman, Dorn, & Chrousos, 1991, who did not find links using linear regressions). It also seems to persist over a 1-year period (Paikoff, Brooks-Gunn, & Warren, 1991). Whether subsequent research will replicate these one-study findings is not known. Recent research by our group is also finding hormonal links with eating problems using the same sample of about 100 girls used in the depressive affect work (Graber, Paikoff & Brooks-Gunn, 1993).

Pubertal status, as assessed by secondary sexual characteristic development (breast and pubic hair growth) and menarche, does not seem to be associated with depressive symptomatology (Graber et al., 1995; Susman et al., 1991). However, links between breast development and eating problems have been reported in one study but not in another (Attie & Brooks-Gunn, 1989; Graber et al., 1993). Breast development may be found to have more indirect affects: For example, dating is associated with breast development, and dating or movement to more intimate behavior may be associated with affective states or perceptions of one's body (Brooks-Gunn, Newman, Holderness, & Warren, 1994; Garguilo, Attie, Brooks-Gunn, & Warren, 1987).

A more direct link is seen between one pubertal process—the increase in body fat—and eating problems. Eating problems increase as girls develop the rounded contours of a women (breast development and body fat), as work in our research group and that of others demonstrates (Attie & Brooks-Gunn, 1989; Garguilo et al., 1987). These effects are probably due to the meaning of body fat, even that associated with normal development, in our society (Faust, 1983). Consequently, we turn to a discussion of the meaning of puberty to girls today.

Meaning of Puberty

Hamburg (1980) has discussed the meaning of puberty to youth as a lottery: Each individual knows that her body will change, but she is not sure about the timing and sequencing of the events, let along the outcome of the process. It comes as no surprise, then, that pubertal changes are scrutinized by the girl as well as her peers. Girls often report that they perceive pubertal events to be private ones that they do not wish to discuss with others (or at least only a few others; Brooks-Gunn & Warren, 1989; Brooks-Gunn et al., 1994; Ruble & Brooks-Gunn, 1982). At the same time, others see the event as public, often commenting on the changes (often to the chagrin of girls; Brooks-Gunn & Reiter, 1990). Girls are embarrassed by their parents' comments about development (Brooks-Gunn & Warren, 1985b). However; they are acutely aware of the status of their friends' development (Brooks-Gunn, Warren, Samuelson, & Fox, 1986). Furthermore, girls are able to provide fairly accurate assessments of the timing of their own development relative to that of their peers (Brooks-Gunn, Petersen, & Eichorn, 1985; Tobin-Richards, Boxer, & Petersen, 1983).

Timing of puberty seems to play a greater role than actual pubertal changes in the occurrence of depressive and eating problems (Attie & Brooks-Gunn, 1989; Brooks-Gunn, 1982; Petersen et al., 1991; Simmons & Blyth, 1987). Early-maturing girls are much more likely to exhibit depressive symptoms than on-time or late-maturing girls. Indeed, in one study on changes in depressive symptomatology over a 4-year period, early puberty was highly predictive of an increase in symptomatology, even controlling for depressive symptoms at age 11, when the early maturers were already exhibiting secondary sexual characteristic development (Brooks-Gunn, 1991). We do not have a good idea of the processes underlying these results, however. The work by Magnusson and Stattin (1990) provides some hints. Early-maturing girls, who were likely to smoke, drink, and have sex earlier than later maturers in Sweden, were also more likely to associate with older peers who presumably were engaging in the behaviors under study. With respect to depressive affect, early-maturing girls, if they have older peers, may be engaging in behaviors and experiencing events for which they are not prepared psychologically. Hence, their movement into older peer groups is stressful due to the multiplicity of events, the lack of support, and the difficulty managing increased expectancies.

The processes underlying links between early puberty and eating problems are probably somewhat different from those for early puberty and depressive problems. It is likely that the ways in which early maturation is perceived by girls (reorganization of body image and mismatch with cultural expectations for a long, linear, lean body in the case of eating problems) are important (Attie & Brooks-Gunn, 1992; Faust, 1983; Palla & Litt, 1988).

Body Image

Body image also plays a role in the emergence of eating and depressive problems. It is difficult to separate the meaning of pubertal change from girls' body images. However, a somewhat separate literature has emerged on body images, using scales that tap how much girls like their bodies, or the specific features of their bodies that they like and dislike. More negative body images are associated with both depressive affect and eating problems (Attie & Brooks-Gunn, 1991; Attie et al., 1990; Post & Crowther, 1985). In the case of eating problems, they seem to have a causal role in that a worsening of body image predicts a change in eating disorders (as demonstrated in one of the few longitudinal studies; Attie & Brooks-Gunn, 1989). Body image is linked to pubertal changes in that girls with more rapid physical growth and with higher weights have worse body images; these effects are intensified in girls who are under pressure to keep their weight low (Brooks-Gunn & Warren, 1985; Brooks-Gunn et al., 1989; Garguilo et al., 1987).

In the case of depressive symptomatology, it is unclear whether poor body images are part of general low self-esteem or are specific to the body in a more physical sense. Low self-esteem is associated with depression and is believed to lead to depressive symptomatology and perhaps clinical depression (Harter, 1990; Renouf & Harter, 1990).

Cognitive Growth

Another milestone of the adolescent experience involves changes in cognitive processes (Keating, 1990). Little literature considers how these changes might result in susceptibility to affective problems. The best-known work is probably that of Nolen-Hoeksma, Girgus, and Seligman, who have been studying attributional styles of thought and rumination as they relate to depression (Nolen-Hoeksema, Girgus, & Seligman, 1991; Seligman, Kamen & Nolen-Hoeksema, 1988). Using stable, general, and internal attributions to explain negative events is associated with higher depressive symptomatology scores in young adolescents (Kaslow, Rehm, & Siegel, 1984; Nolen-Hoeksma, Girgus, & Seligman, 1992). A more inclusive conceptual framework has been proposed by Hammen (1990), who suggests that researchers should consider information processing, attributional, and self-control aspects of cognition as they might impact youth's affective states.

Affective Changes

Affective changes are thought to occur during the transition to adolescence. Often these are subsumed under the broad (and probably misleading) heading of storm and stress (Lerner, 1985). The fact that depressive symptomatology increases during adolescence (in some but all studies) would be evidence of affective change (albeit somewhat circular when considering depression as an outcome [Compas & Hammen, 1994; Petersen et al., 1993]).

What is more interesting is whether the adolescent transition is associated with changes in arousal states (e.g., the sensitivity to external and internal events to trigger increases in arousal, or the lability of arousal states). We (Brooks-Gunn et al., 1994), as well as Buchanan, Eccles, and Becker (1992), have hypothesized that such changes may accompany the initial increases in hormonal output. If so, these changes could be interpreted in various ways by the adolescent girl. Labeling these changes as affective states would occur, as Schacter and Singer (1962) have hypothesized. Events determining how increased arousal is labeled include preexisting personality characteristics (e.g., shyness, novelty seeking), the context in which the girl finds herself during the increased arousal, attributions made to mood state, and the degree to which the girl is physiologically reactive to novel and familiar events. To date, no research has been conducted either on the notion that arousal is one internal process by which hormonal changes and affective states are linked or on the processes underlying such an association.

Interestingly, Bruch (1973) has written about the disturbance of perceptual and cognitive interpretations of feeling states as being one of the three conditions of eating disorders during adolescence. Another approach has been taken by Strober (1991). Cloninger (1987) has put forth a premise related to the personality characteristics of individuals at risk for developing eating disorders. The three are low novelty seeking, high harm avoidance, and reward dependence. These characteristics, while genetically determined, may be moderated by environmental characteristics. Girls with this constellation may be at risk for affect dysregulation that could present as eating (or perhaps depressive) problems. For example, girls who are early maturers, or girls who are experiencing high arousal states associated with the increase in the HPG and HPA axes, and who are also adverse to novelty and change, may find coping with pubertal growth particularly difficult. The result may be a set of ritualized behaviors (such as food restriction or exercising) in an attempt to control or minimize the pubertal influences (Attie & Brooks-Gunn, 1995).

In any case, it is clear that little research had been directed to affective processes, other than describing them, during the adolescent transition (see, as an exception, the work of Csikzentmihalyi & Larson, 1984; Larson & Lampman-Petraitis, 1989; Tobin-Richards et al., 1983).

Contextual Influences

Family Processes and Disorders

Family factors include genetic and environmental influences, which are often difficult to disentangle. It is clear that the major risk factor for clinical depression is having a parent with an affective disorder (Downey & Coyne, 1990; Hammen, 1991; Hammen, Burge, & Stansbury, 1990). Offspring of such parents also are at increased risk for other forms of psychopathology, as well as school problems, peer problems, and other problems. Research not only implicates genetic transmission (Weissman, 1990), but also the interactions among family members and the climate in the family as etiological factors (Burge & Hammen, 1991; Carlton-Ford, Paikoff, & Brooks-Gunn, 1991; Downey & Coyne, 1990). Divorce and economic conditions in the family also are associated with depression (Block, Block, & Gjerde, 1986; Cherlin et al., 1991; Lempers & Clark-Lempers, 1990).

This rich and informative literature has no parallel in the eating disorder literature. This is due in part to the fact that the offspring of eating-disordered women are not followed and that the genetic transmission, while clearly existing, does not seem to be as strong. Unfortunately, almost all family studies focus on the family interactions after an eating disorder has been identified in the adolescent girl. While providing much insight into the functioning of these families, caution must be taken in attributing causality in this research corpus (Attie et al., 1990; Attie & Brooks-Gunn, in press).

Family Processes and Problems

Literature on problems rather than disorders has identified a number of risk factors during the adolescent years. One research line involves direct socialization or parental concern for particular behaviors. Perhaps the best illustration involves the fact that mothers influence girls' eating behaviors in terms of their emphasis placed on body shape and size. Two studies have reported associations between mothers and daughters in terms of body image, weight concerns, and eating (Attie & Brooks-Gunn, 1989; Rodin, Silberstein, & Striegel-Moore, 1984).

Another research tradition involves the transformation of family interactions during the transition to adolescence (Paikoff & Brooks-Gunn, 1991). However, this work does not address depression or eating directly (i.e., it does not look at change in family functioning and effects on problem behavior).

However, work has been conducted on family functioning using cross-sectional approaches. This work suggests that different dimensions of family functioning may be related to different forms of problems. Families who are low in cohesion are likely to have daughters who exhibit eating problems (Attie & Brooks-Gunn; 1989; Paikoff, Brooks-Gunn & Carlton-Ford, 1991). In contrast, a different family climate dimension—family conflict—is associated with depressive affect (Paikoff et al., 1991,). These two dimensions—cohesion and control—have been identified in the clinical literature as being common in families where daughters have eating disorders, on the one hand, and depression, on the other (Attie & Brooks-Gunn, 1992).

We wish to sound a note of caution with respect to these findings. It is possible that family processes are altered following the daughter's behavioral change (Paikoff & Brooks-Gunn, 1991). Reciprocal effects could occur via instigation by the daughter (moving away from the family in the case of eating problems or confrontation with the family in the case of depressive affect). Alternatively, the parents could be providing a milieu in which a particular problem behavior will flourish. In all likelihood, these associations reflect reciprocal effects, such that families who are low in cohesion are probably more likely to provide an environment conducive to eating problems, while the onset of eating problems heightens the effects of the preexisting characteristics of the family or increases the level of family dysfunction directly. The same processes might be at work in families with daughters who exhibit depressive symptoms or clinical depression. Indeed, in an exploratory analysis of the links between family conflict and depressive affect, each measured twice during adolescence, some support for family conflict leading to more depressive symptoms in the daughters was found (i.e., cross-lagged panel analyses; Carlton-Ford, Paikoff, Oakley, Sharer, & Brooks-Gunn, in press). The same criticism could be leveled at the work on family dysfunction and its role in the etiology of eating or depressive disorders.

Another research tradition focuses on early parent child interations, as as a critical foundation for healthy psychological functioning later on. Object relations theory and attachment theory are perhaps the best exemplar of this tradition. Most of what is written is quite speculative vis-à-vis depressive and eating outcomes in adolescence in that samples have not been tracked from infancy through adolescence. The dysregulations in parent–child synchrony captured in work on avoidance attachment patterns, unresponsive parenting, disengagement, and intrusive dyadic interactions during the infant and toddler phases have features that are associated with affect regulation problems later on (Cicchetti, in press; Emde, 1988; Rutter, 1986). Likewise, the scanty but provocative literature on interactional problems in feeding patterns early on may be indicative of subsequent issues about food and control.

Peers

Given the salience of the peer group during adolescence, it comes as no surprise that a vigorous research tradition exists (Brown, 1990; Savin-Williams & Berndt, 1990; Youniss & Smollar, 1985). Not much of this work directly addresses links with depressive or eating problems or disorders, and when it does, the direction of effects is not always clear.

Work on depression suggests that disruptions in peer relationships occur during depressive episodes. However, little research addresses the question of whether social isolation from peers precedes or follows the onset of a depressive problem or disorder. Scanty evidence suggests that these effects might be reciprocal (Vernberg, 1990). At the same time, adult disorders are strongly associated with poor peer relationships in the adolescent years (Sroufe & Rutter, 1984).

Much less is known about peer relationships and eating problems. Perhaps the most interesting work is that focusing on learning unhealthy eating behavior from same-sex peers. Socialization into binge and bulimic cycles has been reported (Crandall, 1988; Killen, Taylor, Telch, Saylor, Maron, & Robinson, 1986). Unlike the literature on mothers and daughters, the literature on the female peer system indicates that the peer group is thought to provide direct teaching about purging techniques. It is unclear how frequently such learning occurs.

Another research thread has to do with how self-perceptions may be altered by the peer system. Harter's work is illustrative. In a recent study, Harter and her colleagues (1992) have suggested that self-worth, being linked to competence domains identified as important by youth, will vary as a function of these domains. Central to middle school students were a peer domain (appearance, peer friendships, athletic ability) and an academic and behavior (school and conduct) self-worth domain. The former was linked to perceived peer support and the latter to perceived parental support, as expected. These domains predicted depressive problems in different ways. Such an approach allows for more specific hypotheses about how peer approval is linked to self-worth, in what domains of competence, and for what subgroups of adolescents.

Developmental Trajectories and Developmental Psychopathology

We have considered the emergence of eating and depressive problems and disorders in the context of adolescence by reviewing what is known about various risk factors, as well as taking a cursory look at biological dysregulation. Almost all of this work is cross-sectional, or, if longitudinal, covers only a brief time span. Many have pleaded for more prospective research focusing on mental health outcomes covering a number of transitional periods, and including multiple risk factors. While few such studies have been conducted, we present the results of two to give a flavor of what might be considered the next generation of studies on the mental health of adolescents. Our illustrations come from our work and that of Petersen. Other groups are following samples of youth into their adult years; notable examples are the studies by Block (1991), Hauser, Borman, Powers, Jacobson, and Noam (1990), and Baumrind (1980).

We hasten to add that the perspective is limited in that it looks at youth gathered from school settings. A comparable prospective approach for examining the emergence of disorders is the study of offspring of affectively disordered parents. Often these studies target the offspring of depressed parents (Hammen, 1991); Weissman, Gammon, John, Merikangas, Prusoff, & Scholomskas, 1987; Weissman, Leckman, Merikangas, Gammon, & Prusoff, 1984). Studies have not followed the offspring of eating-disordered parents.

In our study of eating problems (Graber et al., 1995), approximately 120 girls have been followed for almost a decade: They were first seen in middle school, then in high school, and most recently in the last years of college. The girls attended private schools in Manhattan, were members of professional families, and, for the most part, went to elite college throughout the country. They filled out the EAT-26 at each time point, as well as a variety of scales tapping depressive symptomatology (Center for Epidemiology Study—Depression [CES-D]), behavior problems (Youth Behavior Profile), family climate (Family Environment Scale), and body image (Self Image Questionnaire for Young Adolescents, Satisfaction with Body Parts). At the final assessment point, they were also interviewed about eating disorders.

This sample was chosen because upper-middle-class girls are known to be at risk for eating problems. Our sample was no exception. About 12% of the girls had anorexia or bulimia nervosa over the course of the study. An additional 18% would be classified as having an atypical eating disorder (see also Fairburn & Wilson, 1993). Anorexia and bulimia nervosa were most likely to develop during the high school years, while atypical eating disorders were more likely to develop during the college years.

Girls were classified into risk groups based on whether they experienced any type of eating disorder (anorexia nervosa, bulimia nervosa, or atypical eating disorder) during young adolescence and midadolescence. This categorization resulted in girls who had no disorder during these time periods (Low Risk), girls who had disorders in both time periods (Chronic), and girls with no disorder in young adolescence who had a disorder in midadolescence (Increasing Risk). Girls in the Chronic group had a higher percentage of body fat in young adolescence. At late adolescence, though, physical differences among groups were found, with Chronic girls having a higher percentage of body fat than other girls and having an earlier age at menarche than Low-Risk girls. A risk-group effect was also found for the CES-D measure of depressive affect. Follow-up tests revealed a significant group difference, with girls in the Chronic group reporting the highest levels of depressive affect. A univariate group effect was also found for conflict with and separation from the mother (higher in the Chronic group). It is also noteworthy that the conflict with and separation from father measure was unavailable for half of the Chronic girls because the father was deceased or had had no contact with the young women for over 6 years. This suggests that parental loss may have been an influence in initial group membership.

Similar analyses were conducted for girls classified as having eating problems or not (rather than the existence of an eating disorder). Here, girls in the Chronic group had earlier ages of menarche, as well as more (not less) body fat. Depressive affect was highest in the Chronic group as well, which is not surprising given the high incidence of comorbidity. However, our analyses suggest that depressive affect follows a rise in eating problems rather than appearing concurrently.

In order to chart the development and pattern of depressive affect across the adolescent decade, Petersen and her colleagues (personal communication) followed a group of adolescent boys and girls annually in 6th, 7th, and 8th grades, with follow-up examinations in 12th grade and 4 years after high school (i.e., senior year in college). This sample of nearly 200 adolescents was randomly drawn from suburban schools in the vicinity of a large midwestern city. Adolescents were predominantly white, from middle- to upper-middle-class, well-educated families. The study assessed psychological adjustment and self-esteem, pubertal development, and a variety of family influences on adolescent development.

Depressive affect during early adolescence was assessed using the Emotional Tone subscale (e.g., "I frequently feel sad") of the Self-Image Questionnaire for Young Adolescents (SIQYA) (Petersen, Schulenberg, Abramovitz, Offer, & Jercho, 1984). In order to identify adolescents who experience recurrent affective disturbances, adolescents were categorized based on the pattern of their emotional tone scores. That is, adolescents whose scores were one-half of a standard deviation below the mean for the sample were identified as experiencing distressed affect in that year. Adolescents fell into one of four groups based on their scores across sixth, seventh, and eighth grades: chronic-distressed affect in all 3 years, recurrent-distressed affect in 2 of the 3 years, intermittent-distressed affect at 1 year only, or never distressed.

Patterns of adjustment in early adolescence were predictive of depressive affect both 4 years later (senior year in high school) and 8 years later during the transition to young adulthood. In young adulthood, chronically distressed adolescents were more depressed than other young adults using an independent measure of depression. Early adolescent affective trajectories also predicted five of the nine SIQYA scales such that nondistressed adolescents had the highest self-image and were significantly different from chronically distressed adolescents, with recurrently and intermittently distressed individuals falling in between. In particular, on the Mastery and Coping scale, group differences were stronger for girls than for boys, suggesting that early adolescent patterns of the depressive affect may be more indicative of longer-term adjustment patterns for girls than for boys.

In summary, these analyses are a first step toward identifying the processes by which eating and depressive problems emerge, as well as differentiating those that are chronic from those that are more transitory. Thus far, these studies have not looked at the routes by which girls come to have a clinical disorder or a subclinical problem (see the example by Rutter, this volume). The same is true for how some girls with a problem go on to develop a disorder. Multiple developmental trajectories to the same or similar outcomes are well recognized. However, few studies have charged the existence of such trajectories for eating or depressive problems in adolescent girls. Such information also is necessary if we are to resolve ongoing issues about whether symptoms, problems, and disorders array themselves on a continuum (or the circumstances in which they do and do not).

Conclusion

This brief tour of the literature on the development of eating and depressive disorder clusters in the context of adolescence is meant to be illustrative, not exhaustive. However, several issues need to be highlighted for future research. The first focuses on measurement. In order to chart age and gender trends in eating and depression problems and disorders accurately, more attention needs to be paid to the meaning and expression of these problems. Do changes occur over time? Do meaning and expression vary as a function of gender? Or of ethnicity or social class? Almost no research has been conducted on these issues. We do not know what children or adolescents mean when they say that they have been on a diet, or that they are blue or depressed (Attie & Brooks-Gunn, 1992; Kovacs & Paulauskas, 1984). With respect to dieting, do individuals mean that they have restricted food intake or that they would like to restrict food intake? What is their referent point (a day ago, two weeks ago)? When do children have the self-regulatory ability to restrict food intake in the face of hunger? When are individuals influenced by counterregulatory mechanisms vis-à-vis eating (Heatherton & Polivy, 1992)? What is the definition of a "successful" diet to youngsters of different ages?

The second question involves the nature of the continuity between early adaptational patterns of behavior and interaction and the subsequent development of a problem or behavior. While we have mentioned this issue only in a fleeting fashion, our omission is due in part to the paucity of data. Frameworks have been used to consider links between early forms of problems or, more likely, early patterns of dysregulation that place individuals at risk for psychopathology later on (see the work by Robins, 1972, and Rutter, 1989, using developmental psychopathology frameworks). However, the more normative developmental work needs to consider the form, structure, and meaning of early patterns of interaction and behavior more adequately. It needs to take seriously the call for attention to the coherence of functioning across the life span in the face of changes in behavior and symptomatology, as well as in their meaning.

Our third concern has to do with the perennial issue of continuity between forms of psychopathology. The question is often framed in terms of a continuum or level of severity. Are the risk factors similar or different for the onset of problems and disorders or clinical and subclinical disorders? The question also may be posed in terms of chronicity, as our work and that of Petersen demonstrate.

Related is the issue of how disorder arise. Is it necessary for a disorder to arise as a result of the more normative experience of dieting or depressed mood? Is it possible to distinguish two girls who are restricting food intake in the hope of enhancing their appearance when one continues to diet while the other one goes on to develop bulimic behaviors or an eating disorder? How do we differentiate girls with depressed mood who develop a chronic dysthmia from those who do not?

A slightly different issue arises when we acknowledge that different paths of problems and disorders exist. While the notion of trajectories is well accepted by developmentalists, little research attention has been paid to individual variation in paths. In part, this is due to an over-reliance on regression models, which do not allow for differentiation of groups of girls or of paths. The work discussed by Rutter (this volume) and the work by our group presented in this chapter are exemplars of more individual difference approaches.

When considering risk factors, several different models need to be put forth. Are specific risk factors particularly important, or is the accumulation of risk factors more salient (Liaw & Brooks-Gunn, 1994; Sameroff, Seifer, Baldwin, & Baldwin, 1993)? Do certain risk factors, or their accumulation, have more power at certain developmental transitions or age points than others? Does the accumulation of events influence boys and girls differently?

Finally, the answers to such questions have implications for primary and secondary prevention programs. Developmentalists have not been involved in prevention efforts to any great extent. In part, their hesitance may be due to the number of unanswered questions with respect to why certain problems and disorders emerge during adolescence.

Acknowledgments

Portions of this chapter were presented at a conference on Frontiers of Developmental Psychopathology, Cornell University, Ithaca, NY, March 1993. Portions of this chapter also appear in Brooks-Gunn, Petersen, & Compas, 1995. This work was supported by grants from the National Institutes of Child Health and Human Development, the W. T. Grant Foundation, and the NICHD Child and Family Well-Being Research. We wish to thank Julie Graber for her critical reading of the manuscript. We also would like to thank Anne Petersen and Bruce Compas for their collaboration on research on adolescent depression. Joshua Brown and Diana Scott are to be thanked for their help in manuscript preparation.

Notes

1. We recognize that we are blurring distinctions between chronicity and severity here. Indeed, research should be considering the intersection of chronicity and severity of symptom clusters, as well as their intersection with the symptom-free trajectories during the adolescent period.

2. So little is known about the movement between problems and disorders, the timing of the movement, or the factors associated with variations in movement and timing that we cannot even speculate about the developmental course from normative dieting to problems to disorders (if such a course even exists; Graber et al., in press).

References

Achenbach, T. M. (1991). *Manual for the child behavior checklists/4–18 and 1991 profile.* Burlington: Department of Psychiatry, University of Vermont.

Achenbach, T. M. (in press). The derivation of taxonomic constructs: A necessary stage in the development of developmental psychopathology. In D. Cicchetti (Ed.), *Rochester symposium on developmental psychopathology (Vol. 3)*. Hillsdale, NJ: Erlbaum.

Achenback, T. M., & Edelbrock, C. (1987). *Manual for the youth self-report and profile*. Burlington: University of Vermont, Department of Psychiatry.

Akiskal, H. S., & McKinney, W. T., Jr. (1973). Depressive disorders: Toward a unified hypothesis. *Science, 182*, 20–29.

Alessi, N. E., Krahn, D., Brehm, D., & Wittekindt, J. (1989). Prepubertal anorexia nervosa and major depressive disorder. *Journal of the American Academy of Child and Adolescent Psychiatry, 28* 380–384.

Andersen, A. E., & DiDomenico, L. (1992). Diet vs. shape content of popular male and female magazines: A dose–response relationship to the incidence of eating disorders? *International Journal of Eating Disorders, 11*, 283–287.

Angold, A. (1988). Childhood and adolescent depression II: Research in clinical populations. *British Journal of Psychiatry, 153*, 476–492.

Angold, A., & Rutter, M. (1992). Effects of age and pubertal status on depression in a large clinical sample. *Development and Psychopathology, 4*, 5–28.

Attie, I., & Brooks-Gunn, J. (1989). The development of eating problems in adolescent girls: A longitudinal study. *Developmental Psychology, 25*(1), 70–79.

Attie, I., & Brooks-Gunn, J. (1992). Developmental issues in the study of eating problems and disorders. In J. H. Crowther, S. E. Hobfoll, M. A. P. Stephens, & D. L. Tennenbaum (Eds.), *The etiology of bulimia: The individual and family context* (pp. 35–58). Washington DC: Hemisphere Publishers.

Attie, I., & Brooks-Gunn, J. (1995). The emergence of eating disorders and eating problems in adolescence: A developmental perspective. In D. Cicchetti & D. J. Cohen (Eds.), *Manual of developmental psychopathology, (Vol. 2).* (pp. 332–368). New York: Cambridge University Press.

Attie, I., Brooks-Gunn, J., & Petersen, A. C. (1990). The emergence of eating problems: A developmental perspective. In M. Lewis & S. Miller (Eds.), *Handbook of developmental psychopathology* (pp. 409–420). New York: Plenum Press.

Baumeister, R. F. (1990). Suicide as escape from self. *Psychological Review, 97*, 90–113.

Baumrind, D. (1980). New directions in socialization research. *American Psychologist, 35*, 639–652.

Bird, H. R., Canino, G., Rubio-Stipec, M., Gould, M. S., Ribera, J., Sesman, M., Woodbury, M., Huertas-Goldman, S., Pagan, A., Sanchez-Lacay, A., & Moscoso, M. (1988). Estimates of the prevalence of childhood maladjustment in a community survey in Puerto Rico. *Archives of General Psychiatry, 45*, 1120–1126.

Block, J. H. (1991, April). *Self-esteem through time: Gender similarities and differences*. Paper presented at the 1991 biennial meeting of the Society for Research in Child Development, Seattle, WA.

Block, J. H., Block, J., & Gjerde, P. F. (1986). The personality of children prior to divorce: A prospective study. *Child Development, 57*, 827–840.

Boyar, R. M., Finklestein, J., Roffwarg, H., Kapan, S., Wertman, E., & Hellman, L. (1972). Synchronization of augmented luteinizing hormone secretion with sleep during puberty. *New England Journal of Medicine, 287,* 582–586.

Brand, P. A., Rothblum, E. D., & Solomon, L. J. (1992). A comparison of lesbians, gay men, and heterosexuals on weight and restrained eating. *International Journal of Eating Disorders, 11,* 253–259.

Brooks-Gunn, J. (1982). Methods and models of menstrual research: A sociocultural approach. In A. M. Voda, M. Dinnerstein, & S. R. O'Donnell (Eds.), *Changing perspectives on menopause* (p. 203–208). Austin: University of Texas Press.

Brooks-Gunn, J. (1991). How stressful is the transition to adolescence in girls? In M. E. Colten & S. Gore (Eds.), *Adolescent stress: Causes and consequences* (pp. 131–149). Hawthorne, NY: Aldine de Gruyter.

Brooks-Gunn, J. (1992). Growing up female: Stressful events and the transition to adolescence. In T. Field, P. McCabe, & N. Schneiderman (Eds.), *Stress and coping in infancy and childhood* (pp. 119–145). Hillsdale, NJ: Erlbaum.

Brooks-Gunn, J., Attie, I., Burrow, C., Russo, J. T., & Warren, M. P. (1989). The impact of puberty on body and eating concerns in different athletic and nonathletic contexts. *Journal of Early Adolescence, 9*(3), 269–290.

Brooks-Gunn, J., Graber, J., & Paikoff, R. L. (1994). Studying links between hormones and adaptive and maladaptive behavior: Models and measures. *Journal of Research on Adolescence, 4*(4), 469–486.

Brooks-Gunn, J., Newman, D., Holderness, C. & Warren, M. P. (1994). The experience of breast development and girls' stories about the purchase of a bra. *Journal of Youth and Adolescence, 23*(5).

Brooks-Gunn, J., & Paikoff, R. L. (1993). "Sex is a gamble, kissing is a game": Adolescent sexuality, contraception, and pregnancy. In S. P. Millstein, A. C. Petersen, & E. O. Nightingale (Eds.), *Promoting the health of adolescents* (pp. 180–200). NY: Oxford University Press.

Brooks-Gunn, J., & Petersen, A. C. (1983). (Eds.). *Girls at puberty: Biological and psychosocial perspectives.* New York: Plenum Press.

Brooks-Gunn, J., & Petersen, A. C. (1984). Problems in studying and defining pubertal events. *Journal of Youth and Adolescence, 13*(3), 181–196.

Brooks-Gunn, J., & Petersen, A. C. (1991). Studying the emergence of depression and depressive symptoms during adolescence. *Journal of Youth and Adolescence, 20*(2), 115–119.

Brooks-Gunn, J., Petersen, A. C., & Compas, B. (1995). Physiological processes and the development of childhood and adolescent depression. In I. M. Goodyer (Ed.), *Mood disorders in childhood and adolescence* (pp. 81–109). New York: Cambridge University Press.

Brooks-Gunn, J., Petersen, A. C., & Eichorn, D. (1985). The study of maturational timing effects in adolescence. *Journal of Youth and Adolescence, 14*(3), 149–161.

Brooks-Gunn, J., Phelps, E., & Elder, G. H. (1991). Studying lives through time: Secondary data analysis in developmental psychology. *Developmental Psychology, 27*(6), 899–910.

Brooks-Gunn, J., & Reiter, E. O. (1990). The role of pubertal processes in the early adolescent transition. In S. Feldman & G. Elliott (Eds.), *At the threshold: The developing adolescent* (pp. 16–53). Cambridge, MA: Harvard University Press.

Brooks-Gunn, J., Rock, D., & Warren, M. P. (1989). Comparability of constructs across the adolescent years. *Developmental Psychology, 25*(1), 51–60.

Brooks-Gunn, J., & Warren, M. P. (1985a). The effects of delayed menarche in different contexts: Dance and nondance students. *Journal of Youth and Adolescence, 14*(4), 285–300.

Brooks-Gunn, J., & Warren, M. P. (1985b). Measuring physical status and timing in early adolescence: A developmental perspective. *Journal of Youth and Adolescence, 14,* 163–189.

Brooks-Gunn, J., & Warren, M. P. (1989). Biological contributions to affective expression in young adolescent girls. *Child Development, 60,* 372–385.

Brooks-Gunn, J., Warren, M. P., Samuelson, M., & Fox, R. (1986). Physical similarity of and disclosure of menarcheal status to friends: Effects of age and pubertal status. *Journal of Early Adolescence, 6*(1), 3–14.

Brown, B. B. (1990). Peer groups and peer cultures. In S. Feldman & G. Elliott (Eds.), *At the threshold: The developing adolescent* (pp. 171–196). Cambridge, MA: Harvard University Press.

Brownell, K. D., & Rodin, J. (1994). The dieting maelstrom: Is it possible and advisable to lose weight? *American Psychologist, 49*(9), 781–791.

Bruch, H. (1973). *Eating disorders.* New York: Basic Books.

Buchanan, C. M., Eccles, J. S., & Becker, J. B. (1992). Are adolescents the victims of raging hormones: Evidence for activational effects of hormones on moods and behavior at adolescence. *Psychological Bulletin, 111,* 62–107.

Burge, D., & Hammen, C. (1991). Maternal communication: Predictors of outcome at follow-up in a sample of children at high and low risk for depression. *Journal of Abnormal Psychology, 100,* 174–180.

Carlson, G. A., & Garber, J. (1986). Developmental issues in the classification of depression in children. In M. Rutter, C. E. Izard, & P. B. Read (Eds.), *Depression in young people: Clinical and developmental perspectives* (pp. 399–434). New York: Guilford Press.

Carlton-Ford, S., Paikoff, R. L., & Brooks-Gunn, J. (1991). Methodological issues in the study of divergent views of the family. In R. L. Paikoff (Ed.), *New directions for child development: Shared views in the family during adolescence* (Vol. 51, pp. 87–102). San Francisco: Jossey-Bass.

Carlton-Ford, S., Paikoff, R. L., Oakley, J., Sharer, A., & Brooks-Gunn, J. (in press). Adolescent depressive affect and daughter's and mother's reports of family cohesion and conflict. *Human Development.*

Cherlin, A. J., Furstenberg, F. F., Chase-Lansdale, L., Kiernan, K. E., Robins, P. K., Morrison, D. R., & Teitler, J. O. (1991). Longitudinal studies of effects of divorce on children in Great Britain and the United Sates. *Science, 252,* 1386–1389.

Childress, A. C., Brewerton, T. D., Hodges, E. L., & Jarrell, M. P. (1993). The kids' eating disorders survey (KEDS): A study of middle school students. *Journal of the American Academy of Child and Adolescent Psychiatry, 32,* 843–850.

Cicchetti, D. (1984). The emergence of developmental psychopathology. *Child Development, 55,* 1–7.

Cicchetti, D. (in press). Developmental theory: Lessons from the study of risk and psychopathology. In S. Matthysse, D. Levy, J. Kagan, & F. Benes (Eds.), *Psychopathology: The evolving science of mental disorder.* New York: Cambridge University Press.

Cicchetti, D., & Cohen, D. J. (Eds.). (1995). *Developmental Psychopathology (Vol. 2).* New York: Wiley.

Cicchetti, D., & Schneider-Rosen, K. (1984). Theoretical and empirical considerations in the investigation of the relationship between affect and cognition in atypical populations of infants. Contributions to the formulation of an integrative theory of development. In C. Izard, J. Kagan, & R. Zajonc (Eds.), *Emotions, cognition, and behavior.* London: Cambridge University Press.

Cloninger, C. R. (1987). A systematic method for clinical description and classification of personality variants. *Archives of General Psychiatry, 44*, 573–587.

Colton, M. E., & Gore, S. (Eds.). (1991). *Adolescent stress: Causes and consequences*. Hawthorne, NY: Aldine de Gruyter.

Compas, B. E. (1987a). Coping with stress during childhood and adolescence. *Psychological Bulletin, 101*, 393–401.

Compas, B. E. (1987b). Stress and life events during childhood and adolescence. *Clinical Psychology Review, 7*, 275–302.

Compas, B. E., Davis, G. E., Forsythe, C. J., & Wagner, B. M. (1987). Assessment of major and daily stressful events during adolescence: The adolescent perceived events scale. *Journal of Consulting and Clinical Psychology, 55*, 534–541.

Compas, B. E., & Hammen, C. L. (1994). Depression in childhood and adolescence: Covariation and comorbidity in development. In R. J. Haggerty, N. Garmezy, M. Rutter, & L. Sherrod (Eds.), *Risk and resilience in children: Developmental approaches*. New York: Cambridge University Press.

Compas, B. E., Petersen, A. C. & Brooks-Gunn, J. (in press). *Depression in adolescence*. Newbury Park, CA: Sage.

Crandall, C. S. (1988). Social contagion of binge eating. *Journal of Personality and Social Psychology, 55*, 588–598.

Csikzentmihalyi, M., & Larson, R. (1984). *Being adolescent: Conflict and growth in the teenage years*. New York: Basic Books.

Dahl, R. E., Ryan, N. D., Puig-Antich, J., Nguyen, N. A., Al-Shabbout, M., Meyer, V. A., & Perel, J. (1991). 24-Hour cortisol measures in adolescents with major depression: A controlled study. *Biological Psychiatry, 30*, 25–36.

Downey, G. & Coyne, J. C. (1990). Children of depressed parents: An integrative review. *Psychological Bulletin, 108*(1), 50–76.

Emde, R. N. (1988). The effect of relationships on relationships: A developmental approach to clinical intervention. In R. A. Hinde & J. Stevenson-Hinde (Eds.), *Relationships within families: Mutual influences* (pp. 354–363). Oxford: Clarendon Press.

Fairburn, C. G., & Beglin, S. J. (1990). Studies of the epidemiology of bulimia nervosa. *American Journal of Psychiatry, 147*, 401–408.

Fairburn, C. G., & Wilson, (1993).

Faust, M. S. (1983). Alternative constructions of adolescent growth. In J. Brooks-Gunn & A. C. Petersen (Eds.), *Girls at puberty: Biological and psychosocial perspectives* (pp. 105–125). New York: Plenum Press.

Fendrich, M., Warner, V., & Weissman, M. M. (1990). Family risk factors, parental depression, and psychopathology in off-spring. *Developmental Psychology, 26(1)*, 40–50.

Feldman, S. S., & Elliott, G. (Eds.). (1990). *At the threshold: The developing adolescent*. Cambridge, MA: Harvard University Press.

Garguilo, J., Attie, I., Brooks-Gunn, J., & Warren, M. P. (1987). Dating in middle-school girls: Effects of social context, maturation, and grade. *Developmental Psychology, 23*, 730–737.

Garner, D. M. (1986). Cognitive therapy for bulimia nervosa. *Adolescent Psychiatry, 13*, 358–390.

Garner, D. M., & Garfinkel, P. E. (1979). The eating attitudes test: An index of the symptoms of anorexia nervosa. *Psychological Medicine, 1*, 273–279.

Garner, D. M., & Garfinkel, P. E. (Eds.). (1985). *Handbook of psychotherapy for anorexia nervosa and bulimia*. New York: Guilford Press.

Garner, D. M., Olmsted, M. P., & Polivy, J. (1983). The development and validation of a multidimensional eating disorder inventory for anorexia and bulimia. *International Journal of eating Disorders, 2*(2), 15–34.

Garner, D. M., Olmsted, M. P., Polivy, J., & Garfinkel, P. E. (1984). Comparison between weight-preoccupied women and anorexia nervosa. *Psychosomatic Medicine, 46,* 255–266.

Giles, D. E., Jarrett, R. B., Roffwarg, H. P., & Rush, A. J. (1987). Reduced REM latency: A predictor of recurrence in depression. *Neuropsychopharmacology, 1,* 33–39.

Gjerde, P. F., & Block, J. (1991). Preadolescent antecedents of depressive symptomatology at age 18: A prospective study. *Journal of Youth and Adolescence, 20*(2), 217–232.

Gold, P. W., Goodwin, F. K., & Chrousos, G. P. (1988). Clinical and biochemical manifestations of depression: Relation to the neurobiology of stress. *New England Journal of Medicine, 319*(7), 348–420.

Graber, J. A., Brooks-Gunn, J., Paikoff, R. L., & Warren, M. P. (1994). Prediction of eating problems: An eight year study of adolescent girls. *Developmental Psychology, 30*(6), 823–834.

Graber, J. A., Brooks-Gunn, J., & Warren, M. P. (1995). The antecedents of menarcheal age: Heredity, family environment, and life events. *Child Development. 66,* 346–359.

Graber, J. A., Paikoff, R. L., & Brooks-Gunn, J. (1993, March). *Correlates of eating attitudes and disorders from adolescence to young adulthood.* Paper presented as part of the symposium "The development and course of eating disorders across adolescence and young adulthood," at the biennial meeting of the Society for Research in Child Development, New Orleans.

Gunnar, M. R., & Collins, W. A. (Eds.). (1988). *Transitions in adolescence: Minnesota symposia on child psychology.* Hillsdale, NJ: Erlbaum.

Hamburg, B. A. (1980). Early adolescence as a life stress. In S. Levine & H. Ursin (Eds.), *Coping and health* (pp. 121–143). New York: Plenum Press.

Hammen, C. (1990). Cognitive approaches to depression in children: Current findings and new directions. In B. B. Lahey & A. E. Kazdin (Eds.), *Advances in clinical child psychology* (Vol. 13, pp. 139–173). New York: Plenum Press.

Hammen, C. (1991). *Depression runs in families.* New York: Springer-Verlag.

Hammen, C. Burge, D., & Stansbury, K. (1990). Relationship of mother and child variables to child outcomes in a high-risk sample: A causal modeling analysis. *Developmental Psychology, 26*(1), 24–30.

Harter, S. (1990). Self and identity development. In S. Feldman & G. R. Elliott (Eds.), *At the threshold: The developing adolescent* (pp. 352–387). Cambridge, MA: Harvard University Press.

Harter, S., Marold, D. M. & Whitesell, N. R. (1992). Model of psychosocial risk factors leading to suicidal ideation in young adolescents. *Development and Psychopathology, 4,* 167–188.

Hauser, S. T., Borman, E. H., Powers, S. I., Jacobson, A. M., & Noam, G. G. (1990). Paths of adolescent ego development: Links with family life and individual adjustment. *Psychiatric Clinics of North America, 13*(3), 489–510.

Heatherton, T. F., & Baumeister, R. F. (1991). Binge eating as escape from self-awareness. *Psychological Bulletin, 110,* 86–108.

Heatherton, T. F., & Polivy, J. (1992). Chronic dieting and eating disorders: A spiral model. In J. H. Crowther, D. L. Tennenbaum, S. E. Hobfoll, & M. A. P.

Stephens (Eds.), *The etiology of bulimia nervosa: The individual and family context* (pp. 133–155). Washington, DC: Hemisphere.

Hill, J. P., & Lynch, M. E. (1983). The intensification of gender-related role expectations during early adolescence. In J. Brooks-Gunn & A. C. Petersen (Eds.), *Girls at puberty: Biological and psychosocial perspectives* (pp. 201–228). New York: Plenum Press.

Holmbeck, G. N., & Hill, J. P. (1991). Conflictive engagement, positive affect, and menarche in families with seventh-grade girls. *Child Development, 62,* 1030–1048.

Hsu, L. K. G. (1987). Are the eating disorders becoming more common in blacks? *International Journal of Eating Disorders, 6,* 113–124.

Irwin, M. (1981). Diagnosis of anorexia nervosa in children and the validity of DSM-III. *American Journal of Psychiatry, 138,* 1382–1383.

Jacobs, B. W., & Isaacs, S. (1986). Pre-pubertal anorexia nervosa: A retrospective controlled study. *Journal of Child Psychology and Psychiatry, 27,* 237–250.

Kandel, D. B., Raveis, V. H., & Davies, M. (1991). Suicidal ideation in adolescence: Depression, substance use, and other risk factors. *Journal of Youth and Adolescence, 20*(2), 289–309.

Kaplan, A. S., & Woodside, B. (1987). Biological aspects of anorexia nervosa and bulimia nervosa. *Journal of Consulting and Clinical Psychology, 55*(5), 645–653.

Kaslow, N. J., Rehm, L. P., & Siegel, A. W. (1984). Social-cognitive and cognitive correlates of depression in children. *Journal of Abnormal Psychology, 12,* 605–620.

Kazdin, A. E. (1989). Childhood depression. In E. J. Mash & R. A. Barkley (Eds.), *Treatment of childhood disorders* (p. 135–166). New York: Guilford Press.

Keating, D. P., (1990). Adolescent thinking. In S. Feldman & G. R. Elliott (Eds.), *At the threshold: The developing adolescent* (pp. 54–89). Cambridge, MA: Harvard University Press.

Kendler, K. S., MacLean, C., Neale, M., Kessler, R., Heath, A., & Eaves, L. (1991). The genetic epidemiology of bulimia nervosa. *American Journal of Psychiatry, 148,* 1627–1637.

Keys, A., Brozek, J., Henschel, A., Mickelsen, O., & Taylor, H. L. (1950). *The biology of human starvation.* Minneapolis: University of Minnesota Press.

Killen, J. D., Taylor, C. B., Telch, M. J., Saylor, K. E. Maron, D. J., & Robinson, T. N. (1986). Self-induced vomiting and laxative and diuretic use among teenagers. *Journal of the American Medical Association, 255,* 1447–1449.

Kovacs, M., & Paulauskas, S. L. (1984). Developmental stage and the expression of depressive disorders in children: An empirical analysis. *New Directions for Child Development, 26,* 59–80.

Lancelot, C., Brooks-Gunn, J., & Warren, M. P. (1991). A comparison of DSM-III and DSM-IIIR bulimia classifications. *International Journal of Eating Disorders, 10*(1), 57–66.

Larson, R., & Lampman-Patraitis, C. (1989). Daily emotional states as reported by children and adolescents. *Child Development, 60*(5), 1250–1260.

Lask, B., & Bryant-Waugh, R. (1992). Early-onset anorexia nervosa and related eating disorders. *Journal of Child Psychology and Psychiatry, 33,* 281–300.

Lempers, J. D., & Clark-Lempers, D. (1990). Family economic stress, maternal and paternal support and adolescent distress. *Journal of Adolescence, 13,* 217–229.

Lerner, R. M. (1985). Adolescent maturational changes and psychosocial development: A dynamic interactional perspective. *Journal of Youth and Adolescence, 14*(4), 355–371.

Lerner, R. (1988). Early adolescent transitions: The lore and the laws of adolescence. In M. D. Levine & E. R. McAnarney (Eds.), *Early adolescent transitions* (pp. 1–23). Lexington, MA: Lexington Books.

Lerner, R. M., & Foch, T. T. (Eds.). (1987). *Biological–psychosocial interactions in early adolescence: A life span perspective.* Hillsdale, NJ: Erlbaum.

Lewinsohn, P. M., Clarke, G. N., Hops, H., & Andrews, J. (1990). Cognitive-behavioral treatment for depressed adolescents. *Behavior Therapy, 21,* 385–401.

Lewinsohn, P. M., Rohde, P., Seeley, J. R., & Hops, H. (1991). Comorbidity of unipolar depression: I. Major depression with dysthymia. *Journal of Abnormal Psychology, 100,* 205–213.

Liaw, F. R., & Brooks-Gunn, J. (1994). Cumulative familial risks and low-birthweight childrens: Cognitive and behavioral development. *Journal of Clinical Child Psychology, 23*(4), 360–372.

Lowe, M. R. (1993). The effects of dieting on eating behavior: A three-factor model. *Psychological Bulletin, 114,* 100–121.

Lucas, A. R., Beard, C. M., O'Fallon, W. M., & Kurland, L. T. (1991). 50-Year trends in the incidence of anorexia nervosa in Rochester, Minnesota: A population-based study. *American Journal of Psychiatry, 148,* 917–922.

Magnusson, D., & Stattin, H. (1990). *Pubertal maturation in female development.* Hillsdale, NJ: Erlbaum.

Magnussin, D., Stattin, H., & Allen, V. L. (1985). Biological maturation and social development: A longitudinal study of some adjustment processes from mid-adolescence to adulthood. *Journal of Youth and Adolescence, 14,* 267–283.

Malina, R. M. (1983). Menarche in athletes: A synthesis and hypothesis. *Annals of Human Biology, 10,* 1–24.

Maloney, M. J., McGuire, J. B., & Daniels, S. R. (1988). Reliability testing of a children's version of the Eating Attitude Test. *Journal of the American Academy of Child and Adolescent Psychiatry, 27,* 541–543.

Millstein, S. P., Petersen, A. C., & Nightingale, E. (Eds.). (1991). *Promotion of health behavior in adolescence.* New York: Carnegie Corporation.

Morgan, H. G., & Russell, G. F. M. (1975). Value of family background and clinical features as predictors of long-term outcome in anorexia nervosa: A four year follow-up study of 41 patients. *Psychological Medicine, 5,* 355–371.

Nolen-Hoeksema, S., Girgus, J. S., & Seligman, M. E. P. (1991). Sex differences in depression and explanatory style in children. *Journal of Youth and Adolescence, 20*(2), 233–245.

Nolen-Hoeksema, S., Girgus, J. S. & Seligman, M. E. P. (1992). Predictors and consequences of childhood depressive symptoms: A 5-year longitudinal study. *Journal of Abnormal Psychology, 101,* 405–422.

Offer, D., Howard, K. I., Schonert, K. A., & Ostrov, E. (1991). To whom do adolescents turn for help? Differences between disturbed and nondisturbed adolescents. *Journal of the American Academy of Child and Adolescent Psychiatry, 30*(4), 623–630.

Office of Technology and Assessment (1991). *Adolescent health.* Washington, DC: United States Congress.

Paikoff, R., & Brooks-Gunn, J. (1991). Do parent–child relationships change during puberty? *Psychological Bulletin, 110*(1), 47–66.

Paikoff, R. L., Brooks-Gunn, J., & Carlton-Ford, S., (1991). Effect of reproductive status changes upon family functioning and well-being of mothers and daughters. *Journal of Early Adolescence, 11*(2), 201–220.

Paikoff, R. L., Brooks-Gunn, J., & Warren, M. P. (1991). Effects of girls' hormonal status on depressive and aggressive symptoms over the course of one year. *Journal of Youth and Adolescence, 20*(2), 191–215.

Paikoff, R. L., & Brooks-Gunn, J. (1990). Physiological proceeds: What role do they play during the transition to adolescence? In R. Montemayer, G. Adams, & T. Gullotta (Eds.), *Advances in adoloescent development: Vol. 2, The transition from childhood to adolescence* (pp. 63–81). Newbury Park, CA: Sage.

Paikoff, R. L., Carlton-Ford, S., & Brooks-Gunn, J. (1994). Mother–daughter dyads view the family: Associations between divergent perceptions and daughter well-being. *Journal of Youth and Adolescence, 22*(5), 473–492.

Palla, B., & Litt, I. F. (1988). Medical complications of eating disorders in adolescents. *Pediatrics, 81*(5), 613–623.

Petersen, A. C. (1987). The nature of biological–psychosocial interactions: The sample case of early adolescence. In R. M. Lerner & T. T. Foch (Eds.), *Biological–psychosocial interactions in early adolescence: A life-span perspective* (pp. 35–61). Hillsdale, NJ: Erlbaum.

Petersen, A. C. (1988). Adolescent development. In M. R. Rosenzweig (Ed.), *Annual review of psychology* (pp. 583–607). Palo Alto, CA: Annual Reviews.

Petersen, A. C., Compas, B., Brooks-Gunn, J., Stemmler, M., Ely, S., & Grant, K. (1993). Depression in adolescence. *American Psychologist, 48*(2), 155–168.

Petersen, A. C., Sarigiani, P. A., & Kennedy, R. E. (1991). Adolescent depression: Why more girls? *Journal of Youth and Adolescence, 20,* 247–271.

Petersen, A. C., Schulenberg, J. E., Abramovitz, R. H., Offer, D., & Jarcho, H. D. (1984). A self-image questionnaire for young adolescents (SIQYA): Reliability and validity studies. *Journal of Youth and Adolescence, 13,* 93–111.

Polivy, J., & Herman, C. P. (1987). Diagnosis and treatment of normal eating. *Journal of Consulting and Clinical Psychology, 55,* 635–644.

Post, G., & Crowther, J. H. (1985). Variables that discriminate bulimic from nonbulimic adolescent females. *Journal of Youth and Adolescence, 14,* 85–98.

Puig-Antich, J. (1986). Psychological markers: Effects of age and puberty. In M. Rutter, C. E. Izard, & P. B. Read (Eds.), *Depression in young people: Developmental and clinical perspectives* (pp. 341–381). New York: Guilford Press.

Pumariega, A. J. (1986). Acculturation and eating attitudes in adolescent girls: A comparative and correlational study. *Journal of the American Academy of Child and Adolescent Psychiatry, 25,* 276–279.

Radloff, L. S. (1977). The CES-D Scale: A self-report depression scale for research in the general population. *Applied Psychological Measurement, 1*(3), 385–401.

Radloff, L. S. (1991). The use of the center for epidemiologic studies depression scale in adolescents and young adults. *Journal of Youth and Adolescence, 20*(2), 149–166.

Reiter, E. O. (1987). Neuroendocrine control process. *Journal of Adolescent Health Care, 8*(6), 479–491.

Renouf, A. G., & Harter, S. (1990). Low self-worth and anger as components of the depressive experience in young adolescents. *Development and Psychopathology, 2,* 293–310.

Reynolds, C. F., Gillen, J. C., & Kupfer, D. J. (1987). Sleep and affective disorders. In H. Y. Meltzer (Ed.), *Psychopharmacology: The third generation of progress* (pp. 647–654). New York: Raven Press.

Robins, L. N. (1972). Follow-up studies of behavior disorders in children. In H. C. Quay & J. S. Werry (Eds.), *Psychopathological disorders of childhood.* New York: Wiley.

Robins, L. N., Carlson, B., Bucholz, K. K., Sussman, L. K., & Earls, F. J. (1989). *Intentional and unintentional injury as a black health problem.* Unpublished manuscript, Epidemiological Catchment Area Program.

Robins, L., & Rutter, M. (Eds.). (1990). *Straight and devious pathways from childhood to adulthood.* Cambridge: Cambridge University Press.

Rodin, J., Silberstein, L. R., & Striegel-Moore, R. H. (1984). Women and weight: A normative discontent. In T. B. Sonderegger (Ed.), *Nebraska symposium on motivation: No. 32. Psychology and gender* (pp. 267–307). Lincoln: University of Nebraska Press.

Rosen, J. C., Tacy, B., & Howell, D. (1990). Life stress, psychological symptoms and weight reducing behavior in adolescent girls: A prospective analysis. *International Journal of Eating Disorders, 9,* 17–26.

Ruble, D. N., & Brooks-Gunn, J. (1982). A developmental analysis of menstrual distress in adolescence. In R. C. Friedman (Ed.), *Behavior and the menstrual cycle* (pp. 177–197). New York: Marcel-Dekker.

Rutter, M. (1986). The developmental psychopathology of depression: Issues and perspectives. In M. Rutter, C. E. Izard, & P. B. Read (Eds.), *Depression in young people: Developmental and clinical perspectives* (pp. 3–30). New York: Guilford Press.

Rutter, M. (1989). Pathways from childhood to adult life. *Journal of Child Psychiatry and Psychology and Applied Disciplines, 30,* 23–51.

Rutter, M., Graham, P., Chadwick, O. F., & Yule, W. (1976). Adolescent turmoil: Fact or fiction? *Journal of Child Psychology and Psychiatry, 17,* 35–56

Rutter, M., Izard, C. E., & Read, P. B. (Eds.). (1986). *Depression in young people: Clinical and developmental perspectives.* New York: Guilford Press.

Salisbury, J. J., & Mitchell, J. E. (1991). Bone mineral density and anorexia nervosa in women. *American Journal of Psychiatry, 148,* 768–774.

Sallis, J. F., (1993). Promoting healthful diet and physical activity. In S. P. Millstein, A. C. Petersen, & E. Nightingale (Eds.), *Promotion of health behavior in adolescence* (pp. 209–241). New York: Oxford University Press.

Sameroff, A., Seifer, R., Baldwin, A., & Baldwin, C. (1993). Stability of intelligence from preschool to adolescence: The influence of social and family risk factors. *Child Development, 64,* 80–97.

Savin-Williams, R. C., & Berndt, T. J. (1990). Friendships and peer relations. In S. Feldman & G. Elliott (Eds.), *At the threshold: The developing adolescent* (pp. 277–307). Cambridge, MA: Harvard University Press.

Schacter, S., & Singer, J. E. (1962). Cognitive, social, and physiological determinants of emotional state. *Psychological Review, 69,* 379–399.

Schwartz, D. M., Thompson, M. G., & Johnson, C. L. (1985). Anorexia nervosa and bulimia: The socio-cultural context. In S. W. Emmett (Ed.), *Theory and treatment of anorexia nervosa and bulimia* (pp. 95–112). New York: Brunner/Mazel.

Seligman, M. E. P., Kamen, L. P., & Nolen-Hoeksema, S. (1988). Explanatory style across the life span: Achievement and health. In M. Levine & E. R.

McAnarney (Eds.), *Early adolescent transitions* (pp. 91–114). Lexington, MA: D. C. Heath.

Seligman, M. E. P., Peterson, C., Kaslow, N. J., Tannenbaum, R. L., Alloy, L. B., & Abramson, L. Y. (1984). Attrbutional style and depressive symptoms among children. *Journal of Abnormal Psychology, 93*(2), 235–238.

Shelton, R. C., Hollon, S. D., Purdon, S. E., & Loosen, P. T. (1991). Biological and psychological aspects of depression. *Behavior Therapy, 22,* 201–228.

Simmons, R. G., & Blythe, D. A. (1987). *Moving into adolescence: The impact of pubertal change and school context.* New York: Aldine de Gruyter.

Sroufe, L. A. & Rutter, M. (1984). The domain of developmental psychopathology. *Child Development, 55*(1), 17–29.

Stattin, H., & Magnusson, D. (1990). *Paths through life: Volume 2. Pubertal maturation in female development.* Hillsdale, NJ: Erlbaum.

Stein, D. M., & Reichert, P. (1990). Extreme dieting behaviors in early adolescence. *Journal of Early Adolescence, 10*(2), 108–121.

Story, M., Rosenwinkel, K., Himes, J. H., Resnick, M., Harris, L. J., & Blum, R. W. (1991). Demographic and risk factors associated with chronic dieting in adolescents. *American Journal of Diseases of Childhood, 145,* 994–998.

Striegel-Moore, R. H. (1992). Prevention of bulimia nervosa: Questions and challenges. In J. H. Crowther, D. L. Tennenbaum, S. E. Hobfoll, & M. A. P. Stephens (Eds.), *Bulimia nervosa: The individual and family context* (pp. 203–224). Washington, DC: Hemisphere.

Striegel-Moore, R. H., Silberstein, L. R., Frensch, P., & Rodin, J. (1989). A prospective study of disordered eating among college students. *International Journal of Eating Disorders, 8,* 499–509.

Strober, M. (1991). Disorders of the self in anorexia nervosa: An organismic-developmental paradigm. In C. Johnson (Ed.), *Psychodynamic treatment of anorexia nervosa and bulimia* (pp. 354–373). New York: Guilford Press.

Stunkard, A. J., Sorensen, T. I. A., Hanis, C., Teasdale, T. W., Chakraborty, R., Schull, W. J., & Schulsinger, F. (1986). An adoption study of obesity. *New England Journal of Medicine, 314,* 193–198.

Susman, E. J., Dorn, L. D., & Chrousos, G. P. (1991). Negative affect and hormone levels in young adolescents: Concurrent and predictive perspectives. *Journal of Pediatric Psychology, 7*(3), 253–261.

Takanishi, R. (1993). Changing views of adolescence in contemporary society. *Teachers College Record, 94*(3), 459–465.

Tobin, D. L., Johnson, C. L., & Dennis, A. B. (1992). Divergent forms of purging behavior in bulimia nervosa patients. *International Journal of Eating Disorders, 11,* 17–24.

Tobin, D. L., Johnson, J. C., Steinberg, S., Staats, M., & Dennis, A. B. (1991). Multifactorial assessment of bulimia nervosa. *Journal of Abnormal Psychology, 100,* 14–21.

Tobin-Richards, M. H., Boxer, A. M., & Petersen, A. C. (1983). The psychological significance of pubertal change: Sex differences in perceptions of self during early adolescence. In J. Brooks-Gunn & A. C. Petersen (Eds.), *Girls at puberty: Biological and psychosocial perspectives* (pp. 127–154). New York: Plenum Press.

Vernberg, E. M. (1990). Psychological adjustment and experiences with peers during early adolescence: Reciprocal, incidental, or unidirectional relationships? *Journal of Abnormal Child Psychology, 18,* 187–198.

Warren, M. P. (1986). Anorexia nervosa. In *Precis III. An update in obstetrics and gynecology* (pp. 283–288). American College of Obstetricians and Gynecologists.

Warren, M. P., & Brooks-Gunn, J. (1989a). Delayed menarche in athletes: The role of low energy intake and eating disorders and their relation to bone density. In C. Laron & A. D. Rogol (Eds.), *Hormones and sport* (pp. 41–54). Serono Symposia Publications, Vol. 55. New York: Raven Press.

Warren, M. P., & Brooks-Gunn, J. (1989b). Mood and behavior at adolescence: Evidence for hormonal factors. *Journal of Clinical Endocrinology and Metabolism 69*(1), 77–83.

Warren, M. P., & Brooks-Gunn, J., Fox, R. P., Lancelot, C., Newman, D., & Hamilton, W. G. (1991). Lack of bone accretion and amenorrhea: Evidence for a relative osteopenia in weight-bearing bones. *Journal of Clinical Endocrinology and Metabolism, 72,* 847–853.

Watson, D., & Tellegen, A. (1985). Toward a consensual structure of mood. *Psychological Bulletin, 98,* 219–235.

Weissman, M. M. (1990). Evidence for comorbidity of anxiety and depression: Family and genetic studies of children. In J. D. Maser & C. R. Cloninger (Eds.), *Comorbidity of mood and anxiety disorders* (pp. 349–365). Washington DC: American Psychiatric Press.

Weissman, M. M., Gammon, G. D., John, K., Merikangas, K. R., Prusoff, B. A., & Scholomskas, D. (1987). Children of depressed parents: Increase psychopathology and early onset of major depression. *Archives of General Psychiatry, 44,* 847–853.

Weissman, M. M., Leckman, J. F., Merikangas, K. R., Gammon, D., & Prusoff, B. A. (1984). Depression and anxiety disorders in parents and children. Results from the Yale Family Study. *Archives of General Psychiatry, 41,* 845–852.

Weissman, M. M., Warner, V., Wickramaratne, P., & Prusoff, B. A. (1988). Early-onset major depression in parents and their children. Special issue: Childhood affective disorders. *Journal of Affective Disorders, 15,* 269–277.

Whitaker, A. Johnson, J., Shaffer, D., Rapoport, J. L., Kalikow, K., Walsh, B. T., Davies, M., Braiman, S., & Dolinsky, A. (1990). Uncommon troubles in young people: Prevalence estimates of selected psychiatric disorders in a nonreferred adolescent population. *Archives of General Psychiatry, 102,* 177–180.

Wilson, G. T. (1993). Relationship of dieting and voluntary weight loss to psychological functioning and binge eating. *Annals of Internal Medicine, 119,* 727–730.

World Health Organization (1990). *International classification of diseases and related health problems* (10th revision). Geneva: Author.

Youniss, J., & Smollar, J. (1985). *Adolescent relations with mother, father and friends.* Chicago: University of Chicago Press.

6

Behavioral Research in Childhood Autism

MARIAN SIGMAN

The history of behavioral research in childhood autism parallels the history of developmental psychopathology. Efforts to understand autism have depended on the discovery of developmental concepts and principles of experimental design. For example, the characteristics of autistic children could not be identified until researchers realized the necessity of comparison groups matched on developmental level. The first purpose of this chapter is to elucidate some of the advances made in the discipline of developmental psychopathology as applied to questions about childhood autism.

Developmental psychopathology has emerged as a discipline devoted to the investigation of psychological problems from a developmental perspective. Three main approaches are used in studies of developmental psychopathology. The first approach is to investigate a disorder using as a framework some conception of the typical developmental tasks for children at specified age periods. The two other approaches use longitudinal studies to determine how children with a disorder fare at different age periods and to identify precursors of later development. Most studies of the developmental psychopathology of autism have used the first approach, so the discussion in this chapter will be confined to that literature.

The second purpose of this chapter is to review our current understanding of childhood autism so that new directions for research can be suggested. This analysis will focus on the phenomenology of autism rather than on etiology and intervention. Before discussing current conceptualizations of autism, it is necessary to review briefly the history of research on childhood autism.

The Discovery of Autism

Early infantile autism was first identified as a specific syndrome in a paper by Leo Kanner published about 50 years ago (Kanner, 1943). Quite remarkably, 1 year later, Hans Asperger described a similar syndrome in a paper that did not receive much notice because it was published in Germany during the Second World War (Asperger, 1944). While Asperger focused on milder forms of the disorder in nonretarded individuals, he explicitly recognized that autism exists at all levels of intelligence. Kanner's discover had immediate impact because he was a clinician with a strong reputation and because there was already some incipient recognition of the disorder. Cases of socially isolated, noncommunicative children had long been part of the clinical and popular lore, the most famous being Itard's description of the wild child of Aveyron (Lane, 1977).

In his original description of the syndrome, Kanner focused on the extreme social aloneness of his 11 patients and characterized this aloneness as inborn. However, from the 1940s through much of the 1960s, many papers followed that concurred with Kanner's clinical descriptions but attributed autism to neglectful parenting. One basis for this can be found in Kanner's clinical descriptions; almost every child he mentioned had at least on parent who was socially isolated or eccentric. Currently, this pattern might be seen as evidence for the genetic basis of the syndrome. However, at the time, it was interpreted as evidence for the psychogenic explanation, partly because of the psychoanalytic interpretations of child development that dominated the thinking of the period.

The most immediate and obvious impact of the adherence to a psychogenic explanation was on treatment approaches and on the families of autistic children. Various forms of clinical treatment aimed at undoing the harmful effects of supposedly poor parenting were organized (Bettleheim, 1967). Parents were faced with the double problem of trying to help their children while being haunted by feelings of responsibility that they fluctuated in accepting and rejecting (Park, 1967). The more long-term effect of this early attribution of autism to psychogenic factors has been on subsequent research. The reaction to the psychogenic theories has shaped the scope of the investigations that followed.

Early Investigations

Three different kinds of studies predominated during the 1960s, all of these at least partly motivated by a desire to challenge this dominant theory of autism. First, a number of studies focused on differentiating autism from other forms of psychosis, especially childhood schizophrenia (Kolvin, 1971). This process of differentiating one disorder from another is clearly one of the necessary first steps in all areas of developmental psychopathology, and a great deal of work on diagnosis of childhood disorders has been carried out with this aim. In the case of autism, the differentiation of this disorder from other forms of childhood psychosis led to a change in the name of the principal journal concerned with the syndrome from the *Journal of Autism and Childhood Schizophrenia* to the *Journal of Autism and Developmental Disorders*.

A second line of research investigated the characteristics of the parents of autistic children and compared these parents to those of nonautistic children (De Myer, Pontius, Norton, Barton, Allen, & Steele, 1972; Rutter & Bartak, 1971). The lack of compelling differences between the groups of parents identified in these studies undermined the psychogenic theories of autism.

The third line of research focused on identifying core perceptual and cognitive deficits, with the implicit aim of proving that autism is an innate disorder with a physiological basis. In some cases, this research was based on the assumption that the identification of core psychological problems would lead to the specification of the brain centers that were affected in autistic children. For instance, the attentional responses of young autistic children were examined in order to determine whether the children suffered from disorders in the reticular activating system (Ornitz & Ritvo, 1968).

As this work progressed, researchers began to realize that control groups of nonaffected children were needed in order to identify the characteristics specific to autism. Furthermore, it became clear that groups had to be matched on age since the abilities and behaviors of the subjects changed sharply with maturation. The realization that childhood disorders cannot be studied in the same way as adult disorders because of developmental change has been a key step in the growth of developmental psychopathology.

Research in the 1970s

Recognition that the majority of autistic children are also mentally retarded shaped the next wave of behavioral research, much of which was carried out in Great Britain. It became clear that the characteristics of autistic, mentally retarded children could be identified only if these children were compared to nonautistic, mentally retarded children at the same developmental level. In 1970, two researchers, Beate Hermelin and Neal O'Connor, published a seminal book, *Psychological Experiments with Autistic Children*. They applied the concepts and methods that were being used in the United States during that decade to investigate the perceptual and cognitive abilities of young infants. By adapting the techniques used by Robert Fantz with normally developing infants (Fantz & Nevis, 1967) to young autistic children, Hermelin and O'Connor were able to show that autistic children had more difficulty in extracting meaning from stimuli than mentally retarded children who did not suffer from autism. Moreover, the disorders associated with autism did not seem limited to social situations but could be seen in the patterns of attention shown by autistic children to inanimate objects of various kinds.

Most of the studies on the perceptual and cognitive abilities of young autistic children were carried out with retarded autistic children, partly because it is difficult to locate young, nonretarded autistic children. This is true for several reasons. First, until the recent increase in day-care rearing of young children, the interactions of most young children were limited to their parents, who often lacked broad enough experience to identify subtle difficulties. Thus, the autistic children who were identified early in life tended to be those who had the most obvious developmental delays. The second reason for the especially high prevalence of delay in young autistic children is that even individuals who show average intellectual skills later in childhood and adolescence appear to be slow in developing language and cognitive abilities. For these reasons, autism is almost always confounded with mental retardation in samples of young children.

In older groups, nonretarded autistic children can be identified more easily, although only about one-quarter of autistic children are nonretarded. The advantage of studying nonretarded autistic children is that the effects of autism are not confounded with those of mental retardation. Michael Rutter and his colleagues carried out a series of studies on nonretarded autistic children, comparing them to normal and nonautistic children suffering from language delays (Bartak, Rutter, & Cox, 1975; Lockyer & Rutter, 1970). These studies showed that autistic children had characteristic patterns of intellectual strengths and weaknesses that were not shared with nonautistic, language-delayed children. As an example, autistic children were able to carry out perceptual tasks such as Block Design on the WISC-R with considerable skill but were quite handicapped on subtests such as Comprehension that involve common sense and social judgment. Thus, autism appeared to involve language problems but also some very specific problems in the broader cognitive range.

Current Research on Social and Affective Behaviors in Young Autistic Children

Research in the 1980s shifted from a focus on perception and cognition to the investigation of social and emotional development in autistic children. The impetus for the increasing attention to social development was the tremendous growth in the number of studies of normal social development. Just as Hermelin and O'Connor used the work of Robert

Fantz to investigate perceptual and cognitive abilities, current investigators have had a rich source of concepts and methods to apply in investigations of the social and emotional development of autistic children. In fact, the whole field of developmental psychopathology has benefitted from the growing body of research on normal social and emotional development.

The principal accomplishment of research in the 1980s was to identify and characterize the great difficulty in social understanding shown by autistic individuals of all ages and levels of functioning. This is manifested in young autistic children by a failure to monitor the facial expressions of others or to share attention and emotion with other people. As early as 9–10 months of age, young normal children look up at other people, sometimes with a smile, when they are playing with toys. They point to interesting sights in their world and follow the pointing behaviors of others. In ambiguous situations when an unfamiliar or strange event has occurred, they look to other people quizzically, and their behavior is shaped by this social referencing. When they have accomplished a challenging task, normal 14- to 15-month-olds look to see if their mother has noticed. Although its manifestations may become somewhat more sophisticated, this kind of social sharing and signaling obviously does not disappear in infancy but continues throughout life. Early social sharing and signaling seems to index a beginning recognition by the young child that other people have viewpoints that can be informative or, at least, worthy of attention.

My research group and I have devoted much of the last 12 years to studying these kinds of behavior in young autistic children ranging in age from $2\frac{1}{2}$ to 5 years and comparing their responses to those shown by mentally retarded and normal children of the same developmental level. We have found that autistic children rarely share attention and emotion with their parents or other adults in reference to an interesting event (Sigman, Mundy, Sherman, & Ungerer, 1986). Moreover, they do not often point spontaneously, hold up objects for their parents to see, or follow the pointing behaviors of others (Mundy, Sigman, & Kasari, 1994; Mundy, Sigman, Ungerer, & Sherman, 1986). When they have finished a task, they show pleasure at mastery but do not look to an adult for approval and they frequently look away if praised (Kasari, Sigman, Baumgartner, & Stipek, 1993). If a strange robot moves into the room and the adults show fear of this robot, the autistic children do not look at the faces of the adults (Sigman, Kasari, Kwon, & Yirmiya, 1992). If an unfamiliar adult blocks the hand motion of the child or teases the child by holding a toy out of reach, the autistic child does not look at the adult's face but attempts to obtain the object (Phillips, Baron-Cohen, & Rutter, 1992). Finally, if an adult pretends to be distressed by having hit a finger accidentally, the autistic children do not look at the adult but turn their attention to the toy with which the adult was playing (Sigman et al., 1992).

In contrast to autistic children, nonautistic, mentally retarded children of the same age and intelligence show high levels of attention to others in all these situations. They frequently look at adults with whom they are playing when exploring novel, interesting toys. They point to interesting sights and look to see if the other person is also attending. They follow the pointing behaviors of others. They look to the adult's face after completing a difficult task, when the strange robot moves into the room, and in response to the adult demonstrating distress. These are all very salient situations for nonautistic, mentally retarded children, and they respond with alerting behavior, attention, and some emotion.

One of the questions that can be asked about these results is whether autistic children simply look less at people's faces in all situations. We have not found this to be the case when the other individual makes any attempt to engage the autistic child. Thus, in face-to-face interactions, the autistic children generally look at the experimenter and their mothers as much as the control children do (Mundy et al., 1986; Sigman et al., 1986). In a play situation, they show as much mutual gaze with their mothers as control children and increase their attention to their mothers when involved in a social game. It is true that the autistic children initiate social involvement somewhat less often then other children when the partner does not attempt to engage the child or when the partner withdraws (Kasari, Sigman, & Yirmiya, 1993). Similarly, as noted by Hermelin and O'Connor in 1970, autistic children attend less than other children to nonsocial stimuli in unstructured situations, but their attention increases to normal levels when an adult encourages involvement with objects.

In friendly interactions between young children and experimenters, autistic children generally show emotions like those of normal and mentally retarded children, although they show somewhat more negative or blended emotions (Yirmiya, Kasari, Sigman, & Mundy, 1989). The biggest difference in these situations is the way in which the autistic children combine their attention and affect (Kasari, Sigman, Mundy, & Yirmiya, 1990). They tend not to smile and attend simultaneously to others; smiles are directed elsewhere than to the adult's face (Dawson, Hill, Spencer, Galpert, & Watson, 1990). Since normal children generally smile as part of acknowledging someone else's attention to objects, the failure of autistic children to smile and attend is most clear in situations designed to elicit joint attention.

The social interactions of young autistic children do not seem quite as barren as some clinical descriptions suggest. First, these children are involved in simple social games and do respond positively to maternal initiations of social play. Second, they show some indication that particular individuals can be used as a secure base. Most autistic children do respond to their mothers' leaving them and returning, and their behaviors do not differ from those of nonautistic, mentally retarded children of the same age and intelligence (Sigman & Mundy, 1989; Sigman &

Ungerer, 1984). At least some autistic children even seem to be securely attached, although this attachment is hidden to some extent by their disorganized response patterns (Capps, Sigman, & Mundy, 1994).

In summary, the most marked deficiencies in young autistic children arise in social behaviors and nonverbal communication that rely on the earliest forms of social understanding. These findings have appeared in the work of my research group and in studies by other authors, some of whom have used older autistic children and different kinds of control groups (Curcio, 1978; Loveland & Landry, 1986; Wetherby & Prutting, 1984). Older autistic children continue to show some of the same patterns, so that they appear to recognize protoimperative gestures that make demands on the viewer, just as they were able to respond to and initiate nonverbal requesting behaviors (such as dragging the parent to the refrigerator) at earlier ages. On the other hand, older autistic children still seem unable to comprehend protodeclarative gestures of pointing by others (Baron-Cohen, 1989).

Research on Social Understanding in Older Autistic Individuals

The findings on the social difficulties of young autistic children are paralleled by those of more developmentally advanced autistic children. The now almost classic discovery that autistic children do not seem to understand what is called *theory of mind* (Baron-Cohen, Leslie, & Frith, 1985) seems to mirror the disorders observed in these children at younger ages. The notion of theory of mind is that the child has to develop the concept that other people have views, thoughts, and feelings that are independent of and perhaps different from those of his or her own. Developmental evidence shows that children under 4 years of age are unable to understand that other people have knowledge that is different from their own, although there may be earlier understanding of differing perceptions and emotions. The standard way to test the child's possession of a theory of mind is to have the child view a puppet show in which one doll hides an object, another doll moves the object, and the original doll comes back to find the object, without having seen it moved in the interim. The child is then asked where the doll will look for the object. Young children point to the second location even though the doll does not know that the object was moved to this location. Older children point to the original location and explain their actions in terms of the information possessed by the doll. Most autistic children, even those with mental ages well beyond 4 years, respond like very young children. Only a few very high-functioning autistic children are able to deal with the counterfactual knowledge of the ignorant doll. These children tend to fail more complex, higher-order problems in which one person reflects on the concepts of another.

This problem with understanding other minds, or *mind blindness* as it has been called, is striking. Like the failure of the young autistic child to look where another person is pointing, it severely limits the autistic individual's understanding of social situations. Moreover, mind blindness appears not only in laboratory settings but also in parents' accounts of social interactions with their autistic children (Frith, Happe, & Siddons, submitted).

In our own studies of nonretarded autistic 12-year-olds, understanding of the experiences of others and of the self also seemed limited. Autistic children were less able to label the emotions felt by child protagonists in videotaped episodes designed to show children experiencing certain emotions in appropriate social circumstances (Yirmiya, Sigman, Kasari, & Mundy, 1992). These findings corroborate the observations made earlier by Peter Hobson (1986, 1989). They also were less likely to say that they felt the same emotion as the protagonist and were less able to explain the situation despite having communicative abilities comparable to those of the normal children. To the extent that the autistic children were successful in labeling and empathizing with the emotions of the protagonist, they seemed to do so cognitively, as if they were solving an intellectual puzzle (Capps, Yirmiya, & Sigman, 1992). They showed great concentration and rather long latencies in verbal responses. This was also characteristic of the way they talked about their own emotional experiences. When asked to tell about a time when they felt happy, sad, proud, or embarrassed, autistic children were able to respond appropriately, but their responses were somewhat stereotyped. They were less likely than normal children to refer to an audience in describing situations that made them embarrassed. This failure to describe an audience may be similar to the young child's lack of attention to the faces of others after having completed a puzzle.

The autistic children seemed quite involved in these procedures and were very interested in the videotapes of children in emotionally arousing situations (Capps, Kasari, Yirmiya, & Sigman, 1993). They showed much emotion in response, almost all of it appropriate to the situation portrayed. Those children who showed the most positive affect in positive situations and the most negative affect in negative situations also verbally reported the most empathy. The autistic children showed much more emotion than the control children in this situation. Our conjecture is that normal children 12 years of age have learned social rules that forbid the display of emotion openly in public, particularly when one is being videotaped.

Thus, these studies showed that autistic children at all ages suffer from a deficit in the kinds of responses that index social understanding. Young autistic children do not attend to emotional cues from others or attempt to initiate joint activities or involvement. Older autistic children, even those with good intelligence, have great difficulty in understanding the experiences of others or themselves. Moreover, autistic children do not seem to understand the social rules that develop early on to regulate social interactions. These deficits in social understanding have disastrous consequences, so that even intellectually able autistic children are reported by their parents to have serious difficulties in social adaptation.

Directions for Future Research

The demonstration and definition of lifelong deficits in the social understanding and responsiveness of autistic children is clearly just the first step. There is a great deal more that we need to know if this information is to be useful. In the remainder of this chapter, some of the questions that seem most important to answer with regard to these findings will be outlined.

1. What are the developmental bases for these disorders?

The disorders that have been identified in autistic children are in forms of social interaction that develop normally at the end of the first year of life and the beginning of the second. Moreover, preliminary findings suggest that these deficits can be identified by 12–18 months of age. A central question is whether these difficulties appear de novo or stem from earlier deficits that have not yet been identified. Some theories of infant development suggest that the capacity for sharing attention—called *intersubjectivity, triadic attention,* or *protodeclarative behaviors,* depending on the theory—has developmental roots in an earlier achievement (Hobson, 1989, 1994; Stern, 1985; Trevarthen & Hubley, 1978). This achievement is the ability shown by 3- to 4-month-olds to share attention dyadically in face-to-face interaction with a social partner. The argument is that an infant who was not involved in the intense social sharing of this period would not have developed the basis for moving on to triadic attention in which the infant needs to divide attention between the other person and an additional person or object.

At this point, the evidence for this position is mixed. When we look at dyadic interaction of autistic children and another adult, we see much of the attentional and affective give-and-take that characterizes the interaction of the normal infant and a partner. However, some studies do show lower levels of social initiative and responsiveness even in these situations. Moreover, autistic children do not combine positive affect with attention in the same way as nonautistic children. Thus, there is some basis for concluding that this more immature form of social responsiveness is also impaired and could be tied to the deficits in more mature joint attention and referencing behaviors.

Of course, one way to identify the developmental precursors of the deficits described in autistic children of 2½ to 4 years of age would be to look at younger autistic children. The difficulty with this is that, at present, autism is not clearly diagnosed until about 2½ years of age. For this reason, investigators have been trying to find ways of measuring social behaviors in children, some of whom will later be diagnosed as autistic. Baron-Cohen, Allen, and Gilberg (1992) have recently published a study of 91 18-month-olds, 4 of whom were later diagnosed as autistic. The reason for the high rate of autism in this sample (it usually occurs in only 4 to 8 children in 10,000; see Gilberg, Steffenburg, & Schaumann, 1991) is that 41 infants were the siblings of autistic children, who are at greater risk of autism than nonaffected probands (Folstein & Rutter, 1987). Parents were asked to fill out a nine-item questionnaire, and health visitors were asked to make four observations. The four toddlers later diagnosed as autistic differed from the other toddlers in that they showed deficits in two or more of the following behaviors: pretend play, protodeclarative pointing, social interest, social play, and joint attention. While some of the nondiagnosed children lacked one of these behaviors, none of them lacked more than one.

An even earlier evaluation has used videotapes of 1-year-olds' birthday parties (Osterling & Dawson, 1993). Eleven infants who were later diagnosed with autism differed from 11 normal infants in showing less social behavior and joint attention. However, the two groups were comparable in following directions and in babbling. The variables that contributed to the discriminant function (which classified 91% of the sample correctly) were pointing, showing an object to another person, looking at the face of another, and orienting to his or her name. The autistic infants performed significantly fewer of these behaviors. Because six of the autistic children had IQs over 80, the differences for most of the sample cannot be attributed to developmental delay.

A related question concerns the nature of the bases for the deficit in joint attention and referencing. While I have been describing this deficit as the first manifestation of a problem in social understanding, these behaviors also index social interest. Autistic children may not share attention with others or fixate steadily on the face of someone showing distress because they do not find others to be of interest or concern. Moreover, they occasionally appear to avoid the gaze of others, as if this gaze caused them to be uncomfortable. As an example, some of the young children in our study looked away or even walked away when praised by their mothers for completing a puzzle. This might occur because the autistic children do not know how to read this behavior and thus find it confusing. Alternatively, social attention from others may be overarousing and therefore disturbing. This is a theory that was espoused earlier, and some data to support it have been found.

One approach to these questions would be to examine response systems other than behavior. We plan to study the heart rate responses of young autistic children to some of the emotion display situations described above. If the autistic children show heart rate responses like those of normal and nonautistic, mentally retarded children, then it is less likely that the deficits in social behaviors are attributable to differences in arousal than if the autistic children show less strong autonomic reactions. If the responses are more dramatic, this may support the notion of overarousal. The return from investigations using combined behavioral and psychophysiological measures is likely to be high.

2. What are the developmental consequences of the deficits shown by autistic children in early life and, if there is continuity, are there any moderating variables?

I have been arguing that there are parallels in the social deficits of autistic children at different ages and levels of functioning. However, to my knowledge, no studies have linked these problems in the same children followed over time. One question is whether autistic children followed later in development will continue to show identical or similar problems to those manifested at younger ages.

Another question is whether autistic children who show somewhat more joint attention and referencing behaviors in early life continue to be more socially skilled later in life than autistic children who show less joint attention and referencing. We have found that autistic children who show some joint attention have better language skills concurrently and 1 year later than autistic children who do not show joint attention (Mundy, Sigman & Kasari, 1990; Mundy, Sigman, Ungerer, & Sherman, 1987). The question of continuity of individual differences is important since it would tell us how important it might be to encourage the development of such social behaviors in young autistic children. Of course, in answering this question, we would have to examine whether continuity could be attributed to associated factors such as intelligence. My research group and I are currently conducting a follow-up study on the autistic children whom we have seen over the past 12 years to address some of these questions.

3. To what extent is it possible to improve the social responses and understanding of autistic children?

The major purposes of defining the deficits of any childhood disorder are to improve the detection, prevention, and treatment of the disorder. Research on the social development of autistic children has had some impact on diagnosis and may lead to earlier detection, as mentioned above. The aims for prevention and treatment have to be much more limited, given the severity of the disorder and its usual course. Rather than focusing on treatment, it seems more fruitful to hope that some of the social dysfunctions may be modifiable.

One line of research might attempt to determine if there are any naturally occurring conditions that modify the development of autistic children. These conditions could be other characteristics of the child or possibly of the environment. For example, one interesting issue is whether autistic children who have siblings with whom they interact have as severe social deficits as autistic children without such frequent social partners.

Intervention studies attempting to remediate problems in social responsiveness and understanding are critical. My impression is that many intervention programs wit young autistic children do focus on their social responses. However, I know of only one experimental intervention that has attempted to improve the joint attention behaviors of autistic children by encouraging maternal imitation and interaction (Dawson & Galpert, 1987).

4. Is the problem in social understanding due to a more basic disorder in cognition or executive functions?

This question takes us back to the research of the 1970s that defined some of the specific cognitive deficiencies of autistic individuals. It is clear that young autistic children show much less symbolic play than matched controls. Symbolic play taps the capacity for representational thought and possibly for metarepresentational thought (Leslie, 1987). While autistic children appear to develop adequately through the sensorimotor period, they appear limited in their understanding of concrete operations. Half of the nonretarded autistic children in our study did not show knowledge of conservation despite having mental ages well beyond 5 to 7 years, when this knowledge develops in normal children (Yirmiya, Sigman, Kasari, & Mundy, 1992).

Deficits in executive functions could account for many of the difficulties shown by autistic individuals. Executive functions consist of those mental operations necessary for goal-directed behavior, such as planning and sequential behaviors, maintaining an appropriate set, monitoring the effectiveness of strategies, and inhibiting inappropriate responses. A series of studies have shown that autistic individuals at all developmental levels have difficulty with executive functions (Ozonoff, Pennington, & Rogers, 1991; Ozonoff, Rogers, & Pennington, 1991; Rumsey, 1985; Rumsey & Hamburger, 1988, 1990). For example, young autistic children have more problems with alternation tasks and tasks in which they have to shift cues than nonautistic, mentally retarded children of the same developmental level. Older autistic individuals are less successful on tasks like the Tower of Hanoi and the Wisconsin Card Sort than control subjects. Hughes and Russell (1993) have shown that autistic children are unable to solve problems that require mental disengagement. The autistic subjects in their study continued to point to a box in which they could see that candy was hidden even though they received the candy only when they pointed to the empty box. They were also less likely to use a deferred strategy that was reinforced to obtain a marble, and continued to reach directly for the marble even though they could not receive it this way.

The notion of a dysfunction in executive functions cannot be ruled out. Although one can see how it would apply to problems in joint attention and referencing, it does not explain why autistic children do not look at individuals showing emotion. Furthermore, autistic children are able to carry out some tasks that seem to require mental disengagement. For example, young autistic children can do some sensorimotor tasks, such as using a rake to obtain candy placed in a long tube when they cannot reach it with their fingers.

On the other hand, a deficit in social understanding is not sufficient to account for all of the difficulties in life adjustment shown by autistic individuals. For example, many nonretarded autistic adults have enormous problems in planning their time or carrying out sequential activities to reach a goal.

5. What are the physiological bases for the dysfunctions shown by autistic individuals, and what kinds of genetic malformations or prenatal events account for these physiological characteristics?

Clearly, any account for the enigma of autism will have to identify the neurophysiological characteristics of autistic individuals and the origins of these characteristics. Many researchers believe that autism may be attributable to dysfunctions in the prefrontal and limbic systems, although the strongest morphological and physiological evidence to date points to the cerebellum (Bauman & Kemper, 1988; Courchesne, 1989). The evidence for a genetic basis for autism is increasingly strong. Until we have identified the biological bases for autism, we will be able to do little in the way of prevention.

To end this chapter, I will contrast the questions that I have asked with those that concluded a chapter on language disorder and infantile autism that was published in 1978 and was particularly influential in directing subsequent research (Rutter, 1978). The questions posed by Michael Rutter in 1978 were as follows: First, "Which cognitive processes are disordered in order for the language disability in autism to arise?" Second, "Which brain systems are involved and what is the locus or loci of brain pathology?" Third, "Is the autistic child's relative failure to use speech for social communication simply a consequence of the severe disorder of language or of central coding processes or is some rather different disorder involved?" Fourth, "Obviously the cognitive deficit and the social abnormalities are closely associated, but does one cause the other or are they both different facets of the same basic disability?" Fifth, and last, "Given that autism is associated with a cognitive deficit involving language, is this a sufficient explanation of the genesis of autism?" This last question was tied to the observation that "within families in which several members show a language impairment, usually only one is autistic," as well as to evidence that "various forms of environmental intervention seem to benefit autistic children."

These were not simple questions, and it has not been easy to find the answers. The research discussed in this chapter has addressed primarily the first and third questions. We have shown that there are deficits in symbolic representation and social understanding in the preverbal period that may partly account for the language disabilities. Moreover, the failure to use language goes along with the failure to use nonverbal social and emotional communication. It is not only language that is impaired in autistic individuals, but the whole system of communication and social understanding that normally develops much earlier than verbal abilities.

The investigation of childhood autism has forced us to develop principles of research design that are basic to all of developmental psychopathology. I believe that we have a clearer understanding of the social abilities and disabilities of autistic children than we did 17 years ago, when the chapter by Michael Rutter was published. This understanding may be useful for early diagnosis and intervention. The study of autistic children has also contributed to our appreciation of the social development of normal children. The enormous achievements in social understanding of the young normal child may be overlooked until they are contrasted with the devastating consequences that ensue from their absence, as in the development of the young autistic child.

Acknowledgment

The research for this study was supported by Grant NS 25243 from NINDS and Grant HD 17662 from NICHD. Contributions to this research were made by Lisa Capps, Connie Kasari, Jung-Hye Kwon, Peter Mundy, Judy Ungerer, and Nurit Yirmiya. I also appreciate the assistance provided by Michael Espinosa with data analysis and Margie Greenwald with administration of my research program and preparation of this manuscript.

References

Asperger, H. (1944). Die autistischen psychopathen im Kidesalter. *Archiv für Psychiatrie und Nervenkrankheiten, 117,* 76–136.

Baron-Cohen, S. (1989). Perceptual role-taking and protodeclarative pointing in autism. *British Journal of Developmental Psychology, 7,* 113–127.

Baron-Cohen, S., Allen, J., & Gilberg, C. (1992). Can autism be detected at 18 months? The needle, the haystack, and the CHAT. *British Journal of Psychiatry, 161,* 839–843.

Baron-Cohen, S., Leslie, A., & Frith U. (1985). Does the autistic child have a "theory of mind"? *Cognition, 21,* 37–46.

Bartak, L., Rutter, M., & Cox, A. (1975). Comparative study of infantile autism and specific developmental receptive language disorder: I. The children. *British Journal of Psychiatry, 126,* 127–145.

Bauman, M., & Kemper, T. L., (1988). Limbic and cerebellar abnormalities: Consistent findings in infantile autism. *Journal of Neuropathology and Experimental Neurology, 47,* 369.

Bettleheim, B. (1967). *The empty fortress: Infantile autism and the birth of the self.* New York: Free Press.

Capps, L., Kasari, C., Yirmiya, N., & Sigman, M. (1993). Parental perception of emotional expressiveness in children with autism. *Journal of Consulting and Clinical Psychology, 61,* 475–484.

Capps, L., Sigman, M., & Mundy, P. (1994). Attachment security in children with autism. *Development and Psychopathology, 6,* 249–261.

Capps, L., Yirmiya, N., & Sigman, M. (1992). Understanding of simple and complex emotions in non-retarded children with autism. *Journal of Child Psychology and Psychiatry, 33,* 1169–1182.

Courchesne, E. (1989). Neuroanatomical systems involved in infantile autism: The implications of cerebellar abnormalities. In G. Dawson (Ed.), *Autism: Nature, diagnosis, and treatment* (pp. 119–143). New York: Guilford Press.

Curcio, F. (1978). Sensorimotor functioning and communication in mute autistic children. *Journal of Autism and Childhood Schizophrenia, 8,* 282–292.

Dawson, G., & Galpert, L. (1987). *Mothers' use of imitative play for facilitating eye contact and toy play in autistic children.* Paper presented at the 1987 meeting of the Society for Research in Child Development, Baltimore.

Dawson, G., Hill, D., Spencer, A., Galpert, L., & Watson, L. (1990). Affective exchanges between young autistic children and their mothers. *Journal of Abnormal Child Psychology, 18,* 335–345.

De Myer, M., Pontius, W., Norton, J. A., Barton, S., Allen, J., & Steele, R. (1972). Parental practices and innate activity in normal, autistic, and brain-damaged infants. *Journal of Autism and Childhood Schizophrenia, 2,* 49–66.

Fantz, R. L., & Nevis, S. (1967). The predictive value of changes in visual preferences in early infancy. In J. Hellmuth (Ed.), *The exceptional infant* (Vol. 1, pp. 349–414). Seattle: Special Child Publications.

Folstein, S., & Rutter, M. (1987). Autism: Familial aggregation and genetic implications. *Journal of Autism and Developmental Disorders, 48,* 3–30.

Frith, U., Happe, F., & Siddons, F. (summitted). Theory of mind and social adaptation in autistic, retarded, and young normal children.

Gilberg, C., Steffenburg, S., & Schaumann, H. (1991). Is autism more common now then 10 years ago? *British Journal of Psychiatry, 158,* 403–409.

Hermelin, B., & O'Connor, N. (1970). *Psychological experiments with autistic children.* New York:Pergamon Press.

Hobson, R. P., (1986). The autistic child's appraisal of expressions of emotion. *Journal of Child Psychology and Psychiatry, 27,* 321–342.

Hobson, R. P. (1989). Beyond cognition: A theory of autism. In G. Dawson (Ed.), *Autism: Nature, diagnosis and treatment* (pp. 22–48). New York: Guilford Press.

Hobson, R. P. (1994). *Autism and the development of mind.* Hillsdale, NJ: Erlbaum.

Hughes, C., & Russell, J. (1993). Autistic children's difficulty with mental disengagement from an object: Its implications for theories of autism. *Developmental Psychology, 29,* 498–510.

Kanner, L. (1943). Autistic disturbances of affective contact. *Nervous Child, 2,* 217–250.

Kasari, C., Sigman, M., Baumgartner, P., & Stipek, D. J. (1993). Pride and mastery in children with autism. *Journal of Child Psychology and Psychiatry, 34,* 353–362.

Kasari, C., Sigman, M., Mundy, P., & Yirmiya, N. (1990). Affective sharing in the context of joint attention interactions of normal, autistic and mentally retarded children. *Journal of Autism and Developmental Disorders, 20,* 87–100.

Kasari, C., Sigman, M., & Yirmiya, N. (1993). Focused and social attention in interactions with familiar and unfamiliar adults: A comparison of autistic, mentally retarded and normal children. *Development and Psychopathology, 5,* 401–412.

Kolvin, I. (1971). Psychoses in childhood—a comparative study. In M. Rutter (Ed.), *Infantile autism: Concepts, characteristics, and treatment* (pp. 7–26). London: Churchill Livingstone.

Lane, H. (1977). *The wild boy of Aveyron.* Cambridge, MA: Harvard University Press.

Leslie, A. M. (1987). Pretense and representation: The origins of "theory of mind." *Psychological Review, 94,* 412–426.

Lockyer, L., & Rutter, M. (1970). A five-to-fifteen year follow-up study of infantile psychosis. IV. Patterns of cognitive ability. *British Journal of Social and Clinical Psychology, 9,* 152–163.

Loveland, K., & Landry, S. (1986). Joint attention and language in autism and developmental language delay. *Journal of Autism and Developmental Disorders, 16,* 335–349.

Mundy, P., Sigman, M., & Kasari, C. (1990). A longitudinal study of joint attention and language development in autistic children. *Journal of Autism and Developmental Disorders, 20,* 115–123.

Mundy, P., Sigman, M., & Kasari, C. (1994). Nonverbal communication, developmental level and symptom presentation in autism. *Development and Psychopathology, 6,* 381–401.

Mundy, P., Sigman, M., Ungerer, J. A., & Sherman, T. (1986). Defining the social deficits in autism: The contribution of non-verbal communication measures. *Journal of Child Psychology and Psychiatry, 27,* 657–669.

Mundy, P., Sigman, M., Ungerer, J. A., & Sherman, T. (1986). Defining the social deficits in autism: The contribution of non-verbal communication measures. *Journal of Child Psychology and Psychiatry, 27,* 657–669.

Ornitz, E. M., & Ritvo, E. R. (1968). Neurophysiologic mechanisms underlying perceptual inconstancy in autistic and schizophrenic children. *Archives of General Psychiatry, 18,* 76–98.

Osterling, J., & Dawson, G. (1993). *Early recognition of children with autism: A study of first year birthday home video tapes.* Paper presented at the 1993 meeting of the Society for Research in Child Development, New Orleans.

Ozonoff, S., Pennington, B. F., & Rogers, S. J. (1991). Executive function deficits in high-functioning autistic individuals: Relationships to theory of mind. *Journal of Child Psychology and Psychiatry, 32,* 1081–1105.

Ozonoff, S., Rogers, S. J., & Pennington, B. F. (1991). Asperger's syndrome: Evidence of an empirical distinction from high-functioning autism. *Journal of Child Psychology and Psychiatry, 32,* 1107–1122.

Park, C. (1967). *The siege.* Boston: Little, Brown.

Phillips, W., Baron-Cohen, S., & Rutter, M. (1992). The role of eye contact in goal detection: Evidence from normal toddlers and children with mental handicaps or autism. *Development and Psychopathology, 4,* 375–383.

Rumsey, J. M. (1985). Conceptual problem-solving in highly verbal, nonretarded autistic men. *Journal of Autism and Developmental Disorders, 15,* 23–36.

Rumsey, J. M., & Hamburger, S. D. (1988). Neuropsychological findings in high-functioning men with infantile autism, residual state. *Journal of Clinical and Experimental Neuropsychology, 10,* 201–221.

Rumsey, J. M., & Hamburger, S. D. (1990). Neuropsychological divergence of high-level autism and severe dyslexia. *Journal of Autism and Developmental Disorders, 20,* 155–168.

Rutter, M. (1978). Language disorder and infantile autism. In M. Rutter & E. Schopler (Eds.), *Autism: A reappraisal of concepts and treatment* (pp. 85–104). New York: Plenum Press.

Rutter, M., & Bartak, L. (1971). Causes of infantile autism: Some considerations from recent research. *Journal of Autism and Childhood Schizophrenia, 1,* 20–33.

Sigman, M., Kasari, C., Kwon, J. H., & Yirmiya, N. (1992). Responses to the negative emotions of others in autistic, mentally retarded, and normal children. *Child Development, 63,* 796–807.

Sigman, M., & Mundy, P. (1989). Social attachments in autistic children. *Journal of the American Academy of Child and Adolescent Psychiatry, 28,* 74–81.

Sigman, M., Mundy, P., Sherman, T., & Ungerer, J. A. (1986). Social interactions of autistic, mentally retarded, and normal children with their caregivers. *Journal of Child Psychology and Psychiatry, 27,* 647–669.

Sigman, M., & Ungerer, J. A. (1984). Attachment behaviors in autistic children. *Journal of Autism and Developmental Disorders, 14,* 231–244.

Stern, D. W. (1985). *The interpersonal world of the infant: A view from psychoanalysis and developmental psychology.* New York: Basic Books.

Trevarthen, C., & Hubley, P. (1978). Secondary intersubjectivity: Confidence, confiding, and acts of meaning in the first year. In A. Lock (Ed.), *Action, gesture, and symbol* (pp. 183–229). London: Academic Press.

Wetherby, A. M., & Prutting, C. A. (1984). Profiles of communicative and cognitive-social abilities in autistic children. *Journal of Speech and Hearing Research, 27,* 367–377.

Yirmiya, N., Kasari, C., Sigman, M., & Mundy, P. (1989). Facial expressions of affect in autistic, mentally retarded and normal children. *Journal of Child Psychology and Psychiatry, 30,* 725–735.

Yirmiya, N., Sigman, M. D., Kasari, C., & Mundy, P. (1992). Empathy and cognition in high-functioning children with autism. *Child Development, 63,* 150–160.

III

Developmental Psychopathology

7

Developmental Psychopathology: Concepts and Prospects

MICHAEL RUTTER

During the last two decades, developmental psychopathology research concepts and strategies have increasingly come to the fore as it has become evident that traditional approaches in both psychiatry and psychology have been limited in their ability to tackle certain key questions and because the prevailing major theories did not take account of many crucial features of development and of psychopathology (Cicchetti, 1989; Rutter, 1993a, in press-a; Rutter & Rutter, 1993; Sroufe & Rutter, 1984). Thus, much psychiatric research has been based on outdated disease concepts that have assumed single causes operating in a direct, one-step fashion. Psychologists have often characterized these as "medical models," but such models have long since become outmoded in internal medicine. Depue et al. (this volume) emphasize that neurobiology requires a dynamic perspective that focuses on the study of processes concerned with the interplay of constitutional features and environmental causes. Similarly, Goldsmith and Gottesman (this volume) point to the markedly variable expression of many genetic conditions and the multiplicity of routes by which genetically influenced risks may operate. In somewhat comparable fashion, Brooks-Gunn and Attie (this volume) note the need to consider the extent to which both eating disorders and depressive disorders represent extremes of normal variation rather than some qualitatively distinct psychopathological condition. Cornblatt et al. (this volume), too, emphasize the need to examine similarities and differences between schizophrenic psychoses and schizotypy as an associated personality disorder.

These issues are ones that are pervasive throughout medicine. Two key points are crucial in understanding the causal processes involved in disease. First, most medical conditions are multifactorial in origin. Obviously, this applies to conditions as diverse as myocardial infarction, asthma, and peptic ulcer. Genetic factors are important in susceptibility to myocardial infarction, but low birth weight, obesity, smoking, and lack of exercise all contribute significantly to the risk. The same multifactorial causation applies to most psychiatric disorders. Second, the risk factors for these diseases often involve dimensional features that operate within the normal as well as the abnormal range. That is so, for example, with respect to serum cholesterol levels and the risk of myocardial infarction. An important corollary of both of these points is that it is essential to move beyond the identification of risk factors to an understanding of risk mechanisms and processes (Rutter, 1994e). In doing to, it is necessary to be aware that, even for a single disease, several different risk mechanisms may be operative.

In parallel with these changes in disease concept, there has been a growing appreciation of the limitations of traditional theories and approaches in developmental psychology. For the most part, they have focused on the *universals* of developmental processes. Thus, Freudian views of development focused on children's progression through a series of psychosexual stages, with psychopathology supposedly related to fixation and regression to earlier stages. In similar fashion, Piagetian theory placed emphasis on children's progression through an ordered sequence of cognitive stages. These "big" theories are important in many ways, but they no longer serve a useful role in guiding research. In part, this is because empirical research findings have failed to sustain many of their basic tenets. But, even more important, they have faded from prominence because it has become evident that there are many features of development that require explanation but that were not addressed by these theories. Thus, research has been quite consistent in showing major individual differences in psychological development. These include individual variations in the speed with which children progress in their development, but, even more important, they include major differences in the content of such development. It is necessary to account for the fact that some children are predominantly sunny in mood, whereas others are characteristically dysphoric; some are high in self-esteem and some are low; some are impulsive and some are cautious; some are overly conscientious and full of self-doubt, whereas others seem untroubled by scruples or concern for others. At one time, there was a tendency to assume that these individual differences represented stable personality traits of some kind. Although subject to influence by experience, they were usually considered to have their basis in some type of constitutional "given" (see Kohnstamm, Bates, & Rothbart, 1989). Accordingly, although there was a need to account for changes in such traits, their persistence appeared to require no explanation. It is now evident that this view constitutes a misleading oversimplification (Caspi & Moffitt, 1993; Rutter & Rutter, 1993; Rutter, in press-b). Genetic factors are indeed important in shaping individual differences, but their effects are probabilistic, not deterministic. Traits persist or fade, to a considerable degree, according to the extent to which experiences accentuate or reinforce them, or, conversely, give rise to countertendencies of some kind. *Both* change and stability require explanation, and both involve the operation of genetic and environmental factors. Direct trait persistence is, of course, a reality, but it is clear that indirect links are at least as important in continuities in psychological functioning.

Developmental Psychopathology

Out of these two patterns of change has grown the approach that has come to be termed *developmental psychopathology*. This involves much more than just a broadening of concepts in developmental psychology and psychiatry but, equally, it does not represent a theory. Rather, it comprises a research perspective (Rutter, 1986a, 1993a). Sroufe and Rutter (1984) described it as "the study of the origins and cause of individual patterns of behavioral maladaptation." The focus is on developing an understanding of the causal processes as they operate over time in the initiation, persistence, and desistence of patterns of psychopathology. Characteristically, longitudinal research strategies are employed because the study of intraindividual change provides a powerful means of testing causal hypotheses (Farrington, 1988; Rutter, 1994e). For obvious reasons, such strategies are also crucial for the elucidation of developmental processes. On their own, cross-sectional designs have severe limitations for this purpose (Baltes, 1968; Schaie, 1965). Because the interest is in gaining an understanding of the operation of risk processes, much research in developmental psychopathology has made use of the prospective study of high-risk samples (Garmezy, 1993). This provides a sharp contrast to the cross-sectional and retrospective studies of subjects with some psychopathological disorder that have been usual in so much psychiatric research (Depue et al. [this volume] make the idiosyncratic suggestion that the typical approach in developmental psychopathology is to start with the disorder, rather than with a risk process, but this is the complete antithesis of what has been characteristic of developmental psychopathology).

Continuities and Discontinuities in Development

In essence, developmental psychopathology is particularly characterized by its use of two key research strategies: the study of continuities and discontinuities over the course of development and the study of continuities and discontinuities over the span of behavioral variation (Rutter, 1986a, 1988, 1993a). Thus, research leverage has been provided by age-indexed variations in the incidence of disorder or in susceptibility to environmental hazards. There are many striking instances of both, and elucidation of the mechanisms involved is likely to be valuable in determining the processes involved in the causation of disorder. Brooks-Gunn and Attie (this volume) draw attention to the fact that both depressive and eating disorders increase greatly in frequency over the teenage years and also show an increase in female preponderance over this same age period. But, as they note, the reasons for these age-related changes remain poorly understood. Clearly, age as such provides no explanation (Rutter, 1989). The reasons could lie in factors as diverse as the biological changes of puberty, the switching on of genes, growth in cognitive capacity, culturally influenced changes in patterns of family relationships and peer interaction, reactions to the bodily changes that accompany puberty, or increases in threatening life stressors. There may also be significance in differences in the age of onset of disorders that otherwise appear similar. For example, Patterson, (this volume) notes that there seems to be an important difference between early-onset and late-onset antisocial behavior (see also Moffitt, 1993a). On the whole, seemingly paradoxically, antisocial behavior that begins early in childhood is more likely to persist into adult life than that which begins in adolescence. Probably the early-onset variety is somewhat different in form in that it is more likely to be associated with hyperactivity, attention deficits, and poor peer relations (Farrington, Loeber, & Van Kammen, 1990).

Age-indexed variations in susceptibility to environmental hazards are evident with respect to both brain damage and patterns of rearing. In later childhood and in adult life, lateralized brain lesions result in quite distinctive patterns of cognitive deficit. By contrast, lateralized brain lesions in early infancy do not have this effect (Vharga-Khadem, Isaacs, van der Werf, Robb, & Wilson, 1992). On the other hand, early lesions are probably more likely to result in generally impaired cognitive function. Evidence that this is much more likely if epilepsy exists implies that brain *mal*function may be more influential than a *loss* of brain function. In the psychosocial arena, the evidence that hospital admissions (and other forms of stressful separation from families) tend to be most damaging during the postinfancy preschool years (Rutter, 1979) and the effects on later peer relations of early institutional rearing (Hodges & Tizard, 1989a, 1989b) both exemplify age-related differences in susceptibility. These examples also illustrate how such variations provide valuable clues regarding the likely underlying mechanisms.

Suicide provides another striking example of age-related effects (Diekstra, Kienhorst, & de Wilde, 1995). During recent decades, suicide rates in adolescent and young adult males have been rising in most countries; by sharp contrast, suicide rates in old people have fallen markedly over the same time period. It remains to be determined whether this is a consequence of different causal factors operating at different age periods or of changes in society that have had opposite effects on older and younger ages groups. Either way, elucidation of the reason for these marked differences in secular trends is likely to provide information on causal processes.

Developmental considerations also require attention to the possibility that the factors involved in the initial onset of a disorder may not be the same as those that are most influential on whether the disorder persists or remits later. Also, childhood adversities may be more influential on the first onset of depression than on its recurrence (Kessler & Magee, 1993). For example, there is some suggestion from twin studies that genetic factors play a greater role in the lifetime burden of depressive disorders, whereas environmental stressors play a greater role in the onset of depressive episodes (Kendler, Neale, Kessler, Heath, & Eaves, 1993a). Similarly, high family involvement, with markedly negative expressed emotion, is a well-documented risk factor for recurrence of schizophrenia (Goldstein, 1987), but it is uncertain whether this plays a role in onset or in overall vulnerability to the disease.

Developmental considerations also suggest the importance of bearing in mind that causation of a disorder may be a multiphase process. For example, the Robins et al. study of Vietnam veterans showed that the factors associated with taking heroin in Vietnam were very different from those associated with the persistence of addition on return to the United States (Robins, Davis, & Wish, 1977). In somewhat comparable fashion, the fat deposition associated with puberty in girls plays a substantial role in the initiation of both dieting and dissatisfaction with body image, but individual psychopathology and disturbed relationships may be more important in the long-term persistence of eating disturbances (Attie & Brooks-Gunn, 1989) and, perhaps especially, in the transition to the more serious conditions of anorexia and bulimia nervosa.

A further feature of multiphase causation is that circumstances brought about by people's own behavior may play a key role in the persistence of that behavior. For example, young people choose the peer groups with which they associate, but longitudinal studies show that the characteristics of the peer group influence the individual's own behavior (Rowe, Woulbroun, & Gulley, 1994). Quinton, Pickles, Maughan, and Rutter (1993) and Fergusson and Horwood (submitted) have shown the importance of the peer group in the persistence of antisocial behavior during adolescence. At a slightly later age, the nature of the marital relationship and the characteristics of the spouse are also powerful influences on social functioning (Quinton et al., 1993; Sampson & Laub, 1993). Delinquent behavior may result in incarceration, but imprisonment makes the continuation of criminal behavior more likely because of its adverse effects on employment (Sampson & Laub, 1993). Age difference in remission from disorder are also informative. Thus, it is well known that there are marked individual differences in the age at which children reach all types of developmental milestones—ranging from the eruption of teeth to the ages of walking and talking. The follow-up studies of children who are markedly late in acquiring spoken language indicate that, by the time they reach school age, about half have caught up with their contemporaries and show no significant sequelae of their slow start in speaking (Bishop & Adams, 1990; Bishop & Edmundson, 1987a, 1987b) However, the other half not only continue to show language impairment but also exhibit an increased rate of many educational and behavioral difficulties. Indeed, many of those with a severe receptive language difficulty continue to show substantial social problems even in early adult life (Rutter & Mawhood, 1991). The implication is that the former group probably constitute normal variations of no particular psychopathological significance, even though the language delay initially gives rise to concern. The latter group, by contrast, may well represent a disorder with rather different origins. Certainly, it seems very dubious whether it represents just the extreme of normal variation. Probably the same pattern applies to the acquisition of bladder control. Although the prevalence of nocturnal enuresis falls sharply with increasing age, the likelihood of becoming continent during any given 12-month period does not alter greatly over the middle years of childhood (Oppel, Harder, & Rider, 1968). Once more, the implication is that some instances of very late onset of bladder control represent a form of disorder, whereas others reflect no more than the extreme of normal variation.

It is evident from the examples given that there is no single explanation for age-indexed variations in the onset, persistence, or remission of disorder or in variations in susceptibility to environmental hazards. What is clear, however, is that attention to these variations may provide a most useful research strategy when examining causal processes.

Continuities and Discontinuities in Behavioral Variation

The second key strategy in developmental psychopathology research is provided by examination of continuities and discontinuities over the span of behavioral variation. Traditionally, psychiatrists tend to conduct their research in terms of disorder categories, with the implicit assumption of discontinuities between psychopathology and normal variation. Psychologists, on the other hand, tend to deal with dimensions of behavior and risk, with the implicit assumption of continuities between normality and pathology. Developmental psychopathology differs from both in making neither assumption but, instead, using the examination of continuities and discontinuities to provide research leverage (Rutter, 1986a).

In that connection, it needs to be appreciated that a psychological characteristic may function as both a dimension and a qualitatively distinct category at the same time. Thus, for example, IQ functions as a dimension across the whole of its range with respect to predictions about educational achievement and social functioning. On the other hand, severe mental retardation is undoubtedly qualitatively distinct from normal variations in intelligence. The causes are quite different, and the biological consequences are equally differentiating (with severe diminution in fucundity and life expectancy associated with severe retardation; see Simonoff, Bolton, & Rutter, in press). As already illustrated with respect to developmental disorders of language acquisition and bladder control, there may also be heterogeneity within categories. Thus, Brooks-Gunn and Attie (this volume) raise this issue with respect to depressive conditions and eating disorders. It is likely that some depressive disorders constitute extreme variations of normality, but it is less likely that the same applies to bipolar affective psychoses. Anorexia nervosa, in some respects, appears to be an extreme variation of the dieting behavior that is so common during adolescence, but it carries a significant mortality (about 5%) and its etiology may not be the same. Genetic factors appear to play substantial role in anorexia nervosa (Holland, Sicotte, & Treasure, 1988), but they may be less important in the far more frequent eating disturbances that are so characteristic of adolescence in females.

A somewhat different distinction is provided by the differentiation between individual behavioral traits and constellations of behavior. Magnusson and Bergman (1988, 1990) showed the importance of this differentiation with respect to conduct disorder. Aggressivity has always been considered a risk factor for criminality, and Magnusson and Bergman showed the same in their analyses of the stockhold longitudinal study. However, they went on to show that the risk derived almost entirely from the subsample that showed multiple problems involving aggression, hyperactivity, attentional deficits, poor peer relations, and educational difficulties. When this multiproblem group was excluded, aggressivity no longer predicted criminality. The lesson is an important one because it highlights the fact that combinations of behavior may have a quite different meaning from the same behaviors considered in isolation. Much the same was evident in the analyses undertaken by Hanson, Gottesman, and Heston (1976) with respect to risk factors in childhood for schizophrenic psychoses in adult life. The developmental delays, attentional problems, and social impairment all predicted schizophrenia, but the rate of false positives was enormous because so many nonschizophrenic individuals showed these characteristics. The picture changed entirely, however, when combinations of these three features were considered. These were very common in schizophrenic individuals but quite unusual in normals. Again, the implication is that constellations of behavior may have a different meaning from the individual components considered separately.

A third facet of the concern for behavioral variations concerns the attention to diversity of outcomes from risk experiences. This has been important with respect to many different risk factors. Rutter and Mawhood (1991) showed substantial social problems in adult life for young men who had exhibited serious developmental disorders of receptive language in early childhood. But these adverse outcomes did not fit any particular diagnostic category, according to the prevailing psychiatric classification schemes. A focus on conventional diagnostic categories might well have overlooked the major risk of poor social functioning in adult life, and retrospective studies of adult diagnostic categories would certainly have failed to pick up this risk. Similarly, long-term follow-up of very low birth weight babies had shown a substantially increased rate of neurodevelopmental and psychological impairments but, again, these have not fallen into any well-recognized pattern of diagnoses (Caesar, de Vries, & Marlow, 1991; Reynolds, in press).

Another aspect of the diversity of outcomes is resilience: namely, the fact that some children do *not* succumb when exposed to adversities that lead to disorder in other people (Rutter, 1985a, 1990, 1993b). In part too, of course, this relative resistance reflects the intensity and chronicity of the risks experienced. In part, however, it also reflects the operation of protective factors, meaning variables that do not necessarily have a positive effect on their own but that do ameliorate the risks associated with adversity. Research on protective factors is still in its infancy, but already it is apparent that protective mechanisms do not necessarily reside in hedonically positive experiences. Just as controlled exposure to pathogenic bacteria provides resistance to later infections, overcoming psychosocial adversities may provide protection against later psychosocial risks. Equally, factors may constitute risks for one outcome but may be protective for another. Sickle cell anemia is a well-documented medical example of this kind in terms of the protection of heterozygote status against malaria. Perhaps adoption is something of a psychological counterpart in that although it brings risks of its own (albeit slight ones), it may well be protective for children who come from high-risk backgrounds.

Another aspect of diverse developmental pathways is provided by *heterotypic continuity*. This term refers to an underlying coherence in psychological continuity but variation in its surface manifestations. Thus, for example, attentional and habituation processes in infancy seem to constitute precursors of later problem-solving intelligence (Colombo, 1993; McCall & Carriger, 1993). Similarly, a predisposition to schizophrenia is shown by a combination of neurodevelopmental impairments and social malfunction in childhood of a kind that bears little resemblance to the psychotic manifestations of schizophrenia in adult life (Done, Crow, Johnstone, & Sacker, 1994; Jones, Rodgers, Murray, & Marmot, 1994; Rutter & Garmezy, 1983).

The frequent existence of comorbidity, meaning the co-occurrence of supposedly separate psychiatric disorders, is another focus of developmental psychopathology (Caron & Rutter, 1991). Undoubtedly, some comorbidity is simply an artifact resulting from the mistaken specification of diagnostic criteria and the very varied manifestations of diagnostic categories. Nevertheless, some comorbidity reflects risk mechanisms in which the presence of one disorder constitutes a greatly increased risk for another. The co-occurrence of hyperkinetic disorder and conduct disorder is probably an example of this kind (Taylor, Chadwick, Heptinstall, & Danckaerts, submitted). Hyperkinetic disorder in early childhood results in a marked predisposition to the later development of conduct disorder. Interestingly, the reverse does not apply. Because the causal arrow seems to run in only one direction, it is unlikely that these conditions represent alternative manifestations of the same underlying predispositions. Rather, hyperactivity seems to constitute a risk factor for conduct disorder, and an understanding of how this mechanism works would be extremely helpful in understanding the causal processes leading to conduct disorder.

Finally, research in developmental psychopathology makes use of the abnormal case in order to pull apart variables that ordinarily go together. As is clearly illustrated in Sigman's excellent chapter in this volume, autism provides a good example. In that case, much of the interest has lain in testing the hypothesis that cognitive deficits may account for the social impairments that serve to define autism. As Sigman notes, it became apparent early on that if a specific pattern of cognitive deficits associated with autism was to be identified, it would be crucial to control for the *level* of cognitive functioning. Much of the early research on autism was invalidated by a failure to do that, but it is now generally accepted that mental retardation controls are needed. At present, "theory of mind," executive planning, and psychological coherence deficits seem to be the prime contenders for a cognitive basis of autism (Baron-Cohen, Tager-Flusberg, & Cohen, 1993; Frith, 1989; Ozonoff, 1994). There is good evidence that each of these cognitive features is associated with autism, but there are queries on the nature of their role in the causal processes because autism is ordinarily evident by 18 months or so of age (Happé, 1994) and often by 12 months of age (Osterling & Dawson, 1994). The hypothesis that a reduced information processing capacity is a strong marker for a biological susceptibility to schizophrenia constitutes a parallel example, as is well argued by Cornblatt et al., (this volume). What is important about the developmental psychopathology perspective, however, is that there is an unwillingness to leave this as simply a strong marker for susceptibility. Instead, researchers have to move on to the question of *how* the risk mechanism operates. As Cornblatt et al., indicate, a variety of methodological questions need to be addressed, but even if they are answered satisfactorily, there is still the question of why and how impaired information processing might create a vulnerability to schizophrenia. These authors suggest that it may operate through impaired social processing and that, because of that feature, social isolation may be protective. Further research is needed to test this hypothesis, but the importance of the suggestion lies in its potential to integrate individual susceptibility characteristics with the response to environmental risk factors.

With these considerations in mind, we can turn to some of the specific issues that need to be addressed in certain key domains of developmental psychopathology research.

Genetic Factors

Goldsmith and Gottesman (this volume) provide an eloquent account of modern genetic approaches to psychopathology. They emphasize the grave fallacy of the assumption that genetic influences are fixed and have their maximum impact at birth, before environmental influences have much of a change to operate. It is clear that genetic factors influence developmental change and continuity just as much as individual differences in trait manifestation. Thus, genetic factors are known to be important in the timing of the menarche and in the onset of Huntington's disease in midlife. Although perhaps less well documented, genetic influences almost certainly play a role, too, in the rise of both schizophrenia and affective disorders during adolescence and early adult life. It is not just a question of genes "switching on" at different points of the life span or of genes affecting the vulnerability to later-onset disorders. Developmental changes also derive from genetic influences on the shaping and selection of environments and of individual differences in susceptibility to environmental risks (see below).

Traditionally, genetic research strategies have been seen as a way of partitioning the variance between genetic and environmental components. That is still a useful step, but the separation of nature and nurture is to some extent misleading. That is because, to an important extent, some of the effects derive from the interplay between nature and nurture. Thus, there are important and influential person–environment correlations (Plomin, 1994; Rutter & Rutter, 1992; Scarr, 1992). These take three main forms: passive, evocative, and active. In *passive correlations,* the characteristics of parents, in part genetically influenced, determine the environment they provide for their children. Thus, for example, mentally retarded parents pass on their genes and also are more likely to provide a limited intellectual environment for their children. *Evocative correlations* refer to the fact that people's own characteristics influence the reactions they engender in other people. For instance, there is good evidence that antisocial males are more likely to fall out with their friends, to experience multiple broken marriages, to be unemployed, to be on welfare, and to experience an increased rate of many environmental stressors (Champion, Goodall, & Rutter, 1995; Robins, 1966). *Active correlations* mean that individuals are not simply passive recipients of environmental stimuli. Instead, they take active steps to shape and select their environments. As already noted, this is evident, for example, in people's selection of peer groups (Rowe et al., 1994) and in their choice of marriage partner (Quinton et al., 1993). Up to now, genetic researchers have paid scant attention to these mechanisms. Indeed, some behavior genetic analyses assume that the origins of a risk factor necessarily account for its mode of operation. It is clear that this cannot be the case (Rutter, 1994a). This is perhaps most obvious in the example of cigarette smoking. People choose to smoke for reasons associated with individual personality characteristics, cultural expectations, and opportunity, but the risks of coronary artery disease, chronic bronchitis, and lung cancer have nothing to do with those factors. Rather, the physical hazards (for a wide range of medical disorders) stem from carcinogenic tars, vascular effects of nicotine, carbon monoxide in the inhaled gases, and other physiological rather than psychological processes. One of the challenges for genetic research in the future is to incorporate gene–environment correlations and to use research strategies that enable environmental risk mechanisms to be studied despite the operation of genetic influences on the origin of environmental risk factors.

Goldsmith and Gottesman (this volume) also draw attention to the vary wide psychopathological heterogeneity associated with genetic abnormalities. Cornblatt et al., (this volume) note the problems of phenotypic definition in studying the origins of schizophrenia. The issues are real and the methodological problems are considerable. Moreover, it is obvious that the difficulties are not removed by obtaining reliability in psychiatric diagnosis or by achieving agreement on diagnostic criteria. There are two parallel but rather different scientific concerns. First, there is the problem of defining the boundaries of psychiatric conditions. Genetic research shows that schizophrenia encompasses some schizotypal personality disorders and some paranoid conditions, as well as schizophrenic psychosis as ordinarily diagnosed (Kendler, McGuire, Gruenberg, Ohare, Spellman, & Walsh, 1993a). It is far less clear, however, where to draw the boundaries when the concept of schizophrenia extends into the range of personality disorders. Also, it is evident that, perhaps particularly during the adolescent years, there can be difficulties in differentiating schizophrenic and bipolar affective psychoses (Werry, McClellan, & Chard, 1991). In somewhat comparable fashion, genetic findings indicate that the phenotype of autism includes a rather broader range of cognitive and social deficits than is encompassed by the traditional diagnosis of autism (Rutter, Bailey, Bolton, & Le Couteur, 1993). Again, however, it is less clear how and where to draw the boundaries. There is little doubt that problems in phenotypic definition have hampered molecular genetic research in psychiatry.

Second, it is apparent that single-gene Mendelian disorders and specific chromosomal anomalies can be associated with quite diverse clinical features (Simonoff et al., in press). This is obvious with respect to the immense variation in the clinical manifestations of conditions such as neurofibromatosis and tuberous sclerosis, and it is also evident in the vary wide range of phenotypic manifestations of the fragile x anomaly. Molecular genetics has opened up the scientific possibilities in a dramatic fashion. No longer is it acceptable simply to assume that the identification of some chromosomal abnormality provides a sufficient explanation for a disorder. Rather, it is necessary to go on to ask why, for example, some fragile x individuals show extreme social anxiety, some show the syndrome of autism, some show personality abnormalities, and some appear to be psychologically unexceptional. The discovery of the trinucleotide repeat expansion mechanism now provides the possibility of explaining variety in clinical expression. Further research is needed to identify the gene product and the mechanisms by which the gene product leads to the behavioral phenotype.

In that connection, genetic researchers must consider the range of ways in which genetic factors may create a vulnerability to psychiatric disorder. As Goldsmith and Gottesman (this volume) emphasize, the genetic influence may not be on disorder as such. The genetic factors involved in antisocial behavior may involve impulse control, sensation seeking, activity level, anxiety proneness, or frustration intolerance. Similarly, the genetic contribution to the liability to affective disorder may involve personality features pre-disposing to depression, rather than a direct vulnerability to depressive episodes as such (Kendler, Neale, Kessler, Heath, & Eaves, 1993c). Equally, the vulnerability to anxiety disorders may concern a temperamental attribute such as behavioral inhibition (Rosenbaum et al., 1991). The point is that it is much too confining to restrict attention to disorders; equal attention needs to be paid to the variety of routes by which the risks of disorder may be carried.

Among other possibilities, attention needs to be paid to the possibility of gene–environment interactions. Behavior genetic research so far has provided very little evidence that such interactions are important (Plomin, Defries, & Fulker, 1988). There is, however, much evidence of the widespread operation of interactions in biology and medicine (Rutter and Pickles, 1991). It is likely that they also apply in the field of psychopathology. There are probably several reasons why they have not yet been discovered. To begin with, most of the known examples in medicine apply to subsegments of the population and, moreover, concern responses to specific environmental features. it is not likely that gene–environment interactions will be discovered by "black box" analyses of unmeasured hypothesized genetic vulnerabilities and environmental risks. It is pertinent that several postulated risk factors for psychiatric disorders, such as sensation seeking or frustration intolerance or behavioral inhibition, refer to some sort of responsiveness to the environment. What is needed now is research that examines such responsiveness directly in relation to risk processes. The second, in some respects opposite, alternative is that the genetically influenced vulnerability applies to widely pervasive environmental features. Insofar as that is the case, the lack of substantial environmental variation will make it difficult to detect interactive mechanisms through statistical interaction effects. Thus, the genetically influenced allergic diathesis concerns bodily responses to allergens that are widespread in the environment. The genetic predisposition will not lead to an allergic disorder in the absence of such allergens but, because they are so widespread in the environment, gene–environment interactions may not be obvious. The fact that all research shows huge individual variations in response to all types of environmental stressors makes it highly implausible that gene–environment interactions do not apply in the field of psychopathology. On the other hand, most of the research that has looked for interactions has been concerned with dimensional attributes such as intelligence or neuroticism, and there is no reason to suppose that interactions are likely to be very important in their case.

Another aspect of behavioral variation that warrants attention is the extent to which behavior varies across situations. Thus, the concept of hyperkinetic disorder involves a specification that the overactivity occurs across a range of situations (Taylor, 1994). It may well be that situation-specific overactivity has a somewhat different meaning. Patterson (this volume) also observes that whereas normal boys vary in their behavior across settings, boys showing antisocial behavior do not to the same extent. In a somewhat comparable fashion, Rutter and Quinton (1984) showed that the children of mentally ill parents differed from the children in a general population comparison group in the extent to which their deviant behavior persisted over time (and presumably, therefore, across a range of situations).

Finally, as Wahlsten (1990) pointed out, most forms of multivariate genetic analyses have very weak statistical power for the detection of gene–environment interactions. What is needed is research designed to test specific risk hypotheses rather than searching for interactions in a vacuum. Interactions in themselves have no particular meaning, but they do provide a useful pointer for possible ways in which risk processes my operate.

Psychosocial Risk Factors

Patterson (this volume) summarizes the considerable body of research, both by his own group and others, suggesting that chronic antisocial behavior is the direct outcome of a breakdown in parental family management practices. Antisocial youngsters have coercive styles of interpersonal interaction and are also unskilled in dealing with social encounters. Both the coercive qualities and the unskilled social functioning are a consequence of disrupted parental discipline and management. Nevertheless, there is a two-way interplay in which the children's coercive behavior elicits maladaptive parental behavior, which in turn perpetuates the antisocial qualities in the children's behavior. Of all the documented associations between family characteristics and child psychopathology, these are the best established. Moreover, they have proved useful in planning therapeutic interventions for which there is some evidence of efficacy. Even so, major queries remain on the risk mechanisms involved.

In considering the research agenda for the future, a crucial question is whether the strong, well-replicated statistical associations represent a causal influence of family functioning on child behavior. Two main alternatives need to be examined: (1) that the causal arrow runs in the opposite direction (i.e., that the coercive behavior of the children leads to disruptive family functioning; Bell & Chapman, 1986) and (2) that the association reflects genetic inheritance rather than the operation of environmental risk mechanisms (Rowe et al., 1994; Scarr, 1992).

There is evidence in favor of both modes of mediation, at least as a partial explanation, but it seems unlikely that they provide the whole answer (Plomin, 1994; Plomin & Bergeman, 1991; Rutter, 1985b, 1991). Nevertheless, the empirical findings do not allow any quantification, even rough and ready, of the relative strength of the three alternative mechanisms (i.e., genetic mediation of supposed environmental risk factors, true environmental risk mediation, and the effects of children on parents). The clear need is for the incorporation of high-quality measures of observed environmental risk factors within genetic designs. So far, there have been regrettably few attempts to do this. Psychosocial researchers, for the most part, have not seen the need to use genetic designs to test environmental risk hypotheses, and genetic researchers have not bothered to include rigorous and discriminating measures of the environment in their studies.

An equally important need is to identify the particular features of family adversity that create the risk of antisocial behavior. For good reasons, Patterson (the volume) has placed emphasis on a lack of adequate parental discipline and management. There is little doubt that these are indeed key elements. On the other hand, there is evidence that family discord and hostility are also key features in the risk process (Rutter, 1994b). The very high rate of antisocial behavior in young people reared in residential institutions of some kind suggests, in addition, that a lack of cohesive supportive relationships may be as important as active discord or poor disciplinary management; (Quinton & Rutter, 1988; Rutter, Quinton, & Hill 1990; Zoccolillo, Pickles, Quinton, & Rutter, 1992). Yet another issue is the extent to which the antisocial behavior derives directly from contemporaneous adverse features in the family environment or from an earlier lack of secure selective attachment relationships (Fagot & Kavanagh, 1990; Greenberg & Speltz, 1988; Greenberg, Speltz & DeKlyen, 1993). It is not easy to differentiate among these possibilities because, in most circumstances, children showing antisocial behavior have experienced varying mixtures of all facets of the postulated risk features. Nevertheless, it is essential that we move beyond the identification of risk indices to an understanding of risk mechanisms. For too long, psychosocial researchers have been content to rely on statistical associations with broad environmental features (such as social disadvantage, unemployment, family disruption, or group day care). The real danger is that inappropriate ameliorative actions will be taken because the statistical association with the risk indicator has only an indirect connection with the operative risk mechanism.

Several years ago, Plomin and Daniels (1987) pointed to the evidence from behavior genetic studies that the main environmental influences on both psychopathology and individual differences in psychological characteristics stemmed from nonshared rather than shared environmental effects. In other words, the implication was that it was the differences *within* families that mattered rather than the differences *between* families. Delinquency seems to be somewhat of an exception to this general tendency (Plomin, Nitz, & Rowe, 1990) but psychosocial researchers must still examine the matter more directly. Four different implications apply.

1. Attention must be paid to potential influences outside as well as inside the family. Thus psychosocial research needs to focus on peer group, school, and community influences to a greater extent than has been the case up to now.
2. Attention needs to be paid to comparison effects within families. Dunn and Plomin (1990) have suggested that the fact that one child in the family is systematically favored (or disfavored) over his or her siblings may matter more than whether th overall atmosphere in the home is emotionally warm or cool, or whether the discipline is strict or relaxed. There is no doubt that human beings tend to compare themselves with others and feel resentful if they consider that they have been abused or neglected. It is certainly possible that comparison effects of this kind may influence psychological development, although we do not yet know the extent to which that is actually the case.
3. Even with apparently familywide influences such as discord, overcrowding, poverty, or parental depression, the impact may still vary considerably from child to child. Thus, when parents are depressed, their anger and irritability are often directed against one child, who is scapegoated, rather than spread among all the children in an evenhanded fashion. Similarly, one child may be much more likely to be drawn into parental quarrels, or one child may be especially used as a source of comfort when the parent is feeling low-spirited. Equally, the response of individual children to paren-

tal negative behavior may be an important stimulant for cycles of coercive interchange.
4. Children are likely to vary in the extent to which they react adversely to family stresses and adversities. It is evident that, in the future, much more attention will have to be paid to the investigation of these proximal processes by which children are influenced by environmental risk mechanisms.

A somewhat related question is whether family adversities have their main negative impact on children who are genetically at risk or otherwise constitutionally vulnerable in some way. Reviewers (e.g., Emery, 1982) have noted that the ill effects of family discord are more evident in samples with mentally ill or criminal parents or in samples that are disadvantaged in other ways. This could be because the discord tends to be more severe or more prolonged in such samples or because it is accompanied by multiple other adversities. On the other hand, it may mean that environmental risks mainly affect children who are personally susceptible as a result of constitutional features or prior experiences.

In considering these psychosocial research issues, family influences on antisocial behavior have been used as the example. It is important to note, however, that we know far less about family influences on other forms of psychopathology. Thus, there is limited evidence that life stressors play a role in precipitating depressive disorders in young people (Goodyer & Altham, 1991a, 1991b; Goodyer, Germany, Gowrusankur, & Altham, 1991), but the understanding of environmental risk factors in both depressive and (even more so) anxiety disorders in children and adolescents is decidedly limited. There is a larger literature on comparable disorders in adult life, but it is not known whether the same risk factors apply in childhood.

Another major constraint on psychosocial risk research is that the great majority of studies have focused on the role of life experiences in the *onset* of disorder. Much less is known about environmental mechanisms with respect to the overall lifetime burden of psychiatric disorders. This is a very important omission. The majority of disorders are recurrent or chronic. In addition, in terms of both individual suffering and service implications, influences on the overall burden of illness are more important than those on the timing of particular episodes.

One further gap in research, which is only beginning to be filled, concerns the origins of environmental risk experiences. Such experiences are not randomly distributed in the population, and it is crucial to determine why some individuals go through life relatively untroubled by serious stresses and adversities, whereas others have a seemingly endless sequence of negative experiences (Rutter, Champion, Quinton, Maughan, & Pickles, in press). Part of the explanation lies in the way people act to shape and select their own environments. However, societal influences also put subsegments of the population at a particular risk, and it is necessary to determine how this comes about so that appropriate remedies can be found.

Finally, most psychosocial risk research (like biological research) has focused on the causal question of why one individual shows some particular disorder whereas another does not. That is an important causal question but it is very far from the only one (Rutter, 1994c, 1995a). Thus, for example, there is now much evidence that many psychosocial disorders in young people have increased considerably over the last half century (Rutter & Smith, 1995). Suicide rates have risen, crime rates have gone up markedly, depression has become more common, drug problems have increased, and eating disorders may have gone up somewhat. This constitutes a considerable public health problem, but it has received remarkably little research attention and we know relatively little about the causal factors involved. There is also good evidence that the rates of these disorders are substantially higher in some geographical areas than in others, but our understanding of the mechanisms underlying these area differences is limited (Reiss, 1995).

Developmental Mechanisms

Many of the developmental research issues are implicit in what has already been discussed, but several overriding issues warrant emphasis. Perhaps surprisingly, there has been very little systematic research to determine the mechanisms underlying the well-documented age differences in psychopathology. Affective disorders, eating disorders, antisocial behavior, suicide, attempted suicide, and schizophrenia all rise markedly during the teenage period. In some cases, the sex ratio changes at the same time. For example, during this age period depressive disorders become substantially more frequent in females. Obviously, it should not necessarily be assumed that the same underlying process will explain all these age trends. Indeed, it is very unlikely that this is the case. Nevertheless, what is needed, in each case, is systematic research to test alternative hypotheses about the underlying mechanism.

Somewhat similar issues arise with respect to the apparently changing role of some risk factors with age. Thus, the Isle of Wight surveys some two decades ago showed that reading difficulties were strongly associated with psychopathology beginning in childhood but showed little connection with disorders beginning during adolescence (Rutter, Graham, Chadwick, & Yule, 1976). At that time, it seemed that this differential association was a function of somewhat different types of disorders. The long-term longitudinal study by Maughan and her colleagues in London (in press) suggests that the same age change applies within individuals. In the London study, as in the Isle of Wight survey, reading difficulties were strongly associated with conduct disorders in childhood. The association weakened during adolescence and was scarcely present at the time of follow-up in the mid-20s. This finding needs to be replicated, but it raises important questions about the mechanisms involved. The association has usually been thought to mean that neuropsychological deficits create a direct risk factor for psychopathology (Moffitt, 1990, 1993b). That assumption, plus the fact that both reading difficulties and conduct disorders tend to be remarkably persistent, seem to suggest that the association should continue into adult life. Finding that it did not, at least in the one study investigating the matter, raises queries about the underlying mechanisms. It also illustrates the value of longitudinal research in investigating causal mechanisms.

Another example of an apparent change in the role of risk factors with age is provided by the finding from twin studies that the genetic component is weak in juvenile delinquency but strong in adult criminality (DiLalla & Gottesman, 1989). The quality of the studies leaves something to be desired, but the finding raises the possibility that there may be an important difference between the conduct disorders that persist into adult life and those largely confined to childhood and adolescence.

As already noted, a pervasive issue in developmental research concerns the mechanisms promoting either continuity or discontinuity, persistence or change in behavior characteristics. For obvious reasons, such research requires longitudinal designs that focus on the features associated with intraindividual change or persistence. Longitudinal studies are not preferable in all instances. The are expensive, and they tend to suffer from the fact that the earlier variables will, by definition, have been obtained in an earlier era when both concepts and measures were less advanced. As Baldwin (1960) put it succinctly some years ago, longitudinal designs are absolutely essential for tackling developmental questions, but they are to be avoided at all costs. His tongue was in his cheek in expressing this paradoxical statement, but clearly, what he meant was that longitudinal studies are rarely the first design to use but, once the questions are clear, they are crucial for the adequate testing of hypotheses.

Another pervasive developmental research issue is the internal mechanisms by which risks are medicated and translated into psychopathology. Cognitive features are likely to play a key role in that connection (Rutter, 1987). These may operate in several different ways. Thus, as discussed in the chapters by Sigman (this volume) and by Cornblatt et al. (this volume), it seems highly probable that cognitive deficits or impairments constitute part of the basis for both autism and schizophrenia. The existence of the cognitive abnormalities is well documented, and there are plausible hypotheses about the possible ways in which they may lead to at least some of the social and behavioral abnormalities characterizing these conditions.

It is clear that in some circumstances, early life experiences can have long-lasting effects. One of the key challenges for the future is to determine the mechanisms involved in this carryforward of effects. Currently, there is much interest in the possibility that internal working models of secure or insecure selective attachment relationships constitute a key mediating feature (Bretherton, 1987; Rutter, 1995b). In view of the importance of close social relationships throughout life the possibility is plausible, but there has been very little systematic research testing of the hypothesis; in particular, very few studies have made systematic comparisons with alternative mechanisms. Another alternative is that the persistence lies in the direct learning of maladaptive behavior patterns shaped by family influences (see Patterson, this volume). Still another alternative is that severely negative experiences lead to biased cognitive processing, so that neutral encounters are perceived as having hostile intent (Dodge, Bates, & Pettit, 1990). Other possibilities concern effects on self-esteem or self-efficacy. What is distinctive about each of these possibilities is that they involve some effect that is likely to shape the ways in which individuals deal with both positive and negative future life experiences. They differ in the details of the effects on the self system that are proposed, but in all cases there is the implicit assumption that, with the possible exception of Patterson's concept of learned styles of behavior, the persistence or nonpersistence of the trait will be influenced by the nature of later life experiences. Thus, Caspi and Moffitt (1993) put forward what they have called the *accentuation principle,* by which stressful experiences tend to elicit exaggerated modes of the person's usual style of response and hence serve to reinforce or enhance it. This suggestion is important because it provides one possible way of understanding how sensitization or steeling effects come about. It is clear that people's experiences may render them less or more vulnerable to later stresses and adversities, but little is known about the mechanisms involved. It is generally supposed that, in some fashion, the processes involve either the effects of earlier experiences in shaping the cognitive appraisal of later experiences or the styles of coping with them. The topic is an important one, and it warrants substantially more research than it has received up to now.

So-called turning point effects also require explanation (Pickles & Rutter, 1991; Rutter, 1994d, in press-b). These refer to the observed instances in which there is a major change in life trajectory from better to worse or vice versa. It seems that such effects usually come about when later experiences involve a marked discontinuity with previous experiences and where the change in environmental circumstances is long-lasting. Alternatively, it could come about when an experience leads to a marked change in self-perception or cognitive set.

All of these possibilities underline the importance of considering indirect chain effects in development. Very few experiences with long-lasting effects are independent of later happenings. One of the research challenges for the future is to analyze the principles underlying the various forms of indirect chain reactions. As already noted, one such effect lies in the role of people's behavior in shaping and selecting their own later environment.

One example of age effects that has been subject to little systematic investigation up to now concerns neurobiological differences. Yet, there are reasonably well-documented phenomena that require explanation. For example, although there is very strong and specific continuity between major depressive disorders in childhood and apparently comparable disorders in adult life, neither children nor adolescents show a beneficial response to tricyclic medications, a sharp difference from the situation in adult life (Harrington, 1993). At present, we cannot be sure that the tricyclic-nonresponsive depressive disorders are occurring in the same individuals who show beneficial reactions to tricyclics at a later age, but it is quite possible that there are age-indexed differences in drug response. It is also well documented that autistic individuals with no previous evidence of neurological abnormality tend to develop epileptic seizures in late adolescence or early adult life (Deykin & MacMahon, 1979; Rutter, 1970). What changes in the brain are taking place that make this vulnerability to epilepsy arise at this time? Similarly, children who show precursors of schizophrenia rarely develop schizophrenic psychoses until the late teens or early 20s. What is happening in the brain for this transition to overt psychoses to occur at that time?

Researchers in the field of social development have tended to assume that they cannot use experimental paradigms because so few of the relevant experiences can be reproduced ethically in the laboratory and because so many of the effects are long-term. Although that is true, there has been a growing awareness in recent years that many occurrences in society provide natural experiments that, if properly handled, can provide something approaching the experimental control of laboratory experiments. The genetic designs of the twin strategy and the various forms of adoptee strategy are the best-known examples (Kendler, 1993; Rutter et al., 1990), but there are many other if psychiatric epidemiologists take the trouble to seek them out (Rutter 1994e; Rutter & Rutter, 1992; Rutter & Smith, 1995). For example, geographical moves (West, 1982), twin–singleton comparisons (Rutter & Redshaw, 1991), the various forms of blended families associated with parental remarriage following death or divorce (Hetherington, Reiss, & Plomin, 1994), school transfer (Mortimore, Sammons, Stoll, Lewis, & Ecob, 1988; Rutter, Maughan, Mortimore, & Ouston, 1979), the various forms of assisted or in vitro reproduction (Golombok, Cook, Bish, & Murray, 1995), the variations within age in a single school year because children tend to start school on a given date rather than at a given age (Cahan & Cohen, 1989), the occurrence of accidental brain injuries (Rutter, Chadwick, & Shaffer, 1983), and the rescue of children from severely depriving environments (Skuse, 1984) provide a varied range of examples of this kind. More use needs to be made of them.

Integration Across Levels

The chapter by Depue et al., (this volume) provides an example of some of the things that need to be achieved in this connection (see also Bailey et al., in press; Oades & Eggers, 1994). As they emphasize, it is necessary to adopt a dynamic perspective because the interplay across levels varies over the course of development. It is also important to reject the notion that the interplay simply involves the brain and the mind, with the structure and function of the brain providing the basic "cause" or explanation. To begin with, as already noted, the brain side of the interplay involves the connections among genes, their products, and their influence on neurobiological development place over time. Also, as we have seen, the functioning of the mind cannot be reduced to a single level. The possible interconnections among cognitive deficits or cognitive processing and behavioral, emotional, and social manifestations also have to be delineated. Furthermore, social functioning cannot be seen as taking place within the individual; necessarily, it involves the interplay between two individuals and will therefore be influenced by the characteristics of both as well as by the joint interplay of those characteristics. Moreover, it is a mistake to see the "biology" driving the "psychology" (Rutter, 1986b). Causal arrows run in both directions. Thus, for example, a rise or fall in sex hormone level has predictable effects on behaviors representing dominance and aggression. But equally, humiliation or victory in interpersonal encounters has predictable effects on sex hormone level. In addition, the workings of the mind necessarily have parallels in the functioning of the brain. This has been demonstrated with respect to phenomena such as imprinting (Horn, 1990), and the same is likely to apply to all forms of learning. What is needed is not a search for the single basic biological cause of psychopathology but, rather, an understanding of the workings of a complex, multilevel system.

In considering the neurobiological correlates of psychopathology in childhood, two special considerations apply. First, caution is needed in inferring that lesions in a particular part of the brain are the cause of some disorder simply because they have been found to be statistically associated with that disorder. If what is characteristic is the time in prenatal development when the process goes awry, the locus of the lesion may reflect that timing rather than the localization of the neural basis of the psychopathology. This may be one of the reasons why the brain imaging abnormalities found in autistic individuals have been so inconsistent both from case to case within studies and also between studies (Bailey & Cox, in press). Second, as already noted, there must be considerable caution in extrapolating from findings of adults to those in children. The cognitive patterns associated with lateralized brain lesions are different in early childhood, and the behavioral consequences may also vary. In addition, the part of the brain serving particular psychological functions sometimes changes during the course of development (Goldman-Rakic, Isseroff, Schwartz, & Bugbee, 1983).

Dupue et al. (this volume) argues that longitudinal studies are not necessary for neurobiological studies in the field of developmental psychopathology. Of course, that is correct if they mean that cross-sectional studies have an important place in such research. However, they are clearly wrong if they mean that longitudinal designs are unnecessary. Longitudinal strategies are crucial for testing causal hypotheses in the neurobiological arena, just as in any other domain. Moreover, one of the key issues in neurobiological research has been to differentiate between trait and state markers. The former are associated with vulnerability to a disorder both before the disorder develops and between illness episodes. By contrast, state markers show the abnormality only during illness episodes. For obvious reasons, the meaning of the two is quite different.

Conclusions

The chapters of this volume exemplify a range of research perspectives and include a focus on diverse types of psychopathology. Each provides a useful overview of the current state of play together with pointers on promising concepts and likely leads for future investigations. It is obvious that we have come a long way from descriptive studies of particular psychiatric categories and descriptive charting of changes in psychological characteristics with age. Researchers have moved on to tackle the more difficult questions of the mechanisms involved in the causes and course of psychopathology. It is noteworthy that with the developmental emphasis, attention is not focused on childhood disorders alone. Much of the research leverage has come from examination of the adult outcome of child psychopathology and from charting the origins of disorders with an overt onset in adult life. Equally, the search for the underlying mechanisms of disorder has involved a questioning of the validity of current diagnostic categories in psychiatry, as well as a focus on the role of dimensional risk factors that operate within the normal as well as the abnormal range, factors that can be studied before disorders begin. As all the chapters of this volume make evident, the research concepts and strategies in developmental psychopathology overlap greatly with those that apply in epidemiology, developmental sciences, neurobiology, and clinical psychiatry more generally. In no way does it constitute a separate discipline. But the particular bringing together of developmental and clinical research perspectives in a fashion that creates extra leverage by focusing on continuities and discontinuities across age and across the span of behavioral variation has proved useful and is likely to prove even more valuable in the future.

References

Attie, I., & Brooks-Gunn, J. (1989). Development of eating problems in adolescent girls: A longitudinal study. *Developmental Psychology, 25*, 70–79.

Bailey, A., Phillips W. & Rutter M. (in press). Autism: Towards an integration of clinical, genetic, neuropsychological, and neurobiological perspectives. *Journal of Child Psycholgy & Psychiatry Annual Review.*

Bailey, A. J. & Cox, T. (in press). Neuroimaging in child psychiatry. In S. Lewis & R. Higgins (Eds.), *Brain imaging in psychiatry.* Oxford: Blackwell Scientific.

Baldwin, A. L. (1960). The study of child behavior and development. In P. H. Mussen (Ed.), *Handbook of research methods in child development* (pp. 3–35). New York: Wiley.

Baltes, P. B. (1968). Longitudinal and cross-sectional sequences in the study of age and generation effects. *Human Development, 11*, 145–171.

Baron-Cohen, S., Tager-Flusberg, H., & Cohen, D. (1993). *Understanding other minds: Perspectives from autism.* Oxford: Oxford University Press.

Bell, R. Q., & Chapman, M. (1986). Child effects in studies using experimental or brief longitudinal approaches to socialization. *Developmental Psychology, 22*, 595–603.

Bishop, D., & Adams, C. (1990). A prospective study of the relationship between specific language impairment, phonological disorders and reading retardation. *Journal of Child Psychology and Psychiatry, 31*, 1027–1050.

Bishop, D., & Edmundson, A. (1987a). Language-impaired 4-year olds: Distinguishing transient from persistent impairment. *Journal of Speech and Hearing Disorders, 52*, 156–173.

Bishop, D., & Edmundson, A. (1987b). Specific language impairment as a maturational lag: Evidence from longitudinal data on language and motor development. *Developmental Medicine and Child Neurology, 29*, 442–459.

Bretherton, I. (1987). New perspectives on attachment relations: Security, communication and internal working models. In J. D. Osofsky (Eds.), *Handbook of infant development* (2nd ed., pp.1061–1100). New York: Wiley.

Cahan, S., & Cohen, N. (1989). Age versus schooling effects on intelligence development. *Child Development, 60*, 1239-1249.

Caron, C., & Rutter, M. (1991). Comorbidity in child psychopathology: Concepts, issues and research strategies. *Journal of Child Psychology and Psychiatry, 32*, 1063–1080.

Casaer, P., de Vries, L., & Marlow, N. (1991). Prenatal and perinatal risk factors for psychosocial development. In M. Rutter & P. Casaer (Eds.), *Biological risk factors for psychosocial disorders* (pp. 139–174). Cambridge: Cambridge University Press.

Caspi, A., & Moffitt, T. E. (1993). When do individual differences matter? A paradoxical theory of personality coherence. *Psychological Inquiry, 4*, 247–271.

Champion, L. A., Goodall, G. M., & Rutter, M. (1995). Behaviour problems in childhood and stressors in early adult life: A 20 year follow-up of London school children. *Psychological Medicine, 25*, 231–246.

Cicchetti, D. (1989). Developmental psychopathology: Past, present, and future. In D. Cicchetti (Ed.), *The emergence of a discipline* (pp. 1–12). Rochester Symposium on Developmental Psychopathology, Vol. 1 Hillsdale, NJ: Erlbaum.

Colombo, J. (1993). *Infant cognition: Predicting later intellectual functioning.* Newbury Park, CA: Sage.

Deykin, E. Y., & MacMahon, B. (1979). The incidence of seizures among children with autistic symptoms. *American Journal of Psychiatry, 136,* 1310–1312.

Diekstra, R. F. W., Kienhorst, I. W. M., & de Wilde, E. J. (1995). Suicide and suicidal behaviour among adolescents. In M. Rutter & D. J. Smith (Eds.), *Psychosocial disorders in young people: Time trends and their causes.* (pp.). Chichester, UK: Wiley.

DiLalla, L. F., & Gottesman, I. I. (1989). Heterogeneity of causes for delinquency and criminality: Lifespan perspective. *Development of Psychopathology, 1,* 339–349.

Dodge, K. A., Bates, J. E., and Pettit, G. S. (1990). Mechanisms in the cycle of violence. *Science, 250,* 1678–1683.

Done, D. J., Crow, T. J., Johnstone, E. C., & Sacker, A. (1994). Childhood antecedents of schizophrenia and affective illness: Social adjustment at ages 7 and 11. *British Medical Journal, 309,* 699–703.

Dunn, J., & Plomin, R. (1990). *Separate lives: Why siblings are so different.* New York: Basic Books.

Emery, R. E. (1982). Interparental conflict and the children of discord and divorce. *Psychological Bulletin, 92,* 310–330.

Fagot, B. L., & Kavanagh, K. (1990). The prediction of antisocial behavior from avoidant attachment classifications. *Child Development, 61,* 864–873.

Farrington, D. P. (1988). Studying changes within individuals: The causes of offending. In M. Rutter (Ed.), *Studies of psychosocial risk: The power of longitudinal data* (pp. 158–183). Cambridge: Cambridge University Press.

Farrington, D., Loeber, R., & Van Kammen, W. B. (1990). Long-term criminal outcomes of hyperactivity-impulsivity-attention deficit and conduct problems in childhood. In L. Robin & M. Rutter (Eds.), *Straight and devious pathways from childhood to adulthood* (pp. 62–81). Cambridge: Cambridge University Press.

Fergusson, D. M., & Horwood, L. J. (submitted). The role of adolescent peer affiliations in the continuity between childhood behavioral adjustment and juvenile offending.

Frith, U. (1989). *Autism: Explaining the enigma.* Oxford: Basil Blackwell.

Garmezy, N. (1993). Developmental psychopathology: Some historical and current perspectives. In D. Magnusson & P. Casaer (Eds.), *Longitudinal research on individual development: Present status and future perspectives* (pp. 95–126). Cambridge: Cambridge University Press.

Goldman-Rakic, P. S., Isseroff, A., Schwartz, M. L. & Bugbee, N. M. (1983). The neurobiology of cognitive development. In M. M. Haith & J. J. Campos (Eds.), *Infancy and developmental psychology, Volume 2, Mussen's handbook of child psychology* (4th ed., pp. 281–344). New York: Wiley.

Goldstein, M. J. (1987). Psychosocial issues. *Schizophrenia Bulletin, 13,* 157–171.

Golombok, S., Cook, R., Bish, A., & Murray, C. (1995). Families created by the new reproductive technologies: Quality of parenting and social and emotional development of the children. *Child Development, 66,* 285–298.

Goodyer, I. M., & Altham, P. M. E. (1991a). Lifetime exit events and recent social and family adversities in anxious and depressed school-age children and adolescents—I. *Journal of Affective Disorder, 21,* 219–228.

Goodyer, I. M., & Altham, P. M. E. (1991b). Lifetime exit events and recent social and family adversities in anxious and depressed school-age children and adolescents—II. *Journal of Affective Disorder, 21,* 229–238.

Goodyer, I. M., Germany, E., Gowrusankur, J., & Altham, P. (1991). Social influences on the course of anxious and depressive disorders in school-age children. *British Journal of Psychiatry, 158*, 676–684.

Greenberg, M. T., & Speltz, M. L. (1988). Attachment and the ontogeny of conduct problems. In J. Belsky & T. Nezworski (Eds.), *Clinical implications of attachment* (pp. 177–218).

Greenberg, M. T., Speltz, M. L., & DeKlyen, M. (1993). The role of attachment in the early development of disruptive behavior problems. *Development and Psychopathology, 5*, 191–213.

Hanson, D. R., Gottesman, I. I., & Heston, L. L. (1976). Some possible childhood indicators of adult schizophrenia inferred from children of schizophrenics. *British Journal of Psychiatry, 129*, 142–154.

Happé, F. G. E. (1994). *Autism: An introduction to psychological theory.* London: UCL Press.

Harrington, R. (1993). *Depressive disorder in childhood and adolescence.* Chichester, U.K.: Wiley.

Hetherington, E. M., Reiss, D., & Plomin, R. (1994). *Separate social worlds of siblings.* Hillsdale, NJ: Erlbaum.

Hodges, J. & Tizard, B. (1989a). IQ and behavioral adjustment of ex-institutional adolescents. *Journal of Child Psychology and Psychiatry, 30*, 53–75.

Hodges, J., & Tizard, B. (1989b). Social and family relationships of ex-institutional adolescents. *Journal of Child Psychology and Psychiatry, 30*, 77–97.

Holland, A. J., Sicotte, N., & Treasure, J. (1988). Anorexia nervosa—evidence for a genetic basis. *Journal of Psychosomatic Research, 32*, 561–572.

Horn, G. (1990). Neural bases of recognition memory investigated through an analysis of imprinting. *Philosophical Transactions of the Royal Society, 329*, 133–142.

Jones, P. B., Rodgers, B., Murray, R., & Marmot, M. (1994). Child development risk factors for adult schizophrenia in the British 1946 birth cohort. *Lancet, 344*, 1398–1402.

Kendler, K. S. (1993). Twin studies of psychiatric illness: Current status and future directions. *Archives of General Psychiatry, 50*, 905–915.

Kendler, K. S., McGuire, M., Gruenberg, A. M., Ohare, A., Spellman, M., & Walsh, D. (1993a). The Roscommon family study 3. Schizophrenia-related pesonality disorders in relatives. *Archives of General Psychiatry, 50*, 781–788.

Kendler, K. S., Neale, M. C., Kessler, R. C., Heath, A. C., & Eaves, L. J. (1993b). A longitudinal twin study of 1-year prevalence of major depression in women. *Archives of General Psychiatry, 50*, 843–852.

Kendler, K. S., Neale, M. C., Kessler, R. C., Heath, A. C., & Eaves, L. J. (1993c). A longitudinal twin study of personality and major depression in women. *Archives of General Psychiatry, 50*, 853–862.

Kessler, R. C., & Magee, W. J. (1993). Childhood adversities and adult depression: Basic patterns of association in a U.S. national survey. *Psychological Medicine, 23*, 679–690.

Kohnstamm, G. A., Bates, J. E., & Rothbart, M. K. (1989). *Temperament in childhood.* Chichester, U.K.: Wiley.

Magnusson, D., & Bergman, L. R. (1988). Individual and variable-based approaches to longitudinal research on early risk factors. In M. Rutter (Ed.), *Studies of psychosocial risk: The power of longitudinal data* (pp. 45–61). Cambridge: Cambridge University Press.

Magnusson, D., & Bergman, L. R. (1990). A pattern approach to the study of pathways from childhood to adulthood. In L. Robin & M. Rutter (Eds.), *Straight and devious pathways from childhood to adulthood* (pp. 101–115). Cambridge: Cambridge University Press.

Maughan, B., Pickles, A., Rutter, M., & Hagell, A. (in press). Reading problems and antisocial behavior: Developmental trends in comorbidity. *Journal of Child Psychology and Psychiatry.*

McCall, R. B., & Carriger, M. S. (1993). A meta-analysis of infant habituation and recognition memory performance as predictors of later IQ. *Child Development, 64,* 57–79.

Moffitt, T. E. (1990). The neuropsychology of juvenile delinquency: A critical review. In M. Tonry & N. Morris (Eds.), *Crime and justice* (Vol. 12, pp. 99–169). Chicago: University of Chicago Press.

Moffitt, T. E. (1993a). Adolescence-limited and life-course persistent antisocial behavior: A developmental taxonomy. *Psychological Review, 100,* 674–701.

Moffitt, T. E. (1993b). The neuropsychology of conduct disorder. *Development and Psychopathology, 5,* 135–151.

Mortimore, P. Sammons, P., Stoll, L., Lewis, D., & Ecob, R. (1988). *School matters: The junior years.* Wells, Somerset, U.K.: Open Books.

Oades, R. D., & Eggers, C. (1994). Childhood autism: An appeal for an integrative and psychobiological approach. *European Child and Adolescent Psychiatry, 3,* 159–175.

Oppel, W. C., Harper, P. A., & Rider, R. V. (1968). The age of attaining bladder control. *Pediatrics, 42,* 614–626.

Osterling, J., & Dawson, G. (1994). Early recognition of children with autism: A study of first birthday home videotapes. *Journal of Autism and Developmental Disorders, 24,* 247–259.

Ozonoff, S. (1994). Executive functions in autism. In E. Schopler & G. B. Mesibov (Eds.), *Learning and cognition in autism.* New York: Plenum Press.

Pickles, A., & Rutter, M. (1991). Statistical and conceptual models of "turning points" in developmental processes. In D. Magnusson, L. R. Bergman, G. Rudinger, & B. Törestad (Eds.), *Problems and methods in longitudinal research: Stability and change* (pp. 133–165). Cambridge: Cambridge University Press.

Plomin, R. (1994). *Genetics and experience: The developmental interplay between nature and nurture.* Newbury Park, CA: Sage.

Plomin, R., & Bergman, C. S. (1991). The nature of nurture: Genetic influence on "environmental" measures. *Behavioural Brain Sciences, 14,* 373–427.

Plomin, R., & Daniels, D. (1987). Why are children in the same family so different from one another? *Behavioral and Brain Sciences, 10,* 1–15.

Plomin, R. DeFries, J. C., & Fulker, D. W. (1988). *Nature and nurture during infancy and childhood.* Cambridge: Cambridge University Press.

Plomin, R., Nitz, K., & Rowe, D. C. (1990). Behavioral genetics and aggressive behavior in childhood. In M. Lewis & S. M. Miller (Eds.), *Handbook of developmental psychopathology* (pp. 119–133). New York: Plenum Press.

Quinton, D., Pickles, A. R., Maughan, B., & Rutter, M. (1993). Partners, peers and pathways: Assortative pairing and continuities in conduct disorder. *Development & Psychopathology, 5,* 763–783.

Quinton, D., & Rutter, M. (1988). *Parenting breakdown: The making and breaking of inter-generational links.* Aldershot, U.K.: Avebury.

Reiss, A. J., Jr., (1995). Community influences on adolescent behavior. In M. Rutter (Ed.), *Psychosocial disturbances in young people: Challenges for prevention*, pp. 305–332. Cambridge: Cambridge University Press.

Reynolds, O. (in press). Causes and outcome of perinatal brain injury. In D. Magnusson (Ed.), *The lifespan development of individuals: Synthesis of biological and psychosocial perspectives.* Cambridge: Cambridge University Press.

Robins, L. (1966). *Deviant children grown up.* Baltimore: Williams & Wilkins.

Robins, L. N., Davis, D. H., & Wish, E. (1977). Detecting predictors of rare events: Demographic, family and personal deviance as predictors of stages in the progression toward narcotic addiction. In J. S. Strauss, H. M. Babigian, & M. Roff (Eds.), *The origins and course of psychopathology* (pp. 379–406). New York: Plenum Press.

Rosenbaum, J. F., Biederman, J., Hirshfield, D. R., Bolduc, E. A., Faraone, S. V., Kagan, J., Snidman, N., & Reznick, J. S. (1991). Further evidence of an association between behavioral inhibition and anxiety disorders: Results from a family study of children from a non-clinical sample. *Journal of Psychiatric Research, 25,* 49–65.

Rowe, D. C., Woulbroun, J., & Gulley, B. L. (1994). Peers and friends as non-shared environmental influences. In E. M. Hetherington, D. Reiss, & Plomin (Eds.), *Separate social worlds of siblings* (pp. 159–173). Hillsdale, NJ: Erlbaum.

Rutter, M. (1970). Autistic children: Infancy to adulthood. *Seminars in Psychiatry, 2,* 435–450.

Rutter, M. (1979). Separation experiences: A new look at an old topic. *Journal of Pediatrics, 95,* 147–154.

Rutter, M. (1985a). Resilience in the face of adversity: Protective factors and resistance to psychiatric disorder. *British Journal of Psychiatry, 147,* 598–611.

Rutter, M. (1985b). Family and school influences on behavioural development. *Journal of Child Psychology and Psychiatry, 26,* 349–368.

Rutter, M. (1986a). Child psychiatry: The interface between clinical and developmental research. *Psychological Medicine, 16,* 151–169.

Rutter, M. (1986b). Meyerian psychobiology, personality development and the role of life experiences. *American Journal of Psychiatry, 143,* 1077–1087.

Rutter, M. (1987). The role of cognition in child development and disorder. *British Journal of Medical Psychology, 60,* 1–16.

Rutter, M. (1988). Epidemiological approaches to developmental psychopathology. *Archives of General Psychiatry, 45,* 486–500.

Rutter, M. (1989). Age as an ambiguous variable in developmental research: Some epidemiological considerations from developmental psychopathology. *International Journal of Behavioral Development, 12,* 1–34.

Rutter, M. (1990). Psychosocial resilience and protective mechanisms. In J. Rolf, A. Masten, D. Cicchetti, K. Nuechterlein, & S. Weintraub (Eds.), *Risk and protective factors in the development of psychopathology* (pp. 181–214). New York: Cambridge University Press.

Rutter, M. (1991). A fresh look at "maternal deprivation." In P. Bateson (Ed.), *The development and inegration of behaviour* (pp. 331–374). Cambridge: Cambridge University Press.

Rutter, M. (1993a). Developmental psychopathology as a research perspective. In D. Magnusson & P. Casaer (Eds.), *Longitudinal research on individual development: Present status and future perspectives* (pp. 127–152). Cambridge: Cambridge University Press.

Rutter, M. (1993b). Resilience: Some conceptual considerations. *Journal of Adolescent Health, 14,* 626–631.
Rutter, M. (1994a). Psychiatric genetics: Research challenges and pathways forward. *American Journal of Medical Genetics, 54,* 185–198.
Rutter, M. (1994b). Family discord and conduct disorder: Cause, consequence or correlate? *Journal of Family Psychology, 8,* 170–186.
Rutter, M. (1994c). Concepts of causation and implications for intervention. In A. Petersen & J. Mortimer (Eds.), *Youth unemployment and society* (pp. 147–171). Cambridge: Cambridge University Press.
Rutter, M. (1994d). Continuities, transitions and turning points in development. In M. Rutter & D. F. Hay (Eds.), *Development through life: A handbook for clinicians* (pp. 1–25). Oxford: Blackwell Scientific.
Rutter, M. (1994e). Beyond longitudinal data: Causes, consequences, changes and continuity. *Journal of Consulting and Clinical Psychology, 62,* 928–940.
Rutter, M. (1995a). Causal concepts and their testing. In M. Rutter & D. J. Smith (Eds.), *Psychosocial disorders in young people: Time trends and their causes.* Chichester, U.K.: Wiley.
Rutter, M., (1995b). Clinical implications of attachment concepts: Retrospect and prospect. *Journal of Child Psychology and Psychiatry, 36,* 549–571.
Rutter, M. (in press-a). Developmental psychopathology as an organizing research construct. In D. Magnusson (Ed.), *The life span development of individuals: A synthesis of biological and psychological perspectives.* New York: Cambridge University Press.
Rutter, M. (in press-b). Transitions and turning points in development. *International Journal of Behavioral Development.*
Rutter, M., Chadwick, O., & Shaffer, D. (1983). The behavioural and cognitive sequelae of head injury. In M. Rutter (Ed.), *Developmental neuropsychiatry* (pp. 83–111). New York: Guilford Press.
Rutter, M., Champion, L., Quinton, D., Maughan, B., & Pickles, A. (in press). Origins of individual differences in environmental risk exposure. In P. Moen, G. Elder, & K. Luscher (Eds.), *Perspectives on the ecology of human development.* Ithaca, NY: Cornell University Press.
Rutter, M., & Garmezy, N. (1993). Developmental psychopathology. In E. M. Hetherington (Ed.), *Socialization, personality, and social development: Volume 4, Mussen handbook of child psychology* (4th ed., pp. 775–911). New York: Wiley.
Rutter, M., Graham, P., Chadwick, O. F. D., & Yule, W. (1976). Adolescent turmoil: Fact or fiction? *Journal of Child Psychology and Psychiatry, 17,* 35–56.
Rutter, M., Maughan, B., Mortimore, P., & Ouston, J. (1979). *Fifteen thousand hours: Secondary schools and their effects on children.* London: Open Books (repr. 1994; London: Paul Chapman).
Rutter, M., & Mawhood, L. (1991). The long-term psychosocial sequelae of specific developmental disorders of speech and language. In M. Rutter & P. Casaer (Eds.), *Biological risk factors for psychosocial disorders* (pp. 233–259). Cambridge: Cambridge University Press.
Rutter, M., & Pickles, A. R. (1991). Person–environment interactions: Concepts, mechanisms and implications for data analysis. In T. D. Wachs & R. Plomin (Eds.), *Conceptualization and measurement of organism–environment interaction* (pp. 105–141). Washington, DC: American Psychological Association.
Rutter, M., & Quinton, D. (1984). Parental psychiatric disorder: Effects on children. *Psychological Medicine, 14,* 853–880.

Rutter, M., Quinton, D., & Hill, J. (1990). Adult outcome of institution-reared children: Males and females compared. In L. Robin & M. Rutter (Eds.), *Straight and devious pathways from childhood to adulthood* (pp. 135–157). Cambridge: Cambridge University Press.

Rutter, M., & Redshaw, J. (1991). Annotation: Growing up as a twin: Twin–singleton differences in psychological development. *Journal of Child Psychology and Psychiatry, 32*, 885–895.

Rutter, M., & Rutter, M. (1993). *Developing minds: Challenge and continuity across the life span.* New York: Basic Books.

Rutter, M., Bailey, A., Bolton, P., & Le Couteur, A. (Eds.) (1993). In R. Plomin & G. E. McClearn (Eds.), *Nature, nurture, and psychology* (pp. 433–456). Washington, DC: APA Books.

Rutter, M., & Smith, D. J. (1995). Autism: Syndrome definition and possible genetic mechanisms. (1995). *Psychosocial disorders in young people: Time trends and their causes.* Chichester, U.K.: Wiley.

Sampson, R. J., & Laub, J. H. (1993). *Crime in the making: Pathways and turning points through life.* Cambridge, MA: Harvard University Press.

Scarr, S. (1992). Developmental theories for the 1990's: Development and individual differences. *Child Development, 63,* 1–19.

Schaie, K. W. (1965). A general model for the study of developmental problems. *Psychological Bulletin, 64,* 92–107.

Simonoff, E., Bolton, P., & Rutter, M. (in press). Mental retardation: Genetic findings, clinical implications and research agenda. *Journal of Child Psychology and Psychiatry.*

Skuse, D. (1984). Extreme deprivation in early childhood—II. Theoretical issues and a comparative review. *Journal of Child Psychology and Psychiatry, 25,* 543–572.

Sroufe, L. A., & Rutter, M. (1984). The domain of developmental psychopathology. *Child Development, 55,* 17–29.

Taylor, E. (1994). Syndromes of attention deficit and overactivity. In M. Rutter, E. Taylor & L. Hersov (Eds.), *Child and adolescent psychiatry: Modern approaches* (3rd ed., pp. 285–308). Oxford: Blackwell Scientific.

Taylor, E. Chadwick, O., Heptinstall, E., & Danckaerts, M. (submitted). Hyperactivity and conduct disorder as risk factors for adolescent development.

Vargha-Khadem, F., Isaacs, E., van der Werf, S., Robb, S., & Wilson, J. (1992). Development of intelligence and memory in children with hemiplegic cerebral palsy: The deleterious consequences of early seizures. *Brain, 115,* 315–329.

Wahlsten, D. (1990). Insensitivity of the analysis of variance to heredity–environment interaction. *Behavioural and Brain Sciences, 13,* 109–120.

Werry, J. S., McClellan, J. M., & Chard, L. (1991). Childhood and adolescent schizophrenia, bipolar and schizoaffective disorders: A clinical and outcome study. *Journal of the American Academy of Child and Adolescent Psychiatry, 30,* 457–465.

West, D. (1982). *Delinquency: Its roots, careers and prospects.* London: Heinemann.

Zoccolillo, M., Pickles, A., Quinton, D., & Rutter, M. (1992). The outcome of childhood conduct disorder: Implications for defining adult personality disorder and conduct disorder. *Psychological Medicine, 22,* 971–986.

Index

Adoptees, 24–25, 29, 31, 33
Affective disorders, 67, 131, 134
Affective genotype, 17, 23
Age variations, 211–12, 214, 225–26, 228, 230
Aggression, 6–12, 18, 25–27
Antisocial behavior, 5–11, 15–19, 21, 23, 25–26, 28, 31–33, 81, 84, 86–91, 96–98, 100, 101, 104–7, 109, 110–12, 114–16
Antisocial parents, 88, 94–100, 117
Antisocial personality disorder (ASP), 5, 7–10, 24–27, 36
At-risk status, 125–26, 131, 135, 144
Attention, 125, 126, 141
  deficits (attentional), 126, 134–35
  sustained attention, 126
  triadic attention, 192, 193, 194, 195, 197, 198, 199
Attention deficit hyperactivity disorder (ADHD), 18, 23–25, 27
Autism
  early infantile, 191, 202
  older children, 196–98, 201
  physiological basis of, 192, 200, 202
  psychogenic theory of, 191–92
  young children, 190–96, 198–99

Biobehavioral markers, 125, 128, 130–31, 136
Bipolar affective disorder, 67–69, 71
Broken home, 91, 95–97

California Psychological Inventory Socialization (CPISo), 10
Categories, 214–16, 219, 230
Change, 81–82, 86–88, 92, 109–13, 116
Characterological depression, 70
Children, effects on other people, 222
Chronicity, 88, 95, 113–17
Coercion, 83–84, 87–88, 91–92, 101–11, 115, 117
Coercive cycles, 9, 26,
Cognitive mediation of risk, 226–27
Comorbidity, 23, 25, 212, 215–17
Constitutive genes, 14
Conduct disorder (CD), 7, 8, 18, 23–27, 36
Context, 81, 88, 91–94, 97–98, 117
Contingency, 86–87
Continuities, 209, 211, 214–15, 219, 226
Continuous Performance Test (CPT), 126–27, 131
Criminality, 5, 9, 10, 15, 23, 27–29, 33

Delinquency, 5, 7, 10, 15, 27–29, 32, 36
Deoxyribonucleic acid (DNA), 11–14
Development, 45, 81–87, 91, 100, 104, 109–10, 116–17, 125, 127, 130, 139
Developmental psychopathology, 44–47, 65, 68, 70, 72, 190, 192, 203

Developmental switches, 15
Diathesis, 45, 66, 72
Dimensions, 210, 214–15, 219, 230
Discontinuities, 209, 211, 214–15, 219, 226
Disease genes, 128
Distal causes, 6, 8, 9
Dopamine (DA), 49–72
Dynamic process, 45–47, 57–60, 65, 68–69, 72

Early onset of disorder, 81, 92, 95–98, 113–17
Emergenesis, 23
Emotional system, 47, 48, 63, 64, 65
Emotional threshold, 51, 58
Environment, 44–47, 53, 58–63, 70–72
Environmental effects on overall liability to disorder, 212, 218, 222, 224
Environmental risk experience, origins of, 210, 219, 224
Epidemiology, 7, 9, 18, 36
Escape conditioning, 101
Euchromatin, 13
Experience-dependent learning, 59–72

Family problem solving, 88, 91, 98, 116

Genetics, 5, 6, 11, 15, 18–20, 36, 125, 130
Genetic heterogeneity, 8, 9, 35
Genetic risk, 28, 35
Genotype, 60, 61–62, 69, 71, 125, 128, 131

Heritability, 5, 11, 19–25, 29, 33
Heterochromatin, 13
Heterotypic continuity, 216
High-risk method, 130, 132
Hyperactivity, 23, 24, 27. *See also* Attention deficit hyperactivity disorder (ADHD)

Incentive motivation, 49, 53, 57, 61, 64, 70
Indicators, 97, 98
Information processing, 127, 139, 142
Integration across levels of functioning, 229
Interaction, 49, 54, 57–60, 70, 72

Laboratory analogue, 82, 84–86, 108
Liability, 24, 32–33
Linkage analysis, 130
Longitudinal research strategies, 211, 213, 226, 230

Markers, 130, 133, 143
Matching law, 87, 101, 104
Mediational model, 82, 83, 91, 97, 98, 114, 117
Mental retardation, 192, 193, 194, 195, 199, 201
Methylation, 13
Mind blindness, 197
MMPI Pd scale, 10, 28, 29, 31, 33, 35
Mobility, 98, 99
Monitoring, 88–89, 91, 98, 116
Multiagent indicators, 89, 116
Multidimensional Personality Questionnaire (MPQ) Aggression scale, 28–29, 33
Multifactorial causation, 209–10, 222
Multimethod indicators, 89, 116
Multi-phased processes, 213

Natural experiments, use of for testing causal hypothesis, 211, 228
Neurobehavioral system, 47–48, 62–65, 68
Neurobiology, 44, 60, 64, 72
Neurodevelopmental model and schizophrenia, 143
New York High-Risk Project (NYHRP), 126, 132–33, 134–35, 141
Non-shared environmental effects, 223

Parenting, 83, 87–91, 94–100, 114, 116, 117
Performance model, 81–87, 108, 116
Personality Disorder Examination (PDE), 136
Personality disorders, 137
Personality structure, 63–64
Person-environment correlations, 218–19
Person-environment interactions, 209, 212–13, 218, 220–21
Phenotype, 46, 65, 71, 128, 216, 219, 220
Pleiotropy, 8–9

Prediction, 83–87, 96, 109, 114, 117, 130
Predispositions, 9, 17
Proximal causes, 6–9
Psychobiological model, 46
Psychosis, 127, 131, 137. *See also* Schizophrenia

Reaction range, 15
Reaction surface, 15
Regulated genes, 12, 14–15, 22
Reinforcement, 84, 86–88, 100–106, 116–17
Replicate, 81, 83–90, 116
Risk experiences and diversity of outcome, 209, 211, 213–16

Schizophrenia, 125, 130, 143–44
Schizophrenia-related personality disorders (SRPD), 130–31, 133
Schizotypal features, 128
Schizotype(s), 132, 143
Second order factor, 116
Secular trends and causes for in disorder, 212–13, 228
Sensitization, 51, 54–55, 59–60, 63, 66, 68
Single parent, 88, 92–100, 117
Social competence, 141–42
Social development and social awareness, 193–203

Social disorganization, 91–94, 100, 117
Social isolation, 137–38, 140, 142
Social skills, 126, 141, 143
Societal rates, 92
Stability, 81–82, 87, 105, 110, 112, 116
Stages in psychological development and individual differences, 210
Structural equation model (SEM), 91, 98, 110
Substance abuse, 66, 71

Taxonomy, 7, 27, 36
Temperament, 20–22, 26
Trade-off function, 46–47, 54–58
Trait, 62–71
Transition, 92, 95–98, 100–101
Turning points in development, 213–14, 218, 227
Twins, 7, 15, 18–29, 32–33, 35

Use of abnormal cases to separate variables, 215, 217

Variability in behavior (situation), 210–11, 214, 221, 230
Variable expression of genetic disorder, 209, 211, 216, 218–22
Violence, 95, 115–17